REBELLIOUS RANGER

Rip Ford and the
Old Southwest

REBELLIOUS RANGER

RANGER

{ *Rip Ford and the*
Old Southwest }

BY W. J. HUGHES

Foreword by Walter L. Buenger

UNIVERSITY OF OKLAHOMA PRESS · NORMAN AND LONDON

LIBRARY OF CONGRESS CATALOG CARD NUMBER: 64–11323
ISBN: 0–8061–1084–8

Some years ago J. Frank Dobie wrote the comment that Texas has had three types of occupants: "Texians," the "Old Rock," who came to found a nation and a state; Texans, descended from the original settlers; and "people who live in Texas," Johnnies-come-(relatively) lately. Consistent with his definitions, this account of a Texian is dedicated to Texans by one who has lived in Texas.

Contents

Illustrations

Foreword

By Walter L. Buenger

WITH TIME most histories and biographies fade into oblivion, or onto the shelves of libraries to be consulted only by anxious aspirants for Ph.D.'s and bone-digging genealogists. Occasionally, as in this instance, scholarly presses elect to bring out a new printing and put it before the public for a second chance at a wider readership.

Such a second chance is warranted for William J. Hughes's story of John Salmon Ford. This work, first published in 1964, serves as an historiographic benchmark and reminds us that history changes as society changes. It is a rousing tale, a book for teenagers dreaming of adventure and for those seeking to escape ambiguity. But this is not simply a romantic tale of high adventure. For almost sixty years Ford was closely associated with the most dramatic events in the history of the state. His life is an intimate portrait of the state's history.

Hughes must have been one of those teenagers dreaming of adventure. His daughter recounts: "Dad had a life-long interest in things western. As a boy in Colorado he subscribed to western magazines and read western stories whenever he could (his parents took him to the Cheyenne Rodeo and he spent his time in their lodgings reading westerns rather than witnessing the real thing—they couldn't understand it)."[1]

He continued his interest in books and things western, receiv-

---

[1] Katherine Hughes to John N. Drayton, December 12, 1989, in possession of the author.

ing a Ph.D. from Texas Tech University in 1959, after specializing in frontier and western history. He first taught at Dakota Wesleyan University, in Mitchell, South Dakota, and then, in 1962, joined the faculty at Mankato State University, in Mankato, Minnesota. Students and colleagues admired his ability as a teacher and especially remembered his artful storytelling. After achieving the rank of professor at Mankato, Hughes retired in 1978. He died in 1986. *Rebellious Ranger* was his only book.

While at Texas Tech, Hughes was heavily influenced by Ernest Wallace and, through him, by Walter Prescott Webb and J. Frank Dobie. It is not surprising then that *Rebellious Ranger* glorifies the Texas Rangers. The book also accepts or downplays Ford's racism and violence, ignores women, and treats Indians, Mexicans, and blacks paternalistically, if at all. For some this is reason enough to let the book continue to reside on the back shelf. In another sense, however, the work is useful exactly because of these characteristics. Vietnam, the Civil Rights Movement, the Women's Movement, and the onslaught of New Social history all swept away this kind of history. This gives the book a certain antique quality that reminds us of the extent and rapidity of change in the study of American history. It also should remind historians that in another twenty-five years their well-honed work and up-to-date attitudes will probably be regarded as having antique characteristics.

What is more timeless about Hughes's life of Ford is that it is a well-written tale of adventure. Most descriptions of Ford use adjectives such as colorful, versatile, zestful, and so forth.[2] Trained as a physician in Tennessee, Ford moved to Texas in the summer of 1836. He was probably drawn by the possibility of upward economic mobility and the excitement of the recent revolution. He was also pushed by a failed marriage. Settling first in East Texas among fellow Tennesseans, Ford taught school, worked as a physician, tried his hand at editing a newspaper, fought In-

[2] See, for example, John H. Jenkins, *Basic Texas Books: An Annotated Bibliography of Selected Works for a Research Library*, rev. ed. (Austin: Texas State Historical Association, 1983), 165–68.

dians, and, in the mid-1840s, organized popular support for annexation. After Texas became a state, Ford moved to Austin and
continued to edit a newspaper. He fought with the Texas Rangers
during the Mexican War and was part of the detachment led by
Jack Hayes that protected Winfield Scott's supply lines from
Vera Cruz to Mexico City. While there his outfit earned the sobriquet "Los Diablos Tejanos" for their bloody methods of dealing with Mexican partisans. After the war Ford was mayor of
Austin for a time and continued his efforts as a newspaperman.
He could not leave the life of a Ranger behind him, however.
Throughout the decade of the 1850s he blazed trails westward,
led attacks on Comanches, and fought what Anglo Texans called
Mexican bandits. Along the Rio Grande his most famous skirmishes were with Juan Cortina, who matched him in charisma
and dramatic appeal. In fact, if this were a work of fiction Cortina
would be the perfect protagonist, a chivalrous but complex individual driven by his own set of demons.

The start of the Civil War brought a new series of problems
and a continued foe in Juan Cortina. A supporter of secession
and member of the secession convention, Ford commanded
troops along the Rio Grande during the war. He helped organize
the important export of cotton through Matamoros, Mexico, and
took part in several small battles with Mexican as well as U.S.
troops. The multisided diplomacy required to deal with the various Mexican governments, the state of Texas, the Confederate
government, and Union forces, not to mention the British and
the French, taxed Ford's patience and abilities to the limit. It
must have been with some relief that he learned that his victory
at Palmetto Ranch on May 13, 1865, was the last battle of the
Civil War.

On through Reconstruction, Ford continued as an editor and
an occasional participant in border strife along the Rio Grande.
With the restoration of the Democrats to power in the mid-
1870s, Ford resumed a more prominent role in public life. Even
after retiring to San Antonio, in 1883, to write his memoirs, he
continued to attract attention from those interested in the ro-

mantic past. A knight errant, a man of letters, an active politician, and a physician, few had so varied and so exciting a career.

It was a career that encompassed most of the significant events of nineteenth-century Texas—events in which Ford took a first-hand role. Again and again he was on the scene. Along with Oran M. Roberts he organized a popular move for annexation. Fifteen years later the same two issued a call for a secession convention. His newspaper was a major organ of the early Democratic party. Then in the mid-1850s he was one of the leaders of the Know Nothing movement that convulsed the state. Accepted back into the fold of the Democratic party, he voted in the secession convention to dissolve the Union and then helped organize the seizure of the federal army's men and material in Texas.

Ford spent the war primarily within the borders of his state, and his duties were always political and diplomatic, as well as military. When it looked as if blood would be shed when Republican governor Edmund J. Davis balked at surrendering his office to Democrat Richard Coke, Ford was in Austin and, as a special sergeant-at-arms, helped quell the threat of violence. In 1875, when the redeemer Democrats wrote a new constitution for the state, he was a member of the convention. When Roberts and John H. Reagan, along with Professor George P. Garrison, organized the Texas State Historical Association in 1897, Ford was again present. Over and over again he played a direct role in the most significant political, military, and cultural events in the state. From 1836 to 1897 he not only had a ringside seat, he played a part in every major event within the state of Texas. Thus it is fitting that his story be brought back on center stage by the University of Oklahoma Press.

By Way of Explanation

CHARACTERISTICALLY has Texas delighted in honoring the sturdy men who carved out her history. It is, then, with surprise that one notes an absence of the story of possibly the most "Texian" of them all—"Rip" Ford. One reason may be that in the broad expanse which is Texas there is regional pride of the kind which elsewhere exists in various parts of certain national states; thus, a tendency persists to grant credit to the local figures. The prestige of John S. Ford undoubtedly suffered through some such circumstance. As an illustration in point, early in this century, a veteran of the Comanche campaign of 1858 attended a Ranger reunion and complained over his plate of barbecue, "If you live in Waco, you have the idea that Shapley Ross was responsible for the Canadian River campaign; in San Antonio, folks believe Captain Tobin won the Cortina War. 'Old Rip' doesn't get any credit." It sounds as if the old Ranger had encountered that collection of Texas biographies which in its article on Ross lauds him for his notable raid into Comanche territory with the assistance of "Capt. Salmon Ford of the U.S. Army." Modern scholarship does only slightly better. In a recent (1959) study of army exploration in the West, the Ford-Neighbors trail is established by Major Robert Neighbors "of the Texas Rangers" and John S. Ford, "the federal Indian agent for Texas." While there is always the danger that any account may create as many errors as it rectifies, the purpose of the present one is to remedy the more obvious mistakes where John S. Ford's career is concerned and to attempt to extend to his memory the credit his services rightfully won.

Since no Texas author has undertaken the Ford biography, it is in apologetic fashion that a non-Texan has attempted it. It would have been better had the narrative been dealt with by any one of three Texans: Ernest Wallace of Texas Technological College, who knows not only the big roads but the little trails of Texas history; the late Walter Prescott Webb, who was all the historian the Rangers ever will need; and J. Frank Dobie, who better than anyone else imparts to the outlander the peculiar Texas "flavor." But these gentlemen had, in the old phrase, "other fish to fry."

To three people, specifically, is the writer deeply obligated for assistance in exhuming and organizing the varied materials concerning John Ford. Professor Wallace, in the best scholarly tradition, surrendered his own intention to investigate Ford and likewise gave up time he could ill spare from his own significant research to counsel me. Mr. Frank M. Temple, catalog librarian at Texas Technological College, and Professor John C. McGraw, head of the Social Sciences Division at William Carey College, not only interrupted major projects of their own to turn up important Ford data but also lent constant encouragement.

From unexpected places have come useful facts, such as that which shows "Old Rip" as a dime-novel figure, provided by a most stimulating colleague, J. Leonard Jennewein, in a gratifying deviation from his preoccupation with northern plains history. Certain relatives of John S. Ford, librarians, archivists, and others who assisted will recognize their contributions and will know of my gratitude to them.

W. J. Hughes

MANKATO, MINNESOTA
JANUARY 20, 1964

REBELLIOUS RANGER

Rip Ford and the
Old Southwest

I

"Known to Everyone"

TEXIANS—that folk which built a nation and created a state—came from the far-flung corners of the old Union, but the most of them had origin in the Old South. Of Stephen Austin, T. J. Rusk, Edward Burleson, Sam Houston, and other illustrious names this is true. It is also true of one who, while never achieving higher than the second plateau of eminence, was the most versatile performer of them all—John Salmon Ford, "Old Rip."

John Salmon Ford was born in the Greenville District of South Carolina on May 26, 1815. His ancestry was Virginian, his paternal great-grandparents having left the Old Dominion before the Revolutionary War to take up land against the Appalachian foothills farther south. Their son, Major John Ford, returned home after war service to practice law and manage the family acres. When he died at the age of forty-five of a lung infection acquired by exposure during the war, supervision of the plantation passed into the hands of his son William.

William Ford, the father of John Salmon, was born in 1785. In early manhood he married Harriet Salmon, daughter of George Salmon, Greenville planter and Revolutionary War veteran, also of Virginia stock. Harriet Salmon's union with William Ford resulted in several children, of whom only John Salmon and an older sister, Elizabeth, survived the vicissitudes of infancy and adolescence.[1] In 1817, the Ford family cast themselves adrift into

[1] John Salmon Ford, "The Memoirs of John Salmon Ford" (unpublished MS, Barker History Center, University of Texas, Austin), I, 8. Hereafter cited as Ford,

the westward current of the Great Migration and eventually came aground in Lincoln County, Tennessee, where William Ford acquired land to which he gradually added more than two hundred acres during the following fifteen years.[2]

On his father's homestead, young John Ford flourished in typical western plantation fashion, learning, like Herodotus' youthful Persians, to ride, shoot, and speak the truth. His memoirs reveal an exuberant boyhood:

> John S. Ford, at an early period of existence, exhibited some marked and rather positive traits of character. He possessed the capacity to get into fights with the boys, to fall in love with the girls, and to take a hand in the deviltry set on foot by his playmates. The old ladies of his neighborhood looked upon him as a kind of prodigy, and predicted he would be killed for his general "cussedness" before reaching the age of maturity, or hung [sic] for some infernal mischief he might commit.[3]

With a mind hungry for knowledge and quick in perception, he rapidly exhausted the curriculum of his country school; by the age of sixteen he was, it is said, qualified to teach school himself.[4] An avid reader, he early became familiar with good literature, and his study of the Bible, on which his mother insisted, implemented the vocabulary which later supported his trenchant editorial pen.

Ford's alert mind was not to be permitted to vegetate in plantation life. North of his Lincoln County home lay Bedford County and its small county seat, Shelbyville. At the age of nineteen, Ford was there reading medicine under Dr. James G. Barksdale, following a process of training not unusual for students remote

"Memoirs." Volume and page numbers refer to those of typescript in Archives Division, Texas State Library, Austin. The 1820 census for Lincoln County, Tennessee, shows William Ford as having two children, one male in age group 1–10, one female in age group 10–16.

[2] A list of land grants, Archives Division, Tennessee State Library, Nashville, shows for William Ford, Lincoln County: Grant No. 4440, November 14, 1826, 44 acres; No. 5012, January 4, 1827, 50 acres; Nos. 11,666 and 11, 696, December 20, 1832, 47 and 70 acres respectively.

[3] Ford, "Memoirs," I, 8. [4] Tom Lea, *The King Ranch*, I, 429–30.

from the few medical colleges of the day. He soon attracted his first public mention. One of his friends, Wilkins Blanton, was attacked by smallpox. Frontier residents were terror-stricken by the disease, and victims usually were quickly isolated. As a matter of course, Blanton, with a pair of Negro slaves, was sent to a cabin beyond the town limits to stay until he died or recovered. Fully aware of the dangers of the situation, Ford accompanied his friend to the pesthouse, remaining until he had nursed Blanton back to health. The act was noted: "The young pill-peddler got his name in the newspapers."

Assiduous attention to his medical studies did not diminish John Ford's capacity "to fall in love with the girls," as his marriage to Mary Davis reveals. Who she was, or exactly when the marriage took place, cannot now be determined. That they had two children, a son whose name cannot be ascertained, and a daughter, Fannie, is known, as is the fact that the marriage ended, probably through divorce, by early summer of 1836.[5]

A crisis in a series of events in Texas interrupted Ford's budding medical career in the spring of 1836. During the preceding fall and winter, Anglo-American colonists and a few courageous native citizens of that region stoutly had opposed the unconstitutional edicts and actions of the Mexican dictator-president, Antonio López de Santa Anna. News of a skirmish between colonists and Mexican troops on October 2, 1835, electrified citizens of the United States, particularly those of Tennessee. Tennesseeans, crowded by a rapidly swelling population, had emigrated to Texas in large numbers to acquire broad acres and elbow room. Their letters, describing to friends and relatives the Mexico-Texas political situation, aligned the stay-at-homes with the cause of their kinsmen, and dormant sympathy for those resisting tyranny awoke.

As the "winter of defeat and death" for Texas colonists waned into spring, indignation mounted in Tennessee. Among the most vocally indignant was John Salmon Ford, who began recruiting

[5] Frank Hamilton deCordova (Ford's grandson) to the author, September 17, 1958.

Shelbyville men for a volunteer military company to reinforce the beset Texans. News of the establishment of the Republic of Texas and of the Alamo disaster stirred Ford to prepare an ardent public address which, circulated in handbill form, brought in some forty recruits. Ford hoped to be chosen captain of the organization; however, upon hearing of the Texas victory at San Jacinto on April 21, 1836, he withdrew from the company. But "Texas fever" had infected him, and a few weeks later he was on his way west, accompanied by his small daughter, Fannie, whose custody he had been awarded.

While their route to Texas is not recorded, it was probably that most frequently traveled: by post road to Memphis, thence by steamboat down the Mississippi past the Walnut Hills and Natchez to the mouth of Red River. From that junction a boat struggling up the meandering Red would have deposited them at the busy little port of Natchitoches. Then they would have toiled on through the humid June days by one of the roads which ran west by south to the Sabine and the Texas border. Dr. Ford and Fannie crossed the Sabine either by Patterson's Ferry or by the more congested Gaines' Ferry farther south, and in late June came through the broken hills of the Redlands to San Augustine, soon to be "the great legal and political centre of Eastern Texas."[6]

Ford arrived at a time when able-bodied men were welcome, for rumors were prevalent concerning a possible Indian uprising in support of a Mexican threat to reconquer Texas. The eastern counties raised companies and sent them to General Sam Houston at Nacogdoches. Ford, one of William Kimbro's San Augustine company, spent several days in camp. When the Cherokee leaders, Bowles and Big Mush, reassured Houston that their people had only peaceful intentions toward the Texans, the volunteers returned home before the end of June. Young John Ford, barely a month past his twenty-first birthday, then began the medical practice which he was to follow intermittently for the next fifteen or sixteen years.

[6] Oran Milo Roberts, miscellaneous papers, Barker History Center, University of Texas, Austin (hereafter cited as Roberts Papers); Ford, "Memoirs," I, 10.

For a time, Ford was busy ministering to plague-stricken participants in the "Run-away Scrape" whom the panic of Santa Anna's invasion had swept into the San Augustine area, but, with their departure, undoubtedly he must have been relieved when other employment became available. In February, 1838, the government of the Republic opened a land office, where holders of land script, headright certificates, and other claims against the Republic might be satisfied. Richard Hooper, Shelby County surveyor, made Ford his deputy to survey lands comprising the present Harrison County, then attached to Shelby County. Ford and a a small party spent several months at the task, laying out the area where the town of Marshall now stands. The group occasionally camped with the Caddo Indians at their Big Spring village, several miles northwest of the future site of Marshall. Ford was much impressed with the beauty and fertility of the region, thereafter remembering its straight-boled trees on the timbered uplands, the thicket-fringed creeks, and the small but pleasant prairies. He was later to regret that he had not claimed land there for himself, as the basis of a "moderate fortune."

With summer came the Vicente Cordova *pronunciamento* against the Republic. Apprehensive of a Cherokee-Mexican coalition, East Texas again took up arms, and this time Ford turned out with a San Augustine company commanded by Captain H. W. Augustine. Upon the quick dispersal of Cordova's adherents, the troops were demobilized, their experience, judging by Ford's account, having been much that of a picnic-camping trip with just enough flavor of possible danger to make the affair interesting.[7]

During the winter of 1838–39, Ford was in the midst of community affairs. Not only did he teach a boys' class in the newly formed Union Sunday School, but he also busied himself in helping to organize a Thespian Corps, comparable to a modern Little Theater group. For the Corps, which included such jovial spirits as Lycurgus Griffith, Duncan Carrington, W. R. Scurry, W. B. Ochiltree, and Frank Sexton, Ford wrote two plays. His first, "The Stranger in Texas," was a comedy based on the treatment

[7] Ford, "Memoirs," I, 205–208.

at Texan hands of an unprincipled acquirer of headrights from the "States." The community's enthusiastic reception of his effort spurred him to his next production, "The Loafer's Courtship." A large, delighted audience and the favorable comments of W. W. Parker, then editor of the San Augustine *Red-Lander*, increased the young doctor's "vanity to an alarming extent. He imagined the lightning had stricken him, and developed a genius of sublime proportions."[8]

More serious matters preoccupied San Augustine in the summer of 1839. Resentment caused by the proximity of the Cherokee settlements and the fact that Chief Bowles's people had been visited by Mexican emissaries had agitated Texans since the preceding summer. President Mirabeau B. Lamar had declared that the tribe had no legal rights to land in Texas, and the idea of Cherokee removal had been enunciated widely and vehemently by General Thomas J. Rusk. Popular sentiment supported such opinions, particularly because of the regular depredations against isolated frontier families, although the Cherokees steadfastly proclaimed their innocence in these affairs. When Bowles indicated that his people would migrate if compensated for the improvements on their farms, Lamar in turn asserted that if the Cherokees would make no agreement with Mexico, he would urge the Texas Congress to award the Cherokee Nation a liberal settlement. Secretary of War Albert Sidney Johnston was sent at the head of a commission to negotiate a settlement, and the Texas Army, two divisions totaling some nine hundred men, accompanied the commission as a precautionary measure. Bowles, apparently having changed his mind about leaving Texas, employed dilatory tactics in conferring with the commissioners, hoping to gain time for assembling his warriors. Johnston finally recognized the true situation and ordered the army to march against Bowles's town.

John Ford, meanwhile, had again mustered behind William Kimbro, and his company became part of a command sent to neutralize the Shawnees, camped at the Big Spring village. The Texans accomplished their mission by confiscating the locks of

8 *Ibid.*, 199–201.

the Shawnee flintlock rifles, Linney, the Shawnee chief, apparently co-operating willingly in the business. It is doubtful, however, that the Indians complied with the reported alacrity; Ford's private opinion was that the tribe surrendered only the locks from useless weapons after concealing good firearms in the brush.[9] At any rate, the Shawnees made no effort to aid Bowles's villagers, toward whom Kimbro now marched to join the main Texas force.

The San Augustine company arrived at Bowles's village a day too late for the two-day battle of July 15–16, which ended in the death of the chief and most of his warriors and in the expulsion of the Cherokees. Ford gazed admiringly on the dead Bowles, lying as he had fallen, in a small cornfield, while conducting a rear-guard action for his people, and mused that "Under other circumstances history would have classed him among heroes and martyrs." His admiration waned, however, when the young volunteer found in a Cherokee cabin a Bible inscribed with the names of the white family from whom it had been plundered; the discovery was, to Ford, irrefutable evidence of Cherokee complicity in the depredations of the preceding year.

Having gained no particular distinction in Texas military affairs, Ford perhaps felt that her politics might prove more gratifying to his ambitions. In the summer of 1840, he succumbed to political fever, a chronic Texas inflammation, and sought election to the House of Representatives. Of the two seats allotted San Augustine, one went to H. W. Augustine and the other to Sam Houston. Ford, by his own account, polled seventeen votes fewer than Houston, experiencing a defeat which better judgment might have prevented, for Ford carelessly repeated a story that Houston was on a spree in Nashville and would not return by election day. Houston's constituents, according to Ford, had been only mildly active, but, at the slur on their candidate, rallied indignantly to assure him of a place in Congress. It was, apparently, a typical frontier campaign.

[9] Anna Muckleroy, "The Indian Policy of the Republic of Texas," *Southwestern Historical Quarterly*, Vol. XXVI (July, 1922–April, 1923), 147; *Telegraph and Texas Register* (Houston), July 31, 1839; Ford, "Memoirs," II, 212–14.

Grog-shop bullies, cross-road politicians, and self-inflated shysters, aped their respective favorites. The artificers of bad blood, the Jerry Sneaks and the Rausig Sniffles of that day had a glorious time in blustering and making faces at each other. Duels were frequently talked of, but never came off.[10]

During the winter of 1840–41, Ford again turned to surveying, this time along the upper waters of the Trinity River. Severe weather drove his party into shelter at King's Fort, a frontier station at the site of present Kaufman. Their presence was fortuitous for another young surveyor, John H. Reagan, whose party had depleted its rations. Reagan, leaving his men at what is now Wills Point, in northwestern Van Zandt County, had ridden for supplies. Caught in a sudden norther, he was frozen almost into immobility by the time his stumbling horse brought him into King's Fort. He was revived carefully by Ford and his crew, who thus preserved for Texas a future statesman and for the Confederacy a future postmaster-general.[11]

When summer came, Ford again sought election to the House of Representatives. Of San Augustine County's five candidates for the two seats, he polled the fewest votes, his ninety-two being twenty-four less than those of his closest rival. This defeat was convincing; for the next few years John Ford eschewed politics. Possibly to prepare himself for future political activity, he began to read law and was busily pursuing the study, according to Oran M. Roberts, when the latter young attorney reached Texas in 1841.[12] In due time, after examination and recommendation by Thomas Johnson, David S. Kaufman, and William G. Duffield of the East Texas bar, Ford was granted a license to practice.[13] However, there is no evidence to show that he ever followed the profession in a regular sense.

[10] Ford, "Memoirs," II, 213–14.

[11] John H. Reagan, *Memoirs, With Special Reference to Secession and the Civil War* (ed. by Walter Flavius McCaleb), 40–42.

[12] Roberts Papers.

[13] R. B. Blake, "Sketches of Nacogdoches and Citizens Thereof" (unpublished MS, Barker History Center, University of Texas, Austin), II, 153. Pagination according to typescript, Archives Division, Texas State Library, Austin. Hereafter cited as Blake, "Sketches."

For the next several years, most of John Ford's time seems to have been devoted to his medical practice. That patients were numerous may be indicated by his acquiring a partner, one Dr. Lister, and moving from his Main Street office-residence to an office nearer the center of the business district. The partnership dissolved after a year, however, and Dr. Ford again moved his office, this time to a site just opposite the *Red-Lander* plant on Columbia Street. His business card in the newspaper indicates that he was keeping political ambitions in check: "Dr. John S. Ford having determined to devote his entire attention to the practice of his profession will attend promptly to every call he may receive."[14]

Among Ford's patients in the early months of 1844 were Vice-President J. Pinckney Henderson, Samuel and Wade Horton, and Richard Scurry, prominent in public affairs in East Texas and the Republic. Ford's medical journal for the period reveals that he received two dollars each for house calls, on which occasions he frequently left prescriptions for ipecac, calomel, and quinine. One journal entry shows that he was more than a "pill-peddler": a fifty-dollar charge to a certain Mr. Lewis for removing a fragment of bone from the brain of Lewis' son. The charge included post-operative treatment, suggesting a successful operation.[15]

In 1844, the annexation of Texas became the paramount political issue in the presidential campaign in the United States. Texans, a majority of whom desired annexation, seized avidly upon newspapers from the States and scanned the reports of speeches, debates, and public resolutions printed therein, enthusiastically grateful for the Democratic pronouncements on their behalf and lividly resentful of Whig aspersions against the Republic of Texas and her citizens. Ford's indignant reaction to an article of the latter type projected him into the front rank of Texas' vigorous defenders. The offending article described a Whig meeting at Mil-

[14] *Red-Lander* (San Augustine), May 19, July 7, 1842; July 8, 1843. The references indicate that Ford at those times was not, as has often been assumed, in Ranger service with Jack Hays.

[15] Ford Papers, Barker History Center, University of Texas, Austin.

ford, Massachusetts, at which the chairman, Colonel Orison Underwood, had been vituperative toward Texas and the idea of annexation. Ford's reply, in the *Red-Lander* of June 29, assailed Underwood for applying the adjective "infamous" to the Republic, pointing out that the Texas citizens had come from the United States, bringing with them their native customs, laws, and attitudes. Refuting the assertion that Texas rightfully was still Mexican property, Ford alleged that Texans had acquired their country as had the New England colonists, and asked Underwood, "When . . . did the Indians invite the ancestors of the present population of your own state to come and settle at Plymouth?" Incensed by Underwood's reference to Texans as "ruffian adventurers," Ford listed some of the more unsavory types of immigrants who had contributed to the settlement of the original colonies, and posed the question: "If, sir, *we* have 'ruffian adventurers' among us, they come mostly from your own government, and how can *you* refuse to take back your own coin?"

Averring that although Texans had much more to lose than to gain by joining the Union, they were proud of being Americans and wished to see "the proud banner of the brave and the free . . . wave its omnipotent folds over our heads." Ford further demonstrated what the United States would lose by rejecting Texas:

> She will lose a territory as large as that of France. By means of the commercial treaty we are about to set on foot with Great Britain, she will lose the cotton trade—she will lose a market for her cotton fabrics—she will render the Southern States bankrupt—her manufacturing ones she will impoverish. She will lose a river, a desert for a boundary. She will lose command of the Gulf of Mexico and she will sever the Union.

These considerations, Ford believed, were weighty enough to overcome all feeling based on party, prejudice, or section. His closing comments provided the principle which would underlie a long career of public service:

> As chairman of the Milford meeting, you have appeared before the world as the calumniator of my country and its people. I, sir,

have addressed you in the language of vindication, in the tone of a freeman, and have only to regret that the task devolved not upon abler hands. But, sir, when I conceive my country needs my services, such as they are, my motto has ever been—"Ready; aye ready."

Two weeks after his letter appeared in the *Red-Lander*, during which time he had opportunity to judge its effect on the San Augustine electorate, Dr. Ford announced his candidacy for the House of Representatives. He probably had the assurance of potent political support from R. A. Scurry, who had been elected to the House in both 1842 and 1843. Scurry was ill in the summer of 1844 and was served by Ford in the dual capacity of physician and political scribe. At his request, Ford had prepared a public paper embodying Scurry's political views. It is reasonable to believe that Scurry, not a candidate because of his health, exerted his influence in behalf of his personable, ambitious physician-friend. In any event, Ford captured one of the two seats at stake in the triangular contest, polling 238 votes to 206 for Benjamin Rush Wallace and 176 for Henry W. Sublett.[16]

Representative Ford took his seat when the Ninth Congress convened on December 2, 1844, at Washington-on-the-Brazos. Made chairman of the Committee on Retrenchment, he was also placed on committees on Indian Affairs, Education, Finance, and on a special committee to examine the report of the commissioner of the General Land Office. In dealing with Indian affairs, he came, for the first time, in contact with concerns of the western frontier residents, whose interests he was to promote as long as Texas had a frontier problem. To the *Red-Lander*, for which he served as an almost daily correspondent while in the legislature, he explained his support of an appropriations bill for frontier defense, a type of measure little favored by East Texans since their own frontier problem had been solved. The issue of January 25, 1845, revealed what would be a lifelong criterion for his stand: "Protection and allegiance are reciprocal terms. I care not if a man were placed on the banks of the Rio Grande, and the sands were crumbling from beneath his feet, if he claimed to be a citi-

[16] *Red-Lander* (San Augustine), July 29, September 7, 1844.

zen of Texas, and demeaned himself as such, I would go for protecting him."

Ford aligned himself with the Houston minority in the House, joining in a protest against passage of a joint resolution censuring Houston's attempt to remove the public archives from Austin in 1842. However, he worked with those attempting to restore amity among members of the House when, on February 1, 1845, he voted for a resolution to effect the return to Austin of the executive branch and part of the archives.

After Congress adjourned on February 3, 1845, Ford remained in Washington. There he consulted with Andrew J. Donelson, the United States minister who had brought to Texas the resolution for annexation, and with the British and French ministers, Captain Charles Elliott and the Count de Saligny, passing on the views of the Europeans to Texas Vice-President Kenneth L. Anderson. Ford himself determinedly opposed the negotiation of any Anglo-Texan alliance which might jeopardize annexation. Already he had expressed to Judge J. C. Brooks his fear that further agreements not only would result in British ledgers' ruling Texas elections, but also would enable "The veriest scoundrel that ever sported a *red coat* [to] claim consideration because he was one of the far off minion of royalty."[17]

His apprehensions were needless. Texans soon learned that President John Tyler had approved on March 1 a joint resolution of the United States Congress providing for the annexation of Texas. The final decision now lay with Texas. Although Ford and many others believed President Anson Jones to be hostile to annexation, Jones made no effort to thwart public sentiment. He summoned the Ninth Congress into special session on June 16 to express its views on the subject. Ford was promptly at hand when Speaker John M. Lewis called the House to order, and on the next day introduced a joint resolution that Texas accept the offer.[18] Action on the resolution was suspended until the Senate

17 Ford, "Memoirs," II, 337–45, 363–64.
18 *Texas National Register* (Washington), June 19, 1845. Why Ford, rather than a senior congressman, introduced the resolution is not explained, but the

had considered the Preliminary Treaty, providing for the recognition of Texas independence, which Captain Elliott had persuaded Mexican officials to sign on May 19. Submitted to the legislature at the same time as the United States offer of annexation, the treaty was unanimously rejected by the Senate on June 21, and two days later both houses unanimously approved the resolution for annexation. Congress also approved President Jones's call for a convention to act officially on the United States offer. On June 28, the final Congress of the Republic of Texas adjourned, having done all it legally could do toward making annexation a reality.

The convention delegates assembled in Austin, where, on July 4, with only one dissenting vote, they approved the offer of annexation and then began to draft Texas' first state constitution. Ford witnessed the proceedings as a reporter for Washington Miller's *Texas National Register* at Washington-on-the-Brazos. His signed articles, chronicling the work of the delegates and giving his own views on the debated topics, appeared regularly in the *Register*. In the issue of July 24, he praised the proposed community-property provision, which, he wrote, was "imperatively demanded by the circumstances of the times and the liberal spirit of the age." The issue of a fortnight later expressed his strong disapproval of a proposal for the popular election of judges.[19] The convention adjourned on August 28, having prepared a document which Ford characterized as "the work of statesmen."

Immediately thereafter, John Ford returned to Washington. The matter which so promptly took him back to the Brazos is best explained by a *Register* item of October 2, reporting the marriage on September 26 of Dr. John S. Ford and Mrs. Louisa Lewis.[20] When and under what circumstances the two met is not apparent, but the lady's maiden name had been Swisher, so that she was possibly a relative of Ford's friend, Colonel John M. honor probably was to reward his enthusiastic endorsement of the annexation proposition.

[19] *Ibid.*, July 24, August 7, 1845.
[20] *Ibid.*, October 2, 1845. The *Register* incorrectly refers to her as "Miss" Lewis. She was "Mrs." (Marriage Record, Washington County, I, 9).

Swisher. Ford's memoirs, which might be expected to provide the information, are strangely silent on the subject (indeed, they contain no references to either his first or second marriage). Certainly it seems that this second union, destined to be brief, brought Ford the conjugal happiness lacking in his marriage with Mary Davis.

The newlyweds stayed but briefly in Washington, for already John Ford had decided to return to Austin. He correctly foresaw that, despite the town's frontier location and its scanty population (of less than 250), as the capital of a large and potentially powerful state, it would grow, and business ventures, such as one he now had in mind, would prosper. Ford and Michael Cronican, a *Register* printer and former Galveston publisher, had formed a partnership to purchase the newspaper and publish it in Austin. After the issue of October 9 was out, they took possession of the equipment. Ford moved his family to Austin, found quarters for the enterprise, and began to transfer the equipment from Washington. After five weeks of arduous freighting and reassembling, the *Texas National Register*'s next issue (of November 15, 1845) appeared on the streets of the capital with the name of John S. Ford as editor on its masthead.

Austin was then truly a frontier settlement. Only one year earlier, residents had fled indoors when a migrating buffalo herd had invaded the streets. Shortly before the convention met, Indian raiders had killed a girl and stolen a boy. The high palisade around the capitol grounds was a necessity. During a recess of the convention, delegates had been alarmed when a nude Negro on a galloping mule thundered up Congress Avenue shouting, "Ingens, Ingens!" in what Ford described as a "kind of 'hark from the tombs' intonation . . . , calculated to disturb the nerves of weak-kneed gents and hysterical old ladies."

> There was a gathering of the clans. A motley crowd it was, numbering about one hundred. . . . With bold front and manly strides they moved upon the foe at the mouth of Shoal Creek. A few had guns; some flourished pistols; others had no visible means of shedding blood. Ex-President Lamar was one of the warriors bold. He was asked "Men where are your arms?"—"In my pocket"

was the prompt reply. . . . When we pranced up to the ford of the Colorado, in real warhorse style, not a single red devil dared to show his dirty face. We felt sure they had seen our terrible array, and had stampeded like so many mustangs. . . .

A party of fishermen were sighted on the opposite bank, just above the ford. They excited no little contempt and disgust in our martial breasts by asserting that, "some negroes and white boys had been bathing in the river; and [the Negro] had mistaken the laughter of the crowd for the Indian war-whoop, hence the alarm."

Editor Ford, from the door of his Congress Avenue office, occasionally heard the howling of wolves and the yelping cries of Indians within the town limits. Shortly after the Fords' arrival, "Old Guard" citizen Louis Horst narrowly escaped capture on his way downtown to market. Lipans, Delawares, and Tonkawas camped near the town late in 1845, their conduct finally eliciting editorial complaint against drunken, thieving savages.[21]

If Austin residents experienced the hazards of frontier life, they also enjoyed its pastimes. The society in which the Fords moved amused itself with dancing parties, horse races (for which John Ford seems to have had an affinity), turkey and beef shoots, cockfights, and occasionally a jack-rabbit hunt after the manner of the British fox hunt—shouting riders galloping on the heels of yelping dogs over the low hills along the Colorado. With the stationing in Austin, in 1846, of a United States Army detachment, additional entertainment was provided: periodic concerts by a military band.

The *Register* was received coolly in Austin. Any pro-Houston journal would have been extended a like welcome from a population still vindictive toward the president who had stubbornly opposed Austin as the seat of government, who further had refused to provide frontier protection, and who had precipitated the "Archives War" through his efforts to remove the public archives from a locality unprotected because of his own prejudice. Thus, when the *Register* appeared under the management of a

[21] Ford, "Memoirs," II, 389–90, 400a; *Texas National Register* (Austin), issues during November, 1845, and that of January 10, 1846.

Houston partisan, there was talk of throwing the press and type into the Colorado River, a suggestion which, Ford commented, "met with no encouragement." But Ford's "amiable deportment" and the fact that he had publicly supported the proposal to return the government to Austin, soon overcame the initial hostility. When his father, William Ford, arrived in Austin in the late fall of 1845, having sold his Tennessee holdings after his wife's death, he found his editor son the one member of the community who was "known to everyone."[22]

The expense of the move and the regular costs of operation left the *Register* partners with little money. Ford explained the paper's predicament in a characteristically styled plea to delinquent subscribers:

> Those in arrears for subscriptions will not, we hope take it amiss at being reminded of the long period of indulgence they have enjoyed, and that every instance in which a number was forwarded without having previously received pay, was in violation of the terms "always in advance."

We were disposed to accommodate our friends, our turn has come. We have been at considerable trouble and much expense, in transporting the establishment to this place. It took money to do it. Before long we shall want paper; money alone can procure it. The printers are growing proud, the beasts! they must have money and won't work without it. The fact is, though it shocks our modesty greatly to own it, we want money ourselves, not that we love it, or anything so, but just to rattle—we have grown tired of the jingle of rusty nails, they soil our pockets—and their music is not half so sweet as the dulcet sound of the *dimes*. Certain venders of goods, wares, and merchandize, have looked at us significantly, as much as to say, "stand and deliver." How can we without delinquent subscribers will "come to the rescue?" We adjure them in the name of all that is merciful, kind and obliging, with the fear of "shocking

22 Ed Burleson, miscellaneous papers, Barker History Center, University of Texas, Austin. Hereafter cited as Burleson Papers. The item cited is a list drawn up by Frank Brown, showing the principal Austin residents when the Brown family arrived in the capital on February 10, 1846. After each name appears the year in which the individual came to Austin and some identifying phrase. The notation concerning Ford reads: "John S. Ford, Known to everyone."

bad hats," sleeveless coats, and soleless boots before our expectant eyes, we implore them to *fork over*, forthwith if not sooner.

The plea apparently brought no immediate response, for less than a month later another appeal was made in much more succinct language.[23]

On January 3, 1846, subscribers learned that when the current volume of the *Texas National Register* expired, the journal would become the *Texas Democrat*. The change accorded with Ford's avowed principles of the previous October, when he had stated that since he had been in full agreement with the Democratic party of the United States on the question of Texas annexation, he intended to support the party principles in his editorial columns. The first issue of the *Democrat* came out on January 17, from its new location above the post office in the building occupied by F. Dieterich's store. Regardless of title, the paper now was a feature of Austin life. There were events in plenty to fill its columns, for, in addition to accounts of Indian depredations and the local items so dear to the hearts of small-town citizens, the activities of the legislature drew the attention of the *Democrat's* subscribers. So bountiful a source of news was the lawmaking business that, on March 7, the *Democrat* announced a change to semi-weekly publication "to keep up with the proceedings of the legislature and take advantage of each mail leaving."

Ford's political connections brought benefits to the *Texas Democrat* in the spring of 1846. The legislature, by the narrow margin of forty-one votes to forty, on April 13 elected Ford and Cronican to be the official state printers, in preference to their competitor, former Secretary of State John G. Chalmers, publisher of the *New Era*. The subsequent contract for printing placed the *Democrat* on a sound financial basis for at least the next two years. More indicative of Ford's political prominence was a development which came two weeks later. On the evening of April 27, certain members of the legislature met to organize the Democratic party in Texas and named the editor to the state

[23] *Texas National Register* (Austin), November 22, December 17, 1845.

central committee, along with ten other men, including H. G. Runnels, R. M. Williamson, T. J. Chambers, and Thomas H. Duval.[24]

John S. Ford was now in a happy situation. He was liked and respected by the members of his chosen community, prominent in their affairs, the spokesman for a thriving business, signally honored by the politically eminent of his state, and head of a happy household, wherein for the first time in her memory Fannie Ford knew normal family life. Soon, however, came the first circumstance of a series which was to cast John Ford into the role in which he is best remembered—that of a frontier fighting man. About the first of June, Louisa Ford fell ill.[25] Neither Ford's own medical skill nor that of fellow Austin physicians was adequate for the crisis. Although Ford ignored his editorial duties and faithfully nursed his wife during the humid Austin summer, she died on August 5, 1846, and was buried in what is now designated as Section 1, Old Grounds, Oakwood Cemetery, in Austin.[26]

Accompanied by his grieving daughter, John Ford rode home from the funeral with the bearing of one who "has had the besom of destruction pass over his domestic hearth."[27] Determined to dispel by activity the gloom in which his bereavement immersed him, he looked about for affairs to divert his thoughts. Nor had he far to search. On May 12, the United States Congress had announced a state of war between the nation and Mexico. Texas troopers already had fought along the border and likely would fight again. Herein lay the distraction Ford sought. His decision to add to his previous medical, political, and editorial experiences those of arms launched him, at the age of thirty-one, on a career in which he was to gain his most notable successes—which thereafter would influence Texans, on many occasions, to seek him out when crises required leadership of prudence and attested courage.

---

24 *Texas Democrat* (Austin), April 15, May 6, 1846.

25 *Ibid.*, May 27, 1846. The reference is to Ford's absence from his office. The June 10 issue states: "The editor is still absent on account of sickness in his family."

26 Sexton's Records, Oakwood Cemetery, Austin.

27 Ford, "Memoirs," II, 395–96.

In September, Ford went to San Antonio, visiting there the camp of those Texas Rangers who had been discharged after serving under General Zachary Taylor on the Monterrey line. Ford found them without pay or medical attention, and his prolonged absence from the *Democrat* office may have resulted from his employing his medical knowledge as well as his pen on their behalf.[28] By November he had returned to the capital, but early in 1847, when there arose a military situation calling for the special talents of the Rangers, it was with those case-hardened riders that John Ford cast his lot.

[28] *Texas Democrat* (Austin), September 16, 1846.

2

"Los Diablos Tejanos"

GENERAL TAYLOR'S NEED for Rangers was indisputably impera-
tive. After he had discharged most of them in the fall of 1846,
his rear echelons fell under devastating, incessant guerrilla attack.
Colonel Samuel R. Curtis, commanding Taylor's line of supply
between the Río Grande and Monterrey in March, 1847, appealed
to both the War Department and the state of Texas for mounted
troops to guard the line. In answer to the "Curtis call," as it became
known, Colonel John C. (Jack) Hays during April and May recruited a regiment of six months' volunteers to provide the service.[1]
Thus arose John S. Ford's opportunity. After finding a haven for
Fannie (probably with his father), he rode south toward San
Antonio and Hays's muster. On May 10, 1847, Editor Ford became Private Ford in Captain Samuel Highsmith's company of
Texas Mounted Volunteers.[2]

Four days later, Hays's men marched for the Río Grande. About
the time they left San Antonio, however, General Taylor decided
not to accept any troops enlisted for less than twelve months.
At the Nueces River, the volunteers met a courier from Taylor,
bearing orders for the command to return and muster out all men
unwilling to serve for at least a year. Not included under the order

[1] *Mexican War Correspondence: Message of the President of the United States,
and the Correspondence, therewith communicated, between the Secretary of War
and other officers of the government upon the subject of the Mexican War,*
1145. Hereafter cited as *Mexican War Correspondence.*

[2] Records Group No. 94, Old Army Records Section, National Archives,
Washington, D. C. Hereafter cited as Records Group No. 94.

were four Ranger companies commanded by Major Michael Chevaille and one led by Captain Henry W. Baylor, retained by Taylor after the Monterrey campaign.

But Ford's anticipation of active campaigning was not to be
thus ingloriously dispelled. Acting under War Department authority granted during the winter, Hays began recruiting a regiment for twelve months' service on the Indian frontier. The regiment filled rapidly, many of the Rangers having remained in and
around San Antonio after their previous discharge, and on July 7,
Ford was promoted to a lieutenancy and transferred to Hays's
headquarters staff as regimental adjutant.[3] Three days later, final
enlistments were accepted, and the regiment was mustered into
federal service for twelve months or the duration of the war,
whichever should be the shorter.

During the preceding weeks, Hays not only had been placed in
command of Texas frontier defense, but also, almost immediately
thereafter, had received orders from Secretary of War W. L.
Marcy to take what Rangers could be spared from the frontier
and proceed immediately to join Taylor. To remedy the miserable
frontier situation which had developed under an incompetent predecessor (Captain M. S. Howe), Hays by early August had sent
to the frontier, under command of Lieutenant Colonel Peter H.
Bell, the companies of Captains Middleton T. Johnson, James S.
Gillette, Shapley P. Ross, Henry W. Baylor, and Samuel Highsmith.[4] Ford probably was thankful for his transfer from Highsmith's company, for now he would participate in operations in
Mexico.

On August 12, Hays and five companies left for the Río
Grande, to be followed later by the company of Captain Jacob
Roberts, then resting its mounts after an arduous journey from
the frontier. Hays fully expected to be assigned the task of protecting Taylor's line of communication from the nuisance raids
of José Urrea, Antonio Canales, and other Mexican partisan commanders. Even before the regiment marched from San Antonio,

[3] *Ibid.*
[4] Ford, "Memoirs," III, 403.

however, its destiny had been altered by President James K. Polk.

Conditions along Major General Winfield Scott's line of advance from Vera Cruz to Mexico City had so deteriorated because of guerrilla operations that Scott, unable to defend his rearward stations, proposed to abandon them. Distressed by Scott's decision, Polk himself, after a week of deliberation, provided the solution. He would send Hays, with whom he was personally acquainted and for whose ability he had high regard, to clear the Vera Cruz–Mexico City line for Scott, and, on July 16, he ordered Secretary Marcy to inform Hays and Taylor of the decision.[5] The orders, forwarded via Governor J. Pinckney Henderson of Texas, caught up with Hays at Mier, on the Mexican bank of the Río Grande, where he had halted to await Roberts' company.

The march to Mier revealed among the Rangers a few malcontents whose warlike fervor waned in proportion to the distance from their homes. Instead of suffering silently, "They played 'Home, Sweet Home' on a harp of a thousand strings, and they had listeners." From the dangers of war, they passed on to the paucity of their rations. To these men Captain Alfred M. Truett spoke in blunt but illuminating terms. Private John Glanton, with equally terse language employed on his own initiative and stimulated by liberal quantities of Río Grande "bust-head" whisky, supported Truett sharply enough to send the ringleaders slinking away. The several archobjectors were quickly discharged at Mier and sent packing for Texas, a farewell blast from Truett ringing in their ears.

From Mier, about the middle of September, the Rangers marched downstream to the tiny station of Ranchita, where they camped to await transportation to Vera Cruz. At Ranchita, Colonel Hays detailed an advance party to proceed to Vera Cruz to prepare a regimental camp site. About two weeks later, Adjutant Ford, with Captains Truett, Roberts, and septuagenarian Isaac Ferguson and their companies, boarded a southbound transport at Brazos Santiago. The voyage was eventful. An Irish seaman took

5 James K. Polk, *The Diary of James K. Polk* (ed. by M. M. Quaife), III, 89.

it upon himself to make the trip unpleasant for the Rangers. After a disappointing experience in attempting to appropriate Ford's quarters, he transferred his attentions below decks to the Rangers and their mounts. There he likewise suffered disaster. At San Antonio, Ford had been assigned a perverse beast called "Old Higgins." The steed had been a consistent winner in East Texas races and had proved himself sturdy in the Monterrey campaign, but he was as treacherous as he was speedy. One day roars of laughter from the hold penetrated the misery of seasickness which engulfed Ford. Soon a Ranger came up to explain. The Irishman had been meddling among the horses. "He came in reach of Old Higgins, and the old scoundrel pitched at him, open-mouthed. He took Paddy's ear off as clean as it could have been done by a pair of shears; then chewed it up and swallowed it. He looked all the time like the devilment pleased him."[6]

Major General Robert Patterson, commanding at Vera Cruz, assigned the Ranger advance party to a bivouac area at Vergara, several miles north of the city on the Jalapa road, where a Massachusetts regiment of Brigadier General Caleb Cushing's brigade lay. The area was relatively healthy but damp and open to winds, which annoyed both the Bay State troops and the Texans.[7] Here the Rangers marked off a regimental camping area across the road from the Massachusetts bivouac, mounted a guard, and established regular camp routine. Before the other companies arrived, the advance units found an opportunity to show their New England neighbors how the Ranger reputation had been won.

General Patterson complained to the Ranger officers of the continual raiding outside Vera Cruz by Mexican partisan bands, notably that of a Colonel Zenobia operating from the hacienda of San Juan, some thirty miles from the city. The General believed that even the Rangers could not campaign successfully against Zenobia in the almost impenetrable jungle growth. The Texans immediately requested permission to attempt a reconnaissance.

[6] Ford, "Memoirs," III, 409–10. This is the same Glanton whose scalp-hunting activities aroused furor on both sides of the Río Grande after the war.

[7] Claude M. Fuess, *The Life of Caleb Cushing*, II, 55. Hereafter cited as Fuess, *Cushing*; Ford, "Memoirs," III, 410.

Patterson acquiesced, promising them a guide. When the guide failed to appear at the designated predawn starting time, the Rangers marched out, following verbal directions given them the night before. Ford led the column, made up of the picked men of the advance party.

After a ride of about twenty-five miles along dim trails overgrown by vines and foliage, Ford suddenly saw guerrillas ahead and, without warning his column, spurred for the enemy. A following Ranger glimpsed the Mexicans and fired his rifle at them just as "Old Higgins" stepped in a mudhole, turning a somersault and plunging the impetuous adjutant beneath him in the mire. The Rangers, convinced that Ford had been shot accidentally, pulled up, heaping curses on their innocent and bewildered comrade. Ford arose dripping, his pistol useless because of its dampened percussion cap, and quickly remounted to continue the pursuit. Several guerrillas were shot down as the two parties raced across a small clearing in which a rude hut stood. Hard on the heels of one guerrilla rode Ford, with one hand snapping his useless pistol and the other brandishing a saber. The fleeing Mexican abandoned his horse and dived into the hut. Ford jumped from his mount and pursued hotly, but found only a solitary woman ("good looking," he noted) standing in the middle of the floor. Outside again, the adjutant circled the hunt a time or two, but no enemy appeared. The frustrated Ranger remounted and rode after his party, feeling, as he put it, "very like a fellow who had peeped through a crack, and saw his rival playing yum-yum with the gal of his heart."

A short gallop brought the Rangers to Zenobia's headquarters, a large, marble-floored, finely furnished hacienda. After a brisk fight, during which several Mexicans were killed and the remainder put to flight, the patrol inspected the residence, finding bloodstained garments, forage sacks, and other American articles. To make the place useless as a guerrilla rendezvous, the Texans ordered the family outside and fired the building.

From San Juan the Rangers returned by a circuitous route to Vergara, skirmishing on the way. They reported to General Patterson at sunset, after a reconnaissance of sixty miles. At their arrival the General was inspecting a regiment drawn up for a review. One can imagine the impression made by the casually clad patrol as it cantered by, one of its members wearing with distinction the uniform and hat of a fallen enemy, reputed to have been a general officer.[8]

Colonel Hays and the last of the regiment arrived at Vera Cruz on October 17, accompanied by Major Michael H. Chevaille, a favorite Ranger officer who had resigned his command with Taylor to ride with Hays as quartermaster. Within ten days the Texans were introduced to the weapon which thenceforward was to be associated with Texas Rangers—the Colt six-shooter. Hays and a few others had used the earlier five-shot revolver against Indians, but to most of the Rangers the heavy Colts were mysterious mechanisms which required explaining. Some pistols exploded after their owners crowded the conical bullets in backward; others, when powder was spilled around the cylinder in reloading, discharged their six shots all at once. On one occasion Ford, passing a Ranger's tent, saw a recruit busily cleaning a fully loaded pistol which still retained the percussion caps on the cylinder. Ford paused long enough to suggest removal of the caps, to which the "greeny" assented. However, barely had the adjutant walked away when a shot cracked in the tent, and Ford turned to find that "Greeny had shot his own horse in the head, and put himself a-foot."

Since Hays was the only field-grade officer with the regiment, he ordered an election to provide a major to be second in command. Captains Truett and Gabriel Armstrong and Sergeant Major Gilbert Brush, a former Mier prisoner, were the candidates. The position went to Truett, a firm, just, courageous man, both loved and feared by the Texans. Since the regiment did not inconvenience itself with all of the usages of Regular Army discipline, Truett, when accused of relying over-heavily upon his rank, waived his privileges and invited his critics to meet him man to man. The critics "changed base instanter."

[8] Ford, "Memoirs," III, 410–13.

Constantly General Patterson called on the Rangers to retaliate against guerrilla raids around the city. On one such occasion, Hays ordered out the company of Captain Jacob Roberts to pursue a band which had killed four Ohio volunteers outside Vera Cruz. Roberts overtook and defeated the raiders and returned the next day. He was handier with pistol than with pen; when it came time for him to submit his written report to the Colonel, he called on Ford for help. In relating his account, Roberts numbered the enemy dead at five. His demeanor stirred the adjutant's curiosity. "Look here, Jake," he demanded, "I want the truth, how many did you kill?"

"Not more than twenty-five," came the prompt admission.[9]

Ford was not surprised. The regiment included a few men, who, like Brush, had been captured at Mier; others had been Santa Fe prisoners; and there were several, including young Lewin Rogers, with personal scores to settle. Some years earlier the Rogers family, except for Lewin, had been captured by Woll's retreating forces north of Brownsville. Father, mother, sister, and brother had their throats cut, only the brother surviving. Obviously not all Rangers had enlisted for the sheer love of adventure.

As adjutant, Ford's place was at the headquarters tent; only when the entire command took the field did he have an opportunity to see action. Possibly, then, he was the prime mover behind the activation of a spy company, a detachment of fifty Rangers carefully selected from among the regiment's six companies. Organized at Vergara, the company elected Ford captain and John Glanton lieutenant. The unit operated independently of ordinary routine; instead of pursuing guerrilla raiders after they struck, it went in search of them and, when the regiment moved, rode ahead as scouts. His election by the picked men of a regiment admittedly unequaled as partisan cavalry was a high tribute to John S. Ford's ability and leadership. Good Rangers usually were particular where their officers were concerned.

Among Ford's attributes was a sense of fairness. On one occasion it was to save his life. Patterson had sent the regiment to at-

[9] *Ibid.*, 414–17, 421.

tack a Mexican detachment reported to be encamped near the town of Antigua, about twenty-five miles northwest of Vera Cruz on the Antigua River and about eight miles inland from the Gulf of Mexico. Following the spy company, the Rangers moved up the coast to the mouth of the river, where the scouts dispersed an enemy outpost. The column halted at the town, and Hays ordered Ford to conduct a reconnaissance of the opposite bank, from which a Mexican lancer carefully watched them. The adjutant and fifteen Rangers navigated the crossing in a vessel designed for no more than eight persons.

On the farther shore, Ford's patrol encountered a Spanish-speaking Negro whom the Rangers, believing him to conceal a knowledge of English, talked of killing. Realizing that the Negro had probably been born in the region and perhaps had never before heard English spoken, the adjutant persuaded his men to leave the countryman unmolested and to search for the guerrillas. Exhausted by illness, Ford lay down near the river bank to wait for the men to report. Unintentionally he fell asleep. When he awoke, he was alone except for the Negro, and a prey for any Mexican partisan who might discover him. Ford immediately informed the Negro of his desire to cross the Antigua. The Negro promptly summoned a Mexican, ordered him to row Ford across, and saw the Ranger depart in safety.[10]

Ford's memoirs make no mention of the nature of the occasionally recurring illness which at times kept him from duty. The troops in Mexico suffered from measles, mumps, smallpox, and the various tropical diseases of the *tierra caliente*—the hot, coastal lowlands. The prime scourge was the black vomit, the *vómito*, which most soldiers believed to be yellow fever, although some held it to be a type of disease unidentified by Western medicine.[11] Ford, a practicing physician himself, hardly would have hesitated to comment on his good fortune had he survived that particular affliction. From the recurrent nature of the illness and the fact

[10] *Ibid.*, 419–21.

[11] John R. Kenly, *Memoirs of a Maryland Volunteer: War with Mexico, in the years 1846–7–8*, 293–94n. Hereafter cited as Kenly, *Memoirs*.

that the attacks did not always keep him from his duties, it is possible that he may have been infected with malaria. At least, the successive chills and fever he experienced would so suggest.

Since they were on a constant alert, the scouts were exempt from routine duties in their respective companies. Only one company commander, Captain Gabriel Armstrong, one of the defeated candidates for major, objected to a portion of his command being placed on special duty, but to insure harmony, Colonel Hays deactivated the spy company before leaving Vergara. Armstrong, Ford felt, was not the best type of Ranger officer.[12]

General Scott, in Mexico City since September 13, now anticipated a need for reinforcements. Late in October he ordered General Patterson to march for the capital with all troops not needed to maintain a garrison at the port. The Rangers were now at full regimental strength, about 580 rank and file, having recruited a number of non-Texans. On November 2, as the long column of troops swung past Vergara, the Rangers joined it and set out for Mexico City, more than 260 tortuous miles away.

Northwest through arid, sandy country speckled with scrub growth which provided excellent cover for guerrillas, the Rangers marched with the men from the older states. Hays sent Ford and Chevaille, both ill and irritable, to the rear to prevent straggling. There they found Captain Armstrong and several companions from other units lagging about one hundred yards behind the troops. Armstrong shrugged off Hays's order to close up with the comment that he had placed a lieutenant in command of his company. In the late afternoon, as he and his cronies continued to tag the column, both Ford and Chevaille growled the hope that guerrillas would teach the stragglers a lesson. Hardly had they expressed the wish when partisan muskets banged in the chaparral and the laggards rushed headlong to the safety of the column.[13]

The Rangers camped on the third night under the high arches of the National Bridge, some thirty miles above Vera Cruz. At dusk, Ford sought to relieve a fever by bathing in the Río Antigua beneath the bridge. As he splashed, he became aware of a little

12 Ford, "Memoirs," III, 423.   13 *Ibid.*, 423–24.

man sitting a big horse in the midst of the Ranger mess equipment. Dissatisfied with the reticent replies to his many questions, the small fellow profanely announced that he was the wagon master and assured Ford that "if you get sick, I'll see you in hell before you shall ride in one of my wagons! Whose camp is this any how?" When Ford rejoined, "It is Col. Hays'," the wagon master used "whip and spur to get out of it."[14]

While Patterson's column was nearing the National Bridge, a situation was developing there which was to affect most of the subsequent Ranger operations. On November 3, a Mexican woman had asked to see the camp commander, Lieutenant Colonel George W. Hughes of the District of Columbia and Maryland Volunteer Regiment, garrisoning the site. She informed Hughes and his second in command, Major John R. Kenly, that two guerrilla officers wished to confer under a flag of truce and were concerned lest they not be permitted to depart. Hughes assured her that they need not hesitate, and that afternoon two Europeans, uniformed as Mexican officers, entered under the flag. They were lieutenants of Padre Jarauta, a priest turned partisan leader, who was the most irritating thorn in the side of Scott's Vera Cruz–Mexico City line. Jarauta had sent them to say that the guerrillas would cease operations if there would be no reprisals. Although the American officers had no authority to treat with guerrillas, they saw an opportunity to solve a difficult problem and felt that Scott would approve their negotiations. The two partisans returned the next afternoon to report that Jarauta had agreed to suspend hostilities, subject to Scott's disposition. While Hughes and Kenly talked with the partisans, Patterson rode in with the Vera Cruz column. Colonel Hughes quickly explained to the General the subject of the conference. Patterson summarily ended negotiations thus: "Tell them that if I catch Jarauta I will hang him to the highest tree in the Tierra Caliente." The guerrilla officers left hurriedly, as did Jarauta, who had been just outside the lines waiting to enter.[15] By his words, General Patterson uncon-

14 *Ibid.*, 424.
15 Kenly, *Memoirs*, 328–32.

sciously provided the Rangers with six months' hard riding; Jarauta was to be the protagonist in the dramatic exploits of Hays's men while they remained in Mexico.

On the following morning the Rangers, leading Patterson's troops, left the towering *Puenta Nacional* behind them and took the hilly road forward. A march of about thirteen miles brought them to the village of Plan del Río, where the Texans were greeted with three rousing cheers from the encamped First Pennsylvania volunteer infantry, impressed by the "fine body of men." Plan del Río lay at the edge of the *tierrra caliente* fever belt,[16] and it probably was with great relief that the Rangers marched out for the climb to the temperate plateau.

Hays's men led the advance from Plan del Río, marching over a difficult road which rose steadily toward the watershed near Jalapa. At noon on Sunday, November 7, the Rangers entered the city, a lovely municipality of some eight thousand citizens, and went into camp two miles beyond on the Puebla road. Hays pressed on for Puebla with the companies of Roberts and Armstrong, leaving the remaining companies in camp under Major Truett, who was slightly ill. Adjutant Ford, still not fully recovered, likewise stayed behind, as did the competent Major "Mike" Chevaille. While Hays probably divided the command to provide scouts for the troops which were to march later for the capital, illness among his company commanders may have caused him to leave behind the units of Captains Ferguson, Chaucer Ashton, and Preston Witt. Both Ashton and Ferguson were to succumb to illness in the City of Mexico, Ashton on December 14, and Ferguson on New Year's Day, 1848.[17]

After the enervating heat of the coastal plain, fragrant Jalapa, in a region of perpetual spring, was a veritable Eden to the troops.

---

[16] Justin H. Smith, *The War with Mexico*, II, 42. Hereafter cited as Smith, *War with Mexico*.

[17] Ford, "Memoirs," III, 401. Ford gives no cause for either death, but the combination of arduous marches, advanced age, and possible illness could account for Ferguson's demise. Ephraim M. Daggett succeeded Ferguson as company commander. Alexander E. Handley took over Ashton's company, originally Truett's.

Over the clean, prosperous-looking city hung the scent of countless varieties of flowers, and beyond Jalapa's limits white haciendas gleamed above the orderly ranks of orange groves which provided a pleasant shade for weary, duty-free soldiers. Even in mid-November the days were agreeably warm, although men fortunate enough to have blankets were envied when night fell. Except for the high humidity of the region, the Texans hardly could have found a better place to recruit their health.

But for those Rangers fit for duty Jalapa was not a station for extended relaxation. There, as elsewhere along the sinuous supply line, Jarauta, Zenobia, and other lesser-known partisans were busy. Colonel F. M. Wynkoop of the First Pennsylvania, to whom Hays's rear echelon was assigned temporarily, found work for the Texans. On the night of November 19, he called out Witt's company and in a surprise strike at the partisan village of Jalcomulco, some thirty miles distant, captured several guerrilla officers, including two who were parole violators.[18] Operations of this sort brought the Texans the plaudits of both the military and the civilians, the latter being thoroughly tired of war and of being preyed upon by partisan bands not always motivated sheerly by patriotism. Occasionally, however, Ranger discipline lapsed. While at Jalapa, two Rangers were tried by military court for stealing money and blankets from citizens.[19]

The column tramped out for Puebla on November 24. The diary of the young Pennsylvania Dutch corporal, Jacob Oswandel, recounts the march in some detail. After a short advance, the

[18] John S. Jenkins, *History of the War between the United States and Mexico, from the commencement of hostilities to the ratification of the treaty of peace*, 473–74. Hereafter cited as Jenkins, *U. S. and Mexico*. The parole violators were hanged on the day Hays's rear echelon left Jalapa. Jenkins gives the month as October, an obvious error since none of the Rangers left Vera Cruz before November 2. Witt had become a company commander upon the resignation of Stephen Kinsey in October. Ford, "Memoirs," III, 401.

[19] J. Jacob Oswandel, *Notes on the Mexican War 1846–47–48*, 388. Hereafter cited as Oswandel, *Notes*. These men may have been recruits added at Vera Cruz, rather than native Texans, for Ford wrote, "They [the Texans] . . . loathed petty thievery. . . . Their rule was to pay for any thing to eat or wear. The men of Hays' regiment loved Texas, and they would do nothing to bring dishonor upon their State or themselves." Ford, "Memoirs," III, 418.

force camped at La Hoya, several thousand feet above the Jalapa slopes. During the night the troops huddled about fires and at daybreak set out on a long day's journey through rain, hail, and snow across the bleak uplands stretching toward the continental divide. Dusk found them at the hamlet of Cruz Blanca, a few miles above Las Vigas. By two o'clock on the next afternoon, November 26, the command had encamped at the village of Perote, below the castle so well remembered by some of the Texans. Hard marching, undulating roads, and bitter weather had taxed the troops and they lay two days at Perote. The movement was resumed on the morning of November 29, and the Rangers and Pennsylvanians put some thirty rough miles behind them before bivouacking at Tepeyahualco on the marshy shore of Laguna del Alchichica. On the next day, with the peak of Orizaba shrinking slowly to the rear, the volunteers passed Ojo de Agua and in mid-afternoon halted to camp amid the huge oaks and towering pines around El Pinal.

Thick dusk had fallen when word came to camp that guerrillas were butchering American stragglers back at Tepeyahualco. Wynkoop sent a Ranger company galloping toward the village with orders to show no mercy. In about two hours the Rangers returned. They had killed two partisans, captured two unarmed but suspected natives, and had brought with them, lashed across the back of a baggage mule, two dead Pennsylvania infantrymen, their throats cut. Corporal Oswandel thought it "one of the seven wonders" that the Texans actually brought in prisoners, since they had the reputation for shooting suspected Mexicans on the spot.

The column left El Pinal village on the morning of December 2, following the climbing road past the forests of giant pines to El Pinal pass, an admirable place for an ambush. Probably because the Rangers scouted ahead, no attack delayed the command, and, winding down to the high tableland, it entered the final stage of the journey. That night the troops slept at the settlement of Amozoc and the next day they came to Puebla, where Hays's regiment was reunited.[20]

20 Oswandel, *Notes*, 397–401.

Truett's companies now learned that the advance group had participated in an excursion which gained wide notice for the Texans. At Puebla, Hays had been attached to the brigade of General Joseph Lane of Indiana, and a friendship quickly sprang up between the two commanders. Lane, with a spirit restless enough to qualify him as a Ranger, in late November eagerly grasped an opportunity to meet the Mexicans.

On the evening of November 22, Lane left Puebla for Matamoros de Izúcar, with Hays's Rangers, a Louisiana dragoon company, and a field gun. His mission was to liberate American prisoners reported to be confined there and to destroy military stores supplying Mexican operations. After marching fifty-four miles in twelve hours through a driving rain, Lane's command charged the town at dawn. The demoralized Mexicans fled quickly, losing more than sixty men and leaving behind twenty-three American captives. The only American casualties were three artillerymen, wounded later in the day while destroying enemy munitions.

Early on the twenty-fourth, behind "Jake" Roberts' advance patrol, Lane began his return march, trailed by three captured Mexican guns, his own fieldpiece, and four wagonloads of arms drawn by small Mexican mules. At the long, winding pass of Galaxra, about five miles above Matamoros, a Mexican lancer attack drove in the scouts. Hays spurred to take command of the advance guard and, joined by Lane and his staff, launched a countercharge, the thirty-five Americans repulsing and pursuing some two hundred lancers. Lane returned to the main body while Hays closed on the Mexican cavalry, chasing it over the summit of a small mountain. When Hays's party galloped across the crest, they came face to face with the Mexican reserve, five hundred lancers commanded by a Colonel Rea, one of the largest organized Mexican forces still in the field. Their weapons empty, the Rangers retreated hastily, but in good order, before Rea's charge. Hays, who still had a few rounds in his Colts, carried out a lone rear-guard action, pistoling two lancers and by his accuracy discouraging the enemy from pressing the assault. Lane, seeing the Mexican reserve appear, forced the lancers back to the mountains with a few rounds of canister and grapeshot. Small enemy detachments, however, prudently remaining out of range, shadowed Lane's flanks for several hours. After halting overnight on the road, the Americans arrived in Puebla early in the afternoon of November 25.

Lane profusely praised his own men, but reserved his superlatives for Colonel Hays. Roberts' conduct was also mentioned. His horse was killed in the charge, and, Lane reported, "He exhibited great presence of mind in making his escape." John Glanton, Ford's lieutenant in the short-lived spy company, "attracted general notice for his extraordinary activity and daring throughout the actions both of the twenty-third and twenty-fourth."[21] A streak of sadness, however, tempered the elation of Hays's men. Of Lane's two dead, one was Private Malpass of Roberts' company, shot down in the front rank of the Ranger charge.[22]

The entire regiment heard with approval Lane's official report, but on the night of December 3 the late arrivals listened to their more fortunate comrades humorously drawl the tales too unimportant for official notice. They laughed immoderately over the attempt of a Matamoros citizen to claim as his own the mount of Chaplain Samuel H. Corley, a horse known throughout Texas as an irascible, extroverted beast, and at the preacher's intention to fight before parting with the steed. They learned with interest that "Jake" Roberts' "presence of mind" lay in his seizing the stirrup strap of George White, who had returned to aid him, and of the Captain's bounding beside White's galloping animal until he had acquired sufficient momentum to leap up behind the rider. They heard how Lane had attempted to lighten his bogged wagons by ordering the captured *escopetas* (muskets) thrown out and burned, and how the muskets, being loaded, began to explode as

[21] 30 Cong., 2 sess., *House Exec. Doc. 1*, 86–89. Sometime after 1880, Captain Robert Evans wrote that Lane's command marched through the rain until midnight, when it halted at Atlixco. Ford, "Memoirs," III, 428. Evans probably commanded Armstrong's men, since the latter, after his defeat in the election for major, had been sullen about performing duty. Hays delayed taking action, probably hoping the situation would remedy itself. It did when Armstrong resigned at Mexico City and Evans got the company.

[22] Reported by Lane as "Walpas."

John Salmon ("Rip") Ford, Texian
—in everything the word implies.

John Coffee ("Jack") Hays,
whose adjutant Ford was during the Mexican War.

From Walter Prescott Webb, *The Texas Rangers*

they caught fire, alarming the command and sending Evans' dismounted rear guard splashing through the mud to repel an attack which never came. They paid keen attention to the detailing of the adventure of Bill Hicklin, who

> fell asleep during a halt. When he awoke he felt rather desolate. He wandered about in the mountainous surroundings, not knowing which way the Americans had gone. Impelled by hunger, he went to a Mexican residence. He was treated with extreme kindness, secreted from other Mexicans, and finally sent to Puebla, where he joined his company. Bill was a great wag, and recounted the adventure with much humor. Until his unexpected arrival it was supposed he had been killed.[23]

One night's rest was all the new arrivals got at Puebla. At noon on December 4, the Rangers were the van of the first of two trains to advance toward the capital. They rode out followed by the Pennsylvanians, a Massachusetts and an Ohio regiment, and fifteen hundred recruits under Major F. T. Lally, the last body being replacements for the decimated regiments at Mexico City. Steadily the road climbed until the Texans emerged from the pine-shaded pass a few miles past Río Frío and saw on the next day, through the still winter air, the City of Mexico, sprawling some forty miles away in the lush valley. On December 7, riding quietly at a walk, the Rangers followed Colonel Hays into the suburbs of the city.[24]

The Rangers were a sight to attract notice. Their clothing, long since shredded by strenuous wear, was augmented by whatever garments they had been able to appropriate, including serapes and odd bits of Mexican uniforms. Their headgear was of all descriptions: the leather hunting cap Hays wore was matched by others in the ranks; a few Texans had managed to retain what had once been broad-brimmed hats; others wore fur caps of varying composition and shape, and at least one had acquired in some doubtless

[23] Ford, "Memoirs," III, 425–28. Since Witt's company was with Chevaille, Hicklin probably had been transferred temporarily to one of those which Hays took.

[24] *Ibid.*, 435–36. Scott reported the Texan arrival as being December 7, the date on which Patterson arrived with the second train.

interesting way a high silk hat. Ragged but impressive they were; "Jack Falstaff's recruits would have made a creditable figure beside them, but every man in that battered corps was worthy to combat for thrones or empires."[25]

Hardly had they entered the city when the population learned that the Texans were as deadly as they were carelessly attired. The suburbs housed the *léperos*, thieving, murderous ruffians who menaced both the residents and American occupation troops. As Hays's men marched toward the central plaza, a rock from the hand of a *lépero* knocked off a Ranger's cap. A long Colt rose in the rider's hand and roared abruptly. The *lépero* spun to the cobbled street, a bullet through his head. The Ranger bent from his walking horse, scooped up the cap, and replaced it. Not a word had been uttered.[26]

Along the packed streets where the citizenry had clustered for a sight of "*Los Diablos Tejanos*" (the Texas Devils), the Rangers forged their way. As they rode, a pistol fell from a Texans' belt and discharged upon striking the rocky pavement. A spectator fell with the ball in his leg. Like magic the way opened before the Rangers, and long before they reached the central plaza word had sped ahead that "*los Tejanos sangrientos*" (the bloody Texans) were coming. The column sliced through the massed throng of awed citizens and curious American soldiers into the Zócalo (plaza) and stretched along the south side of the square, opposite the towering cathedral. The officers, indistinguishable in dress from their men, fell out to accompany Hays to the billeting officer to learn where their companies would be quartered.

While the men waited, a candy vendor, his wares in a basket on his head, passed by the ranks. One trooper casually appropriated a handful of confectionary from the basket. As the vendor spluttered his wrath, the Ranger finished the portion and calmly helped himself again. The Mexican, ignorant of the fact that he

[25] Colonel Frank Triplett, *Conquering the Wilderness*, 602–603; James Kimmins Greer, *Colonel Jack Hays: Texas Frontier Leader and California Builder*, 181. Hereafter cited as Greer, *Hays*; Ethan Allen Hitchcock, *Fifty Years in Camp and Field*, 310.

[26] *Democratic Telegraph and Texas Register* (Houston), February 24, 1848.

would be paid—Hays tolerated no petty theft—and certain that he was being robbed, stooped for a pebble which he hurled at the Texan. A bullet from the Rangers' six-shooter dropped the citizen dead on the plaza cobblestones. The watching thousands stampeded, trampling one another underfoot and knocking each other into the open sewers flowing beside the walks, in mad haste to depart from the dangerous contingent. Minutes later another incident distressed the city's residents. When the Rangers rode toward their quarters, one, scarcely more than a boy, became enraged at his recalcitrant mount and belabored the horse about the ears with the butt of a revolver. The weapon discharged and another citizen fell, shot in the stomach. Nor was he the day's final casualty. That evening, while several Texans waited to enter the National Theater, a *lépero* filched a handkerchief from a Texan pocket and fled, the warning to halt only increasing his gait. A ball from the Ranger's pistol overtook him, and the Ranger, after retrieving the handkerchief, sauntered casually back to his place in line.[27] Later the Rangers adopted the habit of pinning their handkerchiefs in their pockets. When they felt the tug of a thief, they turned upon him and usually were content to administer a pistol-whipping by way of a lesson.

During their first few days in the city, exploring Rangers were attacked in the streets by *léperos*. One group of Texans, subjected to a shower of stones from a roof top, killed six of their assailants, an action sturdily defended to General Scott by Colonel Hays. On another occasion, Van Walling and interpreter Pete Gass were attacked by a rock-hurling crowd which soon resorted to knives. The two broke clear, leaving four or five dead and wounded in the street. A showdown came when Adam Allsens of Roberts' company was caught alone in a district the Rangers called "Cutthroat." Allsens' horse brought him out, but he was literally sliced to ribbons. Before he died that night, he identified some of his attackers, and the Rangers, consumed by a dangerous rage, made quiet preparations for revenge.

[27] Ford, "Memoirs," III, 436–37. The candy vendor incident was related to Ford by Captain Parry Humphreys, a witness.

Late that night, while Ford and Captain Parry Humphreys, a friendly acquaintance, sat talking with Hays in the Colonel's quarters, small-arms fire broke out nearby, steadily increasing to skirmish-line proportions. Ford and Humphreys knew it for revolver fire, but Hays deprecated the opinion, blaming the racket on a Horse Marine detachment. Until midnight the three listened to the multiplying reports; then Humphreys, peering from a window, wondered aloud why General Scott's orderly was approaching Ranger headquarters. Hays vanished rapidly through a rear door, calling back, "Ford, if he comes, tell him I am not in." There was, of course, no orderly; Humphreys merely was attempting to learn if Hays actually knew what was taking place.

After one o'clock Humphreys departed, and Ford went in search of his colonel. He found Hays but, he wrote later, "do not ask where?; you will never be told." It was in a place designed for solitude. Humphreys informed Hays the next morning that more than fifty bodies had been brought to police headquarters, and that night reported that the Mexican dead numbered more than eighty. Apparently the Rangers' action had a salutary effect on the *léperos*: "The latter affair ... broke up the murder of Americans almost entirely." Later a rumor spread that city officials had requested General Scott to remove the Texans to quarters outside the city, else there soon would be no civic population.[28]

Whether or not the rumor was true, the end of the month found the Rangers quartered at San Ángel, about six miles south of the city, a more convenient base from which to ride on the expeditions which were in the offing. Here again they had the Pennsylvanians as neighbors. On the night of December 31, Hays and his men rode out to the Contreras battle ground, southwest of the city, searching for guerrillas reported to have slain two Pennsylvanians there, but the search was fruitless. On the next day, Wynkoop took Daggett and Burke and about forty men on an overnight attempt to strike Jarauta's band. Although they missed the padre, they returned with a Mexican general and a colonel. Four days later, on January 6, 1848, a Ranger galloped into camp

[28] *Ibid.*, 437–41.

with word that guerrillas were attacking Americans on the San Angel–Mexico City road. Daggett again took a company and pursued the attackers, "until they had at least twenty laid dead and wounded on the road, and God knows where it would have stopped had not the dark evening stopped the chase."[29]

These activities, however, were but preliminary to a major Texan effort. On the evening of January 11, the entire Ranger command marched from San Ángel on a secret mission, although it was surmised that they were "going in search of the old priest, Jarauta, who [was] lurking around these diggings."[30] The surmise was correct; Jarauta was reported to be at Otumba, about thirty miles northeast of Mexico City, and it was Hays's intention to surprise the renegade cleric.

Guided by an American stage driver known to the Mexicans as "John the Devil," the Rangers trotted out into the winter dusk. Misinformed by natives along the route, the command lost its way in the dark, finally halting on the Vera Cruz road to stand by their horses until sunrise. To preserve secrecy, Hays concealed his men and horses all day in a nearby hacienda and led the regiment forth again at dark. Daylight saw the Texans entering Otumba, only to learn that Jarauta and his band lay at San Juan Teotihuacán, back toward the capital and ten miles off the Otumba–Mexico City road. Hays pushed his men hard for San Juan, but the bird had flown before him. Two sleepless nights and hard riding now were telling on both horses and men, particularly on Adjutant Ford, who had been ill when the regiment left San Ángel. Hays accordingly took his command into a huge stone structure which occupied almost an entire side of the large plaza, which was entirely enclosed by buildings. The horses were led into a fenced enclosure off the main room of the building and the men stretched out on benches and on the floor. Like Ford, most of them were soon deep in the sleep of exhaustion.[31]

[29] Oswandel, *Notes*, 434, 436–38, 441.

[30] *Ibid.*, 449. Oswandel said the Rangers "went out at full strength." Some must have been left behind, for Ford gives the number at San Juan as sixty-five, while Daggett mentions eighty-four.

[31] Ford, "Memoirs," III, 443–44.

An exception was Lieutenant Daggett. Sleep lay but lightly on his huge frame, and he was soon awakened by a low roaring sound. A question to an old woman passing through the *cuartel* (barracks) brought the answer that the noise was that of the Rangers' horses fighting outside. Uneasily, Daggett stepped out into the enclosure, mounted a block, and peered over the high wall. He saw citizens scattering in terror and, beyond them, Jarauta and his lancers coming at full gallop. Yelling, as he put it, "like a panther or a Comanche Indian," he leaped into the barracks to warn the Texans and to seize his pistols. Before he could buckle his pistol belt around him, guerrillas were at the door and he sprang to engage them. Blinded temporarily by powder from a shot fired in his face by Jarauta's lieutenant, Daggett fired rapidly at random, one shot striking Jarauta's wrist and causing the partisan chief to drop his sword, a second shot boring through the guerrilla lieutenant's shoulder, and a third shot, as Jarauta turned to withdraw, catching the priest in the "beefsteak." Shooting desperately, without hope of surviving, Daggett had determined to give the Mexicans a "coon fight."

The thunder of the heavy Colts and the loud shouting brought Hays and his men to their feet, weapons in hand, and several Rangers joined Daggett in turning back the rush from the door. In a moment Jarauta assembled his men for another charge. Now Ford and Daggett and about a dozen other Rangers advanced into the plaza to meet the lancers. Ignoring the musket fire from the housetops around the plaza, the Ranger line broke the lancer charge. Daggett fired at a particularly active officer with no apparent result. Ford then fired, and the officer dropped. As Ford and Daggett argued about who had hit the enemy, the officer sprang to his feet and ran madly through a nearby doorway. Another Mexican officer, refusing to be turned back, spurred into the Ranger line, where Major Chevaille's bullet pitched him head foremost from his horse and into the wall of the *cuartel*. As the charge broke up, Rangers whom Hays had posted on the barracks roof began to take their toll. Jarauta aligned his men for a third charge, but a long shot toppled him from his mount and his men, abandoning the fight, bore their wounded leader away.

Ford returned to the *cuartel* just in time to prevent a fight between two heated Ranger marksmen. A conspicuous enemy had been felled by a long shot from the top of the barracks, and both men claimed the kill. One insisted he had shot the Mexican in the breast. The other was as positive he had dealt death with a shot through the head. "After the Rangers had driven the enemy from the town the dead man was examined; he had a ball in his head and another had penetrated his breast."

Ford felt that had Jarauta dismounted his men and moved in cautiously on foot, the guerrillas could have annihilated the entire command. As it was, the adjutant credited Daggett and a few men with saving the force.[32] Daggett himself saw the six-shooter as instrumental in repulsing the partisans:

> One thing that contributed to save our command in this affair was the holy awe and superstition entertained by the untutored greaser in regard to the "revolver." They understood the term to mean a turning around and about—a circulator; and were led to believe the ball would revolve in all directions after its victim, run around trees and turn corners, go into houses and climb up stairs, and hunt up folks generally.[33]

Adjutant Ford estimated the enemy losses at about twenty; the nearest thing to a Ranger casualty was Daggett's powder-speckled face. Ammunition, however, had been dangerously depleted, and lack of it prevented Hays from riding to attack a band of about five hundred guerrillas reported by his spies to be but a short distance away. Early in the afternoon the command set out for the capital. They took the officer shot by Chevaille for a short distance, attributing his incoherent ravings to drunkenness, but after a few hours on the road they discovered that the delirium resulted

[32] *Ibid.*, 444–47.
[33] E. M. Daggett, "Adventures with Guerrillas," Isaac George, *Heroes and Incidents of the Mexican War, containing Doniphan's Expedition,* 213. Hereafter cited as Daggett, "Adventures."

from a severe skull fracture and they deposited him at a convenient hacienda. About ten o'clock that night they marched into Mexico City. Ford, so weak on that morning that he hardly could lift his saddle, was again a prey to his recurring illness. He was promptly ordered to bed in his quarters, under a physician's care. Five days later, when the Rangers rode out with Lane on another strike, John Ford lay staring disconsolately at the ceiling of his room.[34]

Four Ranger companies, two of Third Dragoons, and one of Tennessee Mounted Rifles left with Lane for Puebla on the morning of January 18. Santa Anna, discredited in both political and military spheres but unreconciled to a peace—and so still the center of resistance sentiment—was reported to be with his family at Tehuacán, some seventy miles southeast of Puebla, guarded by one hundred regular Mexican cavalry and an undetermined number of guerrillas. It was, then, no small prize the Rangers sought as they left Puebla in a chilling rain on the night of January 21.

Two nights out of Puebla, Lane's scouts halted a heavily guarded coach. Since the owner bore a safeguard issued by General Persifer Smith, Lane rejected Hays's advice to keep the party in custody and permitted it to pass on. At Tehuacán, at four o'clock in the morning, the command was fired upon. Immediately the Tennesseeans and the Dragoons surrounded the town while Lane and the Texans charged for the plaza. Santa Anna and his family were gone, however. His residence gave evidence of a hasty departure, and Lane found later that a rider had brought a warning two hours before the Americans arrived. The courier, it was learned, was of the party which Lane had examined on the road.

On February 3, Lane's raiders were back in Puebla after a series of marches which had taken them more than halfway to the Gulf Coast and during which they had received the surrender of the populous towns of Tehuacán, Orizaba, and Córdoba, at the latter freeing six American prisoners. Word that the Rangers were out must have preceded the command, else it hardly would have been

34 *Mexican War Correspondence*, 1067; Ford, "Memoirs," III, 445, 448, 460; Oswandel, *Notes*, 457, 464.

possible for only 350 men, unsupported by artillery, to have moved unopposed so far through territory into which United States troops had not hitherto penetrated.

From Puebla, Lane sent two Ranger companies toward Mexico City on February 5 as a wagon escort, and with the rest moved northward on the same day toward Tlaxcala in search of a foe. On February 8, he fell in with a Mexican force under Colonel Manuel Falcon at San Juan Teotihuacán. After defeating Falcon and destroying a store of small arms, Lane rested his command overnight and returned to Mexico City.

An incident on the march from Tehuacán marred the satisfaction that Hays's men felt over the operation. Three Rangers had been apprehended robbing a Mexican civilian mule train. On his return to Puebla, Lane saw that the three were dishonorably discharged. Some of the sting of the disgrace was removed, however, when he reported officially, "In justice to the Texas Rangers, I take pleasure in stating that the three individuals specified were not Texans by birth or adoption, but joined the regiment upon this line of operations of our army."[35]

Adjutant Ford doubtless was happy to see his comrades return. His memoirs do not tell how he spent his convalescence. If his strength permitted, he may have attended a performance of an American circus in Mexico City.[36] With other officers, possibly he visited the palace of Chapultepec and the battlefields over which Scott's forces maneuvered during the campaign against the city. Ill or otherwise, he probably joined in celebrating the treaty of peace signed on February 2 at the little village of Guadalupe Hidalgo, about five miles north of the capital. The return of his brother officers to their mess at the Inn of the National Theater permitted the adjutant to learn the details of their campaign. He joined them in facetious criticism of the astute bargaining ability exhibited by "Mike" Chevaille. At Córdoba the Major had made a sharp trade for an Englishman's saddle. The Briton appeared before Lane, complaining, "General, Maj. Chevaille has been beating me."

[35] 30 Cong., 2 sess., *House Exec. Doc. 1,* 89–95.   [36] Kenly, *Memoirs,* 381.

Lane was solicitious. "Did he beat you badly?"

"Yes," said the victim, "quite badly."

Solemnly Lane advised him, "Keep a sharp look out or he will beat you again."

How John Ford must have laughed when E. M. Daggett, Captain Daggett now, paraded in his prize trophy of the Tehuacán raid, Santa Anna's dress coat.[37] The garment by an actual test weighed fifteen pounds, principally because of the elaborate gold braid which almost covered it. The coat, made for Santa Anna's short, somewhat deformed torso, hardly confined the massive captain, whose bulk was ample for his more than six feet of height.

When the Rangers returned to San Ángel, the United States had been at peace with Mexico for exactly a week.[38] But not all who had been in the field against the Americans were willing to accept the provisional Mexican government's agreement to capitulate. Among those refusing to lay down their arms were two whose activities had been particularly obnoxious to Scott's army, General Mariano Paredes, described as being "cut from the same cloth as Santa Anna but of lesser talents,"[39] and the seemingly ubiquitous guerrilla-priest, Padre Celedonio de Jarauta.[40] These men and their adherents continued their depreda-

37 Ford, "Memoirs," III, 458, 460. 38 30 Cong., 2 sess., *House Exec. Doc. 1*, 94.

39 Thomas Ewing Cotner, *The Military and Political Career of José Joaquín de Herrera, 1792–1854*, 98. Hereafter cited as Cotner, *De Herrera*.

40 Jarauta had been a priest in Aragon, but left Spain because of his implication in the guerrilla activities of Cabrera's Carlists. When the Mexican War began, he was attached to the cathedral at Vera Cruz, but either as a result of an altercation with his bishop or in answer to the Mexican government's call for partisan warriors, he left his calling to organize a guerrilla band of Europeans. His chief rival between Perote and the gulf was the Mexican leader Zenobia. As a result of a battle between adherents of the two chieftains in the fall of 1847 (which probably prevented an ambush of the Rangers on their Antigua expedition), Jarauta negotiated with Colonel Hughes. After his rebuff by General Patterson, Jarauta continued in the field after the treaty was signed, participating with General Paredes in a revolt against the Mexican provisional government. The revolt was suppressed in May, 1848, and Jarauta was captured. He was executed in June, before his wounds received at Zacualtipán had healed, to the great indignation of many of the common people of Mexico. Jenkins, *U. S. and Mexico*, 289, 472–73; Smith, *War with Mexico*, II, 171; Cotner, *De Herrera*, 182; Daggett, "Adventures," 209–10; *Diccionario Enciclopédico, U. T. E. H. A.*, VI, 527.

tions, preying not only on American supply trains and small detachments but also on their fellow citizens who were inclined to welcome the treaty. The Rangers could now serve the cause of peace as they had served that of war. Accordingly, after a week's rest, they looked again to their saddles and guns. Behind Jack Hays and Joe Lane, with part of the Third Dragoons and Mounted Rifles as *compañeros*, they rode northeastward on the night of February 17, with partisan spies as guides. This time Adjutant Ford rode in the van with Hays and Chevaille.

A short way from the capital, Lane left the Vera Cruz road and angled toward the village of Tulancingo, where, he had been told, he would find Paredes, Jarauta, and Juan Almonte, a former Mexican ambassador to the United States and, more recently, a privateer and a general. After an all-night ride he reached his destination only to discover that Jarauta had departed a few days earlier. General Paredes was still there, but escaped when mistaken for his brother.[41] Jarauta had retired to Zacualtipán, seventy-five miles northward in the mountains. Lane paused briefly at Tulancingo and late in the afternoon of February 24 set out on a forced night march over the mountainous terrain toward Zacualtipán. At daybreak the command reached the edge of the town, and Lane launched his charge, Hays and the Rangers leading the way.

As the raiders swept into Zacualtipán, a Mexican officer stepped from a doorway into the street. Lane's Mexican guide grasped the officer's arm, held it across his saddle bow, and the command "went into the town on a run, the officer dangling like a wet blanket, who directed us to Jarauta's headquarters."[42] A blast of musketry from an unnoticed *cuartel* ripped over the rushing column. Hays promptly detached Truett and Ford with a Ranger squad to deal with that distraction while the main body of riders raced for the plaza. Truett's detachment burst down the heavy doors to the patio before the *cuartel* and stormed inside, to be met by a heavy fire from more than fifty Mexican regulars, part

41 Ford, "Memoirs," III, 462.
42 Daggett, "Adventures," 209.

of a government force under a Colonel Montaña who had remained faithful to Paredes. The fire came from a two-story structure, protected across the front by a high stockade. A lower wall of stone ran across the courtyard, paralleling the stockade, providing cover for Truett and his band. The accurate Texan marksmanship soon caused the Mexicans to seek a way of escape, and some began to disappear through an opening at the end of the stockade. Ford was the first to discover the enemy movement. He and Private Jacob Horn climbed atop the wall, ran along the top through a blazing fire from the enemy only thirty yards distant, and stationed themselves above the gap. Under heavy volleys from the Mexican *escopetas*, at this point only twenty yards away, the two turned back a large party of the enemy attempting to evacuate the *cuartel*.

Hardly had they sealed the breach when Horn fell with a dangerous chest wound. Ford paused long enough to assure his companion that the wound was not necessarily fatal and then returned to the work at hand. Alone he stood up to the concentrated musket fire, and with each gutteral report of his long Colt a sharpshooter dropped on the long gallery across the *cuartel* or sought safety in the recesses of the building. Attracted by the shots, "Mike" Chevaille, Lieutenant Dan Grady, Jem Carr, and another Ranger came hurrying to take a hand. About this time Truett set out for the plaza in response to a message that a heavy lancer attack threatened Hays's command, and as he left, Private G. M. ("Old Frazzler")[43] Swope came sprinting with a handful of comrades. Ford, now in command of this hastily assembled contingent, forced a gate, which permitted his men to open fire on the enemy's right and rear. Their retreat blocked by a burning

---

[43] Ford, "Memoirs," III, 463–64. Ford defined the term "frazzler" as the equivalent of the Civil War epithet "bummer," applied to expert foragers. Returning from Tulancingo, when the command halted at a hacienda, someone (and judging from Ford's style in the "Memoirs," one suspects it was he) discovered a large cask of wine. Swope was called in to identify it. To the satisfaction of all concerned, the proprietor excepted, Swope pronounced it excellent Madeira. The cask was not quite empty when the Rangers rode on.

wooden structure attached to the left of the stone building, the Mexican troops hung out a white flag. Major Truett, returning from his unnecessary journey to the plaza, found nothing left to do but take charge of the prisoners. There were about twenty of them, including their hard-hit commander, Colonel Montaña, dying of a bullet from Ford's pistol.[44]

Mexican losses in this skirmish were eleven dead and one nearly so, at least four of whom had fallen to Adjutant Ford's guns; eleven more wounded; and additional unwounded prisoners. Horn, who was to die in the Pachuca hospital on the return march, was the only serious Texan casualty. "Pete" Gass had been slightly wounded, and Major Chevaille had been bruised by a spent ball. The remaining Rangers, exhausted but unscathed, began to seek out their own companies, except for a few kept by Ford to extinguish the fire roaring in the wooden building nearby.

Meanwhile, Hays and Lane had driven into the heart of the city, encountering in the streets and *cuartels* a strong lancer force and a small infantry detachment. Here the attackers divided, Hays and his command waging a running battle with the enemy for over a mile outside the city. Informed by a prisoner that Jarauta's headquarters were in a church on the plaza, the Texans returned to attempt his capture. At the plaza a courier reported that Lane was in danger of being ridden down by a superior force. Hays immediately sent Daggett's company to Lane's aid until he could bring up the others. The fight became a house-to-house conflict at point-blank range. After some thirty of the enemy had fallen, the remainder made their escape through the rear of a disputed *cuartel.*[45]

Jarauta again escaped, this time in his nightshirt, so Daggett was told.[46] His band, however, had been shattered irretrievably, and his chief lieutenant, Padre Martínez, lay dead. With nothing further to do, Hays and his staff established regimental head-

[44] *Ibid.,* 465–66; 30 Cong., 2 sess., *House Exec. Doc. 1,* 102–103.
[45] 30 Cong., 2 sess., *House Exec. Doc. 1,* 98–100, 103.
[46] Daggett, "Adventures," 209.

quarters across the street from the scene of Ford's fight and went out to view the city under more favorable circumstances, leaving their unsaddled horses in the headquarters building. Ford, who had remained with the mounts, was suddenly aware that fire had spread to the building adjoining headquarters, and that the roof above him was beginning to blaze. Eight horses had to be saddled and led out, and he was almost exhausted by his recent skirmish. Working frantically, he saddled six before aid came. Then, so weak that he barely succeeded in mounting "Old Higgins," he rode out with the flaming roof falling about him.[47]

In his subsequent report of the raid, Lane set the number of Mexican dead at 150, slightly more than the total estimated by a citizen of the town. One Ranger arrived at an entirely different figure.[48] "A wag used his pencil, and went from place to place, he put the boys on the stand, took an account of the number each man had killed, and reported that eighteen hundred Mexicans had ceased to feast on tortillas."

Lane's men left Zacualtipán on the morning of February 26 and retraced part of their route toward the City of Mexico. At a hacienda where they had camped on the outward march, the Rangers stopped to apply their aptitude for foraging. As Bill Hicklin and the proprietor vociferously disputed possession of a hen, another Texan hurled a stone at a fleeing pig. The rock ricocheted up to strike General Lane severely on the chin. "He used ugly expressions, and actually avowed his willingness to see the landlord, the hens, and the pigs, settled where the thermometer never reached zero. He stopped the foraging."[49] The halt at the hacienda was short, to the great relief of the inhabitants, and the march was resumed through the rich silver mining district of Real del Monte, on past Pachuca, and down to the capital, where the troops arrived on the night of March 1. On the next morning the Rangers, laden with trophies and booty, rode out to their San Ángel camp.[50] Three days later, American and Mexican military

47 Ford, "Memoirs," III, 483.
48 *Ibid.*, 485; 30 Cong., 2 sess., *House Exec. Doc. 1*, 97. A Mexican account reported 126 dead.
49 Ford, "Memoirs," III, 483–85.

commanders agreed to an armistice. This meant that any further operations the Rangers might conduct would be against those chieftains now considered outlaws by both governments.

Early in March, Hays was ordered to move his regiment out on the Vera Cruz road to perform police action against the depredating bands, thus permitting General Scott to obtain maximum benefit from the Ranger services before they should be mustered out at Vera Cruz when their enlistment expired. Minor skirmishes enlivened the patrol activity, and at the village of San Carlos, connoisseurs of revolver artistry were given a masterful exhibition by Sergeant Major William Hewitt, Brush's successor. Firing deliberately, he struck down three guerrillas skulking at the edge of the hamlet. When the guerrillas had been driven off, Ford and others measured the distance of Hewitt's shots and found it to be more than 120 yards. Ford, equally proficient, hailed the feat as superlative shooting.

Patrols rode out at every rumor of guerrilla concentrations. After one such report, Hays dispatched Adjutant Ford with two native guides and twelve Rangers to San Juan de los Llanos, about sixteen miles from Tepeyahualco. At dusk the party arrived at the roped-off plaza of the town, where some four thousand people were gathered for a religious *fiesta*. Ford's demands for quarters and rations for his men were grudgingly honored until the civic officers were informed that the detachment was a part of Hays's command. Then immediately came a dinner invitation, tendered by the prefect of police. Following a bold course, Ford accepted. After arranging for defense of the stone building in which the patrol was quartered, at nine o'clock that night he, interpreter "Pete" Gass, and Miguel, one of his guides, all heavily armed, arrived at the host's residence. Fear of treachery prevented Ford's full appreciation of the handsomely served sixteen-course dinner, and the adjutant returned to his men in time to

[50] Oswandel, *Notes*, 509. Oswandel, a Pennsylvania Dutch corporal, watched them return at noon, March 2, 1848. He commented that "Some of them made out well, having large rolls of linen and black velvet." And what, one wonders, about Hays's strictures against petty theft?

avert an incipient panic. The entire party spent a sleepless night and rode back to the regiment on the following morning to find Hays keenly concerned over their prolonged absence, ignorant of the fact that the patrol had covered almost three times the distance he had estimated.

Scouting the country in thorough, deliberate fashion, the Rangers moved down the Jalapa road and late in March went into camp about two miles outside that city. Here occurred an incident which fell short of reaping catastrophic consequences only through the strenuous efforts of Ford and Major Truett. The Napoleon of the West, Santa Anna, realizing that his star of destiny had waned almost to the point of invisibility, had received permission to leave Mexico and was traveling toward the coast with his entourage. Colonel Hughes, commanding the Jalapa garrison, invited Santa Anna's party to dinner at the hacienda of General José Durán, six miles above the city, and the ill-starred chieftain accepted. The Ranger camp soon buzzed with the rumor that the route of Texas' most despised enemy would lie past the Ranger bivouac.

On the morning of March 28, Colonel Hughes's party met Santa Anna and his family and escorted them to the Durán residence. Hays, who had arrived in Texas too late for the San Jacinto campaign, had never seen the Mexican dictator and took the opportunity to do so, riding out with several other Ranger officers. Ford and Truett also left camp but took their way into Jalapa to witness the spectacular, sentimental demonstration the citizens were preparing in honor of their fallen hero. They had been but a short time in the city when two Rangers came hurriedly with word that most of the regiment, eager for revenge, were determined to kill Santa Anna as he passed the Texan camp. The two officers spurred in haste to frustrate the design.

Upon their arrival at camp, Ford and Truett found the men in what the former described as the "white heat" of anger. Knowing their men, the officers made no threat of punishment against out-of-hand action; instead, their appeals were made toward the honorable sentiments of the Rangers. Skillfully opposing argument

Artist Frederic Remington's portrayal of the attack
by Jarauta's Lancers on the Rangers
at San Juan Teotihuacán.

From *Harper's Monthly* (December, 1896)

"Old Gritter Face"—Joe Lane,
under whom Hays and his Rangers rode in Mexico.

with counterargument, the two pointed out that Santa Anna was traveling under a safeguard issued by the United States commander-in-chief, and that to violate its guarantee would degrade their conduct to the level of that of their erstwhile enemy. Not only would the participants be considered no more than mere murderers, but such a deed perpetrated by Texans would also cast a blemish upon the honor of their native state. Once that point had been made, there came the prompt answer, "Then we will not do it." Ford also refused the request of the Rangers to speak with Santa Anna, fearing that conversation might rekindle the wrath of the Texans. He did, however, assure the men that they might line up along the road and have a close look at their old enemy.[51]

Meanwhile, Colonel Hughes grew uneasy as the dinner seemed to prolong itself unduly. Since he was responsible for Santa Anna's safe passage through his district, he wished to get the party on its way but without appearing to hurry his guests. Hearing that Colonel Hays was at the hacienda, Hughes sent for him and led him to where the Mexican General sat placidly puffing his cigar. When he presented Hays to Santa Anna, a deathly silence fell over the group at the sound of the Ranger's name. Hays bowed in his characteristically modest manner and retired to the rear of the throng. His appearance served Hughes's purpose. Members of the Mexican party quickly signified their desire to be on their way. At that moment the United States officers learned of the uproar at the Ranger camp. Without further delay the Mexican escort formed, Santa and his wife and daughter entered their carriage, and Major Kenly placed himself in advance of the short procession. At a rapid trot the escorted vehicle rumbled down the Jalapa road toward the Texan encampment. In less than an hour the group reached the Ranger area and passed between what appeared to Major Kenly to be two ranks of grim statuary.[52]

Adjutant Ford, keenly watching everywhere for indications of possible trouble, was impressed by the silence of the scene:

[51] Ford, "Memoirs," III, 487–93.
[52] Kenly, *Memoirs*, 491–93.

The "ununiformed" representatives of Texas stood motionless and silent—not even a whisper disturbed the air. They had made up their minds to let the president-general, who prosecuted a war of extermination, of rapine and plunder, upon them in bygone days—who had reaped the benefits of a leniency and a mercy he did not merit by his antecedent actions and examples, again trust to the magnanimity of Texans and go his way unharmed.

So again Santa Anna passed from the scene. His party halted for the night at his hacienda of Encerro, some fourteen miles below Jalapa on the Vera Cruz road, and then took up the journey for Antigua. From that port he sailed on April 4 into voluntary exile aboard a Spanish vessel reportedly bound for Venezuela. Ford later recalled that it was a Ranger company which provided the protective escort to Antigua.[53]

Hays and most of the command rode on toward Vera Cruz, leaving a part of Daggett's company at Jalapa to preserve order in the district. Word of Hays's departure apparently circulated among the bandits, for two days after Santa Anna's passage the Texans at Jalapa had an opportunity to dispel some of the frustration engendered by Santa Anna's escape. On March 30, a bandit gang waylaid and looted a Mexican goods train at Paso del Bobo, near the city. Colonel Hughes called on the combative, durable Daggett to pursue. The latter and a Ranger platoon trailed the depredators and caught them at the village of Desplobade. The fight was brief. Of the fourteen raiders, one escaped; the rest were captured and shot. The swift retaliation appreciably reduced marauding about Jalapa.[54]

Hays returned to Mexico City on April 19 and soon afterward received orders to take his regiment to Vera Cruz for mustering out. Escorting an army wagon train, the Rangers once more marched down the winding road toward the Gulf Coast and on April 29 again pitched their tents on the sandy flat at Vergara. Early in May the command, except for Hays and Ford, who intended to join the frontier battalion in Texas,[55] was mustered out

53 *Ibid.*, 397; Ford, "Memoirs," III, 494.
54 Jenkins, *U. S. and Mexico*, 497.
55 Ford, "Memoirs," III, 499.

of United States service. Ford and his colonel, in company with Daggett, Truett, and other discharged comrades, took passage on a Texas-bound vessel and a few days later disembarked at Port Lavaca, where jubilant citizens organized a ball in their honor.[56]

On the homeward voyage, Ford suddenly decided to leave the Ranger service. His memoirs offer no explanation for the decision, but he may have learned that Hays intended to resign his command and perhaps did not choose to serve under another commander. From Port Lavaca, then, he proceeded to a Ranger post at Enchanted Rock, northwest of Austin on the Gillespie–Llano County line, where he was mustered out on May 14, 1848.[57] Mid-May found him facing toward a lonely Austin home.

The John S. Ford who rode down Congress Avenue on "Old Higgins"[58] in May of 1848 was, in certain respects, a different individual from the physician-politician-editor who had taken the San Antonio road a year earlier. He was now a proven soldier-Ranger. Had there been any doubt about his capacities, Hays never would have appointed him adjutant. Hays's judgment had been vindicated, for in the San Juan and Zacualtipán fights, Ford had demonstrated his courage among men who regarded that virtue as commonplace. He had also been the object of laudatory official comment. Truett had praised Ford highly to Hays, after Zacualtipán, and Hays had reiterated that praise in his own report to Lane. Lane in turn had mentioned Ford in his report to General Walter O. Butler, Scott's replacement as commander-in-chief, and all three reports had reached the Adjutant General in Washington. Major Kenly wrote approvingly of the quickness and skill with which the Ranger officers had quieted the tumult at the camp on the day of Santa Anna's passage.[59] Ford, in displaying a flair for combat leadership, had thus opened for himself the portal to a long career of armed service to Texas.

---

[56] *Ibid.*, 395; Greer, *Hays*, 213.

[57] Records Group No. 94.

[58] Ford, "Memoirs," III, 499. Probably Ford purchased the horse from the army Quartermaster Department.

[59] 30 Cong., 2 sess., *House Exec. Doc. 1*, 95; Kenly, *Memoirs*, 397.

The restlessness brought on by his domestic misfortune still stirred him, so much so that it drew an admonition from his father.[60] Although Ford attempted to adjust himself to a relatively passive, urban routine, he kept himself alert for the chance to take part in any adventure which might arise. Before the year expired, a keen-eyed Californian would forge the first link in the chain of circumstances which was to call John Ford from the editor's cubicle to the vast, dangerous reaches of the West Texas frontier.

[60] Ford, "Memoirs," III, 395–96. Ford says by a "relative." His only known relative then in Texas, other than his daughter, was his father, William Ford. It is unlikely that John Ford would have been admonished by his thirteen-year-old daughter for tending toward "desperadoism."

3

Blazing the Ford–Neighbors Trail

In the spring of 1849, John S. Ford was again in the saddle. Austin citizens, eager to capitalize on a new economic opportunity, summoned him for another public duty fully as arduous as his Mexican War service: to lay out a practicable wagon road across Indian-infested, little-explored West Texas to El Paso.

By the Treaty of Guadalupe Hidalgo, February 2, 1848, Mexico had ceded her New Mexico and California provinces to the United States. In that same month, an employee of entrepreneur John A. Sutter discovered gold on the South Fork of the American River in the Sacramento Valley of northern California. When the news leaked out, there was a mad rush to the California gold fields. The California population soared from 20,000 in December, 1848, to an estimated 100,000 one year later.[1]

On the eastern edge of the Great Plains, civic groups seeking commercial advantages had begun to discuss the possibilities of wagon roads west from their communities. In Texas, interest was heightened by an item in the Houston *Democratic Telegraph and Texas Register* of February 15, 1849, which estimated that more than five thousand people from east of the Sabine would pass through Texas in 1849. Nowhere in the state were citizens more interested than in Austin, where enthusiasm for the opening of an Austin–El Paso road had been kindled by Dr. Joseph K. Barnes, S. D. Mullowney, and other civic-minded men. That Dr. John S. Ford was an interested and able party is best attested to by the

[1] Hubert Howe Bancroft, *The History of California*, VI, 27–34.

fact that it was to him the Austin citizens turned to bring their plans to fruition.[2]

Ford was both available and willing. The former Ranger had returned to pick up the editorial reins of the *Texas Democrat* from the uncertain grasp of his "practical printer" partner, Michael Cronican. The restraint of editorial duties lay heavily upon Ford after the vigorous activity of the Mexican campaign, and he welcomed a new opportunity to escape their routine. Already he had organized a small Ranger company for the purpose of intercepting the Indian raiding parties that had been using the Colorado River Valley as an avenue for depredations upon settlers south and west of Austin. On one occasion, the company of about twenty men, reinforced by Rangers from Captain Henry E. McCulloch's company, moved out on the trail of a returning party of Tonkawa marauders. After following the track for two days and camping in a heavy rain during the second night out, the expedition came in with only hard riding to show for its efforts. Ford later learned that during the rain he had halted near the Tonkawas, who, when they had seen the fires over which the Rangers were boiling coffee, stole away.[3]

This fruitless pursuit probably occurred soon after Ford and Cronican had sold the *Texas Democrat*, early in January, 1849, to William H. Cushney, one of the two men who previously had published the newspaper at Washington-on-the-Brazos under the name of the *National Register*.[4] The press possibly was experiencing financial difficulties. The public printing contract awarded by the legislature in April, 1846, had expired, and the poor postal service, of which Ford had made editorial complaint in almost every issue,[5] had caused a steady decrease in the number of *Demo-*

---

[2] Ford, "Memoirs," III, 529; Frank Brown, "Annals of Travis County and the City of Austin (From the Earliest Times to the Close of 1875)," (unpublished MS, Barker History Center, University of Texas), Ch. XIII, 42. Hereafter cited as Brown, "Annals." Pagination follows typescript in Archives Division, Texas State Library, Austin.

[3] Ford, "Memoirs," III, 528.

[4] Brown, "Annals," Ch. XI, 44.

[5] This is particularly true of the issues of 1846 and 1848.

crat subscribers. The interruption in his journalistic career left Ford available for public service.

Eager to benefit by the California situation, Austin citizens held a public meeting at the capitol on the night of February 20, 1849, to discuss ways and means of achieving their aims. Finally the group chose a committee, including Ford, to prepare a report showing the advantages of a direct, practicable overland route to California by way of El Paso, one with relatively little difficult terrain and with water available at comparatively frequent intervals. Ford and Mullowney, as a subcommittee, prepared the report and submitted it two nights later.[6] They drew heavily on a report of Colonel Jack Hays, who had left San Antonio the previous fall to determine the best route for a San Antonio–El Paso railroad. Misled by an inept guide, Hays's party had become lost in the Big Bend region, finally emerging at Ben Leaton's residence-fort on the Río Grande just below present-day Presidio. Hays's report, published in the *Democratic Telegraph and Texas Register* of December 28, 1848, left a number of questions unanswered but it contained a distinct note of encouragement: the Pecos River was the only difficult obstacle to wagon traffic.

While Austin was studying the Ford-Mullowney report, a more practical proposal was being considered in San Antonio. Major Robert S. Neighbors, supervising agent for the Texas Indians, had foreseen the value of an El Paso wagon road for both civilian and military use. In February, he conferred in San Antonio with the commander of the Military Department of Texas, General William Jenkins Worth, concerning the feasibility of making a personal reconnaissance of the area to be spanned. Having secured Worth's sanction, Neighbors set out for North Texas to obtain Indian guides, stopping in Austin on his way. While he was in the city, Ford, at the urging of the citizens' group, secured the agent's permission to join him in the project. The big, tireless major was glad to have the company of the courageous former adjutant, whose medical, Ranger, and surveying experiences would be useful.

[6] *Texas Democrat* (Austin), April 15, 1846.

Neighbors hoped to begin the journey on or about March 2 from the trading house operated by the Bernard and Torrey brothers on Bosque River near its junction with the Brazos, at a spot now part of a Waco suburb. Late in February, Ford saddled "Old Higgins" and rode northward from the capital, accompanied by a young friend, Thomas C. Woolridge, who later led "Old Higgins" back to Austin since Neighbors had decided to mount his party on mules. The two men crossed the San Gabriel River, bore eastwardly to the crossing of Little River, and from that point, after a long day's ride, came to the house of John Harry, a Delaware Indian, on the Bosque. Guided through the night by the accommodating Delaware, the travelers at daylight climbed stiffly from their saddles at the door of the trading house.

Neighbors had persuaded his Comanche charges to provide guides for the party, but the Indians were tardy. While the agent impatiently reinspected his supplies and reviewed his preparations, Ford passed the time at the home of Captain Shapley P. Ross, several miles down the Brazos, where he met the other two frontiersmen who were to make the journey. They were inseparable companions of about twenty years of age, Alpheus D. Neal and Daniel C. ("Doc") Sullivan. The latter had served with Ross on the frontier during the Mexican War, and while yet a lad had been a Mier prisoner. Mrs. Ross, who had known the two from boyhood, described them to Ford in terms which later circumstances verified. The chunky Sullivan, who never neglected the opportunity for a practical joke, was "insensible to the feeling of fear; brave to a fault—a kind and accommodating friend, and a bitter and dangerous enemy."[7]

When the Comanches, led by Chief Owl, finally rode in, Neighbors hastily gathered up loose ends and on March 23 set out on his history-making trek across West Texas.[8] In addition to the white men and Comanches, the party included Delawares John Harry and Interpreter Jim Shaw; two Shawnees, Joe Ellis and

[7] Ford, "Memoirs," III, 503–506.

[8] "Report of Dr. John S. Ford—upon the practicability of a Route from Austin to El Paso del Norte," *Texas Democrat* (Austin), June 23, 1849. Hereafter cited as "Report of Dr. Ford."

Tom Cooshattee; and Choctaw Patrick Goin. To transact agency business en route, Neighbors detoured northward to the Comanche camps on the headwaters of the Leon River. While the party rode north, Ford experienced the first of a number of diverting incidents which occurred during the excursion. About an hour before sunrise on the third day of the journey, the party was awakened rudely by a Comanche rendition of a medicine song. "It stirred up recollections of boyhood—the calling of hogs—the plaintive notes of a solitary bull frog—the bellowing of a small bull, and all that sort of noises. Anon the awful melody of the sonorous gong was reproduced. . . ."

On the next day the travelers reached Owl's camp, where the chief had agreed to provide Neighbors with a guide for the march west. The Texans created a sensation among the women and children, most of whom had never seen a white person. One frequent, curious visitor to Neighbors' bivouac was a withered old woman said by the Comanches to have seen more than one hundred winters. After lengthy parleying, the agent finally secured the services of Buffalo Hump, the celebrated Comanche war chief and morning songster, as his guide. Neighbors had to pay in advance, a condition which was to be costly.

Dr. Ford, who wore knee-high boots, soon won Comanche admiration. Knowing that rattlesnakes coil when suddenly disturbed, Ford astounded the Indians by leaping atop an unsuspecting rattler and springing off before it could strike. As the Indian horde and the expedition moved through the Cross Timbers, the Comanche scouts came upon a large diamondback rattlesnake, and waited for the "snakeman" to come up. Ford gazed at the ten-foot coil of brilliant serpent, its head swaying about three feet above the ground and its rattles vibrating. He listened respectfully to the Delaware guide's hurried warning that the snake could strike to a distance slightly in excess of its own length. To the disappointment of the Comanches, Ford urged his mule away, and from that time forward he refrained from jumping on "even a garter snake."

Owl's band turned aside in the Cross Timbers, and Neighbors' men rode forward with Buffalo Hump's people. Before they had traveled far, Ford was astonished to see an Indian woman gallop past, her husband rapidly pursuing and belaboring her with a ramrod when he could ride within reach. Neal offered the explanation: Sullivan had gratified the curiosity of the women about the white man by "giving a lecture," and the fleeing woman had been one of his audience. A wife of Buffalo Hump also had witnessed the performance, and a thoroughly frightened Jim Shaw appeared at Neighbors' tent shortly after dark, predicting an attack by the enraged chief before morning. Ford, Neighbors, and their Indian followers spent an alert, wakeful night while the roundly berated Sullivan slept soundly. In the morning, Buffalo Hump sent his main band westward and resumed the southerly march with but one wife and her children as his entourage. In a few days the group reached the Colorado River, about 140 miles above Austin as Ford supposed, and turned up the stream. On April 2 they struck the mouth of Spring Creek and found encamped there the bands of Shanaco, Yellow Wolf, and Buffalo Hump, an assemblage estimated by Ford at approximately ten thousand savages.

By this time, Sullivan had gained a reputation for insanity among the Comanches, who regarded his unpredictable conduct as the work of an evil, though not dangerous, spirit. "He took full advantage of the supposition, and was seldom out of devilment. He stuck pins into warriors, and made them cut capers very unusual for braves to perform." For the benefit of the village, "Doc" gave performances the Indians could appreciate. He imitated the movements of a buzzard near a carcass, went through the antics of a lizard by scuttling on all fours behind a log and peeping ludicrously over it at his convulsed audience, and, in a lisping voice, delivered a song containing the chorus "Miss Julia is very peculiar." While the entranced Comanches understood not one word of English, they applauded and laughed so immoderately that one uninhibited young brave was borne to his lodge by friends who feared he had made himself ill.

Neighbors was delayed at the Spring Creek encampment for at

least a week in an effort to procure another guide when Buffalo Hump decided against going further. Still incensed at Sullivan and not wishing to make the trip, the chief readily acquiesced to the protests of his friends that his life would not be safe among the revenge-seeking Mexicans of the El Paso area. He kept, however, the articles he had taken as payment for the entire trip. With the help of Jim Shaw, the agent at last persuaded a warrior, whose name Ford variously gave as Guadalupe and Tall Tree, to guide the party. On April 15, the brave, with his sister and her female companion, led the group across to Brady Creek and westward toward its headwaters.

Two incidents, one serious, the other both irritating and amusing, occurred along the Brady Creek route. Alpheus Neal got lost while hunting and failed to rejoin the party. Upon his return to San Antonio, Ford learned that Neal, after wandering for several days, had been found by a Comanche band, with whom he remained until he could reach the settlements. Neighbors' people lost one night's sleep during this phase of the journey when they camped near the bivouac of a Mexico-bound war party, whose members sang and danced most of the night.

Leaving the head of Brady Creek, Neighbors' party struck west for the Main Concho. The way led gradually higher across open land trenched by small streams angling northward into the Concho. A long ride brought the party to Kickapoo Creek, whence the wayfarers passed quickly by Potato Springs and climbed to a low pass in the hills. Emerging from the gap, the group continued briefly westward to a stream the leaders named Antelope Creek, and crossed from it to the Boiling Fork (South Fork) of the Main Concho. Tramping onward through the tall prairie grass, the mules left behind them in rapid succession Dove Creek, Good Spring Creek, and Lipan Camp Creek, and came in time to the elevated twin landmarks known as the Green Mounds, not far from the Concho. A two-hour ride brought the explorers to the river. From a camp at this point, Major Neighbors' party made a long upstream march through a pleasant late April day, passing the mouths of North Fork and Kiowa Creek, to the head of the

Concho, crossing then to the Mustang water holes where Neighbors halted to make camp in the gathering gloom.

An incident occurred here which could well have left the party on foot. A herd of mustangs alarmed Neighbors' mules at sunrise, and nearly all of the mounts vanished over the horizon, followed by the pointed imprecations of the travelers. Several of the Indians scrambled onto steeds which had been unable to escape and rode after the recalcitrants. As the hours passed, most of the wrath focused upon Ford's mule, Tantrybogus. An irritating beast at best, despite his hobbles and his notorious laziness he was credited with having led the stampede. When the Indians returned at noon, driving the runaways before them, Tantrybogus "had not a single friend in camp."

Having recovered their stock, the party set out for the Pecos River across a sterile plain sparingly dotted with mesquite and an occasional clump of hackberry growth. From Mustang water holes to Flat Rock water holes was only a few hours' ride, but to the next supply at Wild China water holes was the better part of a day's travel. Past the Flat Rock water holes a wet norther unexpectedly struck the party, but Neighbors led his group stumbling onward through the snow and sleet. Sullivan, whose coat was rolled up in the blankets, suffered intensely but bore the cold bravely, not wishing to open the pack and expose the blankets to moisture. At last the wayfarers reached a thicket of stunted hackberries. Here was material for a fire, about which they huddled, cold, wet, and cheerless, and further distressed by the knowledge that their supplies were almost exhausted.

From the Wild China water holes, the men could see the Castle Mountains lying to the west. They were now, so Guadalupe informed them, on the great Comanche war trail which stretched from the Wichita Mountains in Indian Territory across the Río Grande into Chihuahua. On the next day, Ford rode slightly in advance of the party. As he threaded Gapwater Pass through the mountains, he saw a mounted Indian approaching along the trail from the Pecos. The Indian signaled in sign language and, when Ford failed to reply, lowered his lance and charged. Ford reined Tantrybogus up the side of the pass for advantage of position and awaited the charge, six-shooter leveled. As the warrior came near, Ford raised both hands to indicate peaceful intentions. The savage skidded to an abrupt halt and immediately lost his belligerence, thinking, as Ford later learned, that the white man's gesture meant, "I have ten men at my back." The two sat staring at each other until Ford's companions rode up. Guadalupe immediately recognized the stranger, who was a Comanche warrior homeward bound with his wife and a prisoner taken on a successful plundering raid into Mexico. That night the warrior camped with Neighbors, providing for the explorer a feast of fat mule meat which all devoured "with gusto."[9]

Dropping down the gentle slope of gravel and red sand to the Pecos, the party swam their mounts at Horsehead Crossing. Here they consumed the last of their bacon and glumly anticipated a time of hunger, since game, plentiful at first along Brady Creek,[10] had become increasingly scarce. From this camp they launched into previously unexplored country. Where Hays's party of the previous year had gone southwest, Guadalupe led his charges northwest up the Pecos for a day and then struck west by south, past salt lagoons and over high tableland, to Toyah Creek. As they rode up the stream, on probably the third day from Horsehead Crossing, they found an abandoned, lean, broken-down horse. Guadalupe excitedly announced that horse meat was a real delicacy, and promised his companions a rare feast when they should halt. That evening the travelers encamped beside the bubbling waters of Mescalero Springs, at the head of the Toyah, and Guadalupe made good his promise.

Tempers worn thin by long marches and short rations flared up after camp was pitched. While the horse meat roasted over a bed of coals, the Comanche peremptorily demanded that Sullivan bring him water from the spring. For several days the two had been antagonistic, the Indian becoming more and more incensed

---

[9] *Ibid;* Ford, "Memoirs," III, 506–15.

[10] Game consisted of "buffalo, bear, panther, deer, turkies [*sic*], &c, &c." "Report of Dr. Ford."

at Sullivan's teasing. Guadalupe's order, delivered in no respectful fashion, aroused Sullivan to swift wrath.

A large sized row commenced then and there. Sullivan gesticulated and swore in English, Spanish, Soc, and a sprinkling of Caddo. Tall Tree [Guadalupe] called down anathemas upon Sullivan in pure Comanche, bad Spanish and English, besides in tongues unknown to all of us. The quarrel progressed until a resort to arms was purposed, when Maj. Neighbors and others interfered. The fuss did not take off the keen edge of Tall Tree's appetite. He stowed away meat enough to feed a family of buzzards.

Ford, however, could not share Guadalupe's enthusiasm for horse meat, which tasted "like a sweaty saddle-blanket smells at the end of a long day's ride." By holding his nose he was able to swallow a few small bites of odorous liver.

Leaving Mescalero Springs, the short procession pivoted around the northern shoulder of the Pah-cut Range [Davis Mountains] and moved westward down a great valley past the terminus of the Apache Mountains to the left. After long hours in the saddle, Shawnee Joe Ellis found a water hole and campsite about equidistant from the point of the Delaware Mountains to the east and the westerly Sierra del Diablo, a few miles north of present-day Van Horn. Here Ford's voracious appetite was in no way appeased by the colic pains he suffered after a hearty breakfast of half-roasted mescal cactus. The group was now down to what he described as "starving man's luck." Each one had a cup of coffee and a thirteenth part of a quart of *pinole* (a mush made of corn meal), augmented by unsavory roasted stalks of the maguey plant, a diet made the less appetizing by the sight of an occasional deer or antelope above the horizon but always well out of range. "No one contracted gout," Ford remembered, along this stretch of the route. Major Neighbors had hoped to trade for food with Apache bands, but no aborigines appeared; the trade trinkets remained uselessly stowed in the packs.

Westward Guadalupe led them, toward the gaunt, scarified Carrizo Mountain which appeared to block the way, but through its southern extremities Carrizo Pass lay like a crooked knife wound. From the pass the weary riders emerged into a flat valley walled in by other ranges. Away to his right Ford could see the outlines of another mountain gap which he learned later was the *Puerto de la Cola del Aguila* (the "Pass of the Tail of the Eagle," now called Eagle Pass, at the north end of the Eagle Mountains). Ford wanted to make for the Río Grande by that pass, but Guadalupe bore off to the southwest and Neighbors thought it best to follow. The Comanche now led them over a series of rocky ridges, each seeming higher and more precipitous than its predecessor. Night caught the party among the twisted outcrops, and the group went supperless and waterless to bed, where Ford writhed with a stomach agony brought on by green maguey stalks.

At dawn the party again rode after the now befuddled Guadalupe. Word soon came to Ford and Sullivan, at the rear of the column, that the way was blocked ahead. Members of the party in the rear swung southward over the least difficult terrain into an open valley, where the tracks of shod horses showed a trail. One of the women, who had followed after Ford and Sullivan, now raised a series of shrieks which guided the remainder of the group to the trail, which led about a mile farther to the bank of the Río Grande. Ford, ill and exhausted, was so lethargic that he was unaware that they had reached the river. At Sullivan's mention of the stream, Ford aroused enough to ask where it lay. "Doc" brusquely informed him, "You confounded fool, you have been riding along its banks for more than two miles."[11]

In council that night it was decided that the two men whose mules were strongest should ride on to a settlement and send back food to the others. Neighbors and Sullivan left early in the morning. Ford and Jim Shaw were to conduct the party more leisurely up the river toward El Paso, about eighty miles distant. Ford pushed the animals to their limit, with the discredited and grumbling Guadalupe and the women trailing behind, "over a loose, sandy, chaparral country—full of gullies, ravines, sand hills and quick sand."[12] In a day or two the journeyers found cart tracks

[11] Ford, "Memoirs," III, 516–19.   [12] "Report of Dr. Ford."

and soon saw a cart manned by a peon. Upon sighting the Indians, the Mexican vanished abruptly among the cacti, where he remained in spite of Ford's cajoling.

Not far below San Elizario the group met citizens bringing food sent by Neighbors. Ignoring Ford's admonition counseling moderation, some of the band gorged themselves to illness. At San Elizario, the party rested for several days before advancing the remaining twenty-odd miles to El Paso. The inhabitants of that frontier outpost were very hospitable. On their first day there, Ford and Sullivan accepted one invitation after another to dine. That evening they estimated that in addition to three regular meals, they had consumed three and a half dozen eggs. Ford also paused at an establishment offering a variety of refreshments. On the Texas side of the river, "an American woman, known as the Great Western, kept a hotel. She was tall, large, and well made. She had the reputation of being something of the roughest fighter on the Rio Grande; and was approached in a polite, if not humble manner by all of us—the writer [Ford] in particular."[13]

During their brief stay in El Paso, Ford and Neighbors discussed at length their route from the Pecos. After reflecting upon the paucity of water holes, the difficult terrain, and the fact that in some places wagons would bog inextricably in rainy seasons, Neighbors pronounced the route impracticable for wagon passage and determined to make the return journey by another course. He took his party, enlarged by the addition of a Texas frontiersman named Johnson, back to San Elizario, incidentally finding it necessary to assume a firm position with Guadalupe, who wished to remain at El Paso and raid the Mexicans. After procuring supplies and a guide, an elderly Mexican named Zambrano, to take them by a different route to the Pecos, the explorers in early May marched northeast from San Elizario on the homeward trip.[14]

13 Ford, "Memoirs," III, 521. This woman was well known to American soldiers on the Río Grande during the Mexican War. In the 1870's she was operating a brothel in Arizona and was noted there for her pistol dexterity.

14 "Report of Dr. Ford." Kenneth F. Neighbours, "The Expedition of Major Robert S. Neighbors to El Paso in 1849," *Southwestern Historical Quarterly*, Vol. LVIII (July, 1954 to April, 1955), 54, gives the date as May 6.

Neighbors' first camp was made at the Waco (Hueco) Tanks, about a day's ride east of El Paso in the tangled jumble of granite ridges called the Waco Mountains, where one of the "natural tanks, situated in a cave," contained "perhaps 50,000 gallons of water."[15] Another half-day's ride brought the band to the trio of cottonwoods which marked the eight springs of the Alamo Mountains, where grass was abundant but wood was not. After bearing slightly north of east for another twenty miles or so, they came to the jagged, red granite Cornudas del Alamo peak, where they found water among the crumbling ravines. The grass there was good, and among the rocks there was sufficient firewood. Wood was scarce, however, at the next camp, forty-odd miles to the south in an open plain, where a sulphurous spring identified by Zambrano as Ojo del Cuerpo (Crow Spring) gushed forth.[16]

From Crow Spring, Zambrano led the group farther south, skirted the southern point of the Guadalupe Mountains, and turned left to make the easy ascent of the great pass which opened between the Guadalupes and the Delaware Mountains. From the east end of the pass they moved a short way to Guadalupe Spring and then turned eastward to San Martin Spring at the head of Delaware Creek. Neighbors had now covered that portion of his route which, four months later, Captain R. B. Marcy was to traverse and recommend at the end of his Dona Ana–Fort Smith journey.[17] From San Martin Spring the party rode to the head of Walnut Creek, followed it down to Savin Creek, and marched along the latter stream to its juncture with the Pecos, near the present-day city of Carlsbad, New Mexico. There Zambrano left the party to return to El Paso. Except for anxiety over the dwindling food supply, the journey thus far had been uneventful. To conserve rations, the men had eaten a panther, which, Ford recorded, had a "peculiar fresh taste, very difficult to get rid of."[18]

Southeastward the party followed down the meandering Pecos

[15] "Report of Dr. Ford."

[16] "Report of Captain R. B. Marcy," *Report of the Secretary of War*, 31 Cong., 1 sess., *Senate Exec. Doc. 64*, 63.

[17] *Ibid.*, 198–201, 223.

[18] Ford, "Memoirs," III, 522.

toward Horsehead Crossing, where on May 20 they encountered a California-bound emigrant group blindly following a confused leader, a Captain Duval. Johnson, the El Paso recruit, agreed to turn back to guide the emigrants to the Río Grande. Three days later, on the high prairie between the Pecos and the head of the Concho, Neighbors met a train of forty-five wagons guided by Captain B. O. Tong of Seguin. The meeting was fortunate for both groups. Neighbors obtained badly needed supplies and in return sent the Delaware John Harry to conduct the train over the route just traversed from El Paso. Two more companies were encountered on May 24, one at the head of the Concho, led by a Captain Murchison of Fayette County, and a second about ten miles downstream, commanded by a Captain Smith of Houston.[19] Five days later on the San Saba, the wayfarers came abruptly upon a solitary, elderly traveler leading a pack animal. The old man, certain he had fallen in with a band of cutthroats, begged hard to avoid confiscation of the worthless accumulation his animal bore. He was in no danger anyway; the men of the party "had hardly strength enough to commit larceny on a hen roost." This meeting came just prior to that with the large, well-equipped company of Persifer Smith, whose emigrants employed "Doc" Sullivan to guide them to El Paso.[20] At this point, most of the Indians left Neighbors to take a more direct route to the trading house, while the Major, Ford, Guadalupe, two other braves, and the women rode down the emigrant trail to Fredericksburg and on toward San Antonio.

In San Antonio, Neighbors, with Ford's aid, prepared his report and bore it away to department headquarters. Ford, left to his own devices, appeared on Alamo Plaza, attracting considerable attention. He wore, as he remembered, "a pair of old drawers and a breech-clout—no coat, and a shirt chock full of the free soil element." Friends escorted him into a restaurant-saloon, disregarding the loud protests of the proprietor. They intimidated the host by relating in gory detail a catalog of murders attributed to the tat-

19 *Ibid.; Texas Democrat* (Austin), June 15, 1849.
20 Ford, "Memoirs," III, 522–23; *Texas Democrat* (Austin), June 15, 1849.

tered traveler, and the owner immediately began to ply the companions with free drinks to purchase their quiet behavior.[21] Guadalupe too attracted much notice and became, during his brief stay in the city, something of a municipal pet. He was given a hat, coat, and other accessories of civilization. Trousers, too, he received and wore proudly, but astonished and probably somewhat dismayed the citizenry by his practice of invariably shedding the pants whenever he sat down to a meal.[22]

From San Antonio, Ford proceeded to Austin, where the *Texas Democrat* on June 10 published his report to the citizens. His account not only delineated clearly the most practicable wagon route but also pointed out the moderate cost of constructing a railroad along the thirty-second parallel (thus anticipating the recommendations of a War Department survey of several years later). He had been twenty-two days by mule from San Elizario to San Antonio, and estimated that a horse could travel the route from Austin to El Paso in the same time. The distance, via the mouth of the San Saba, he calculated at 601 miles, but admitted the estimate might be high since he had computed it on the three and one-half miles per hour mule gait, which was slower than that usually maintained by horses.[23]

The value of the expedition became more evident later in the summer. On August 3, "Doc" Sullivan arrived in Austin from El Paso with fifteen men and a wagon, having made the trip in twenty-three days' actual traveling time. Sullivan further reported that when he left El Paso, twelve to fifteen hundred emigrant wagons were outfitting there for the long haul west across New Mexico Territory.[24] Obviously the route traced in the reports of Ford and Neighbors, up the Pecos from Horsehead Crossing by Guadalupe Pass to El Paso, already was showing signs of becoming the great highway of western Texas traffic, a route which

[21] Ford, "Memoirs," III, 523.

[22] *Texas Democrat* (Austin), June 30, 1849.

[23] "Report of Dr. Ford." According to Ford, his map of the expedition was published in the *Texas Democrat*. The files fail to show it.

[24] *Texas Democrat* (Austin), August 4, 1849.

retained its predominance for a generation, until wagons disappeared in the smoke of roaring locomotives.

Significantly, the opening of this California route brought about crucial developments for Texas. The El Paso road brought within comparatively quick and easy reach of the Texas government the eastern New Mexico region claimed by Texas since 1836 but never actually under Texas administration. It made possible the extension of Texas jurisdiction over the area between the Río Grande and the Staked Plains, and Ford's reporting of the fertile soil and other natural resources of the region might be expected to touch off a westward movement of Texans into the country.[25] The Texas legislature at its next session, partly anticipating such a development, confirmed an 1848 proposal to organize the western area into counties and also approved sending Major Neighbors as the state's organizing agent. By March, 1850, having completed the organization of El Paso County, Neighbors rode north to continue the work at Santa Fe. There the frustration of his intentions by federal authorities resulted in the mutual recriminations and threats of war which were resolved later in the year by the Compromise of 1850.

Dr. Ford, meanwhile, returned to medical practice, although at the moment Austin seemed to promise little for the profession. The *Texas Democrat* on July 21 reported only six or seven deaths from illness during the preceding year, most of them among newly arrived immigrants who apparently had brought their ailments with them. The issue of August 4 did report the death of a resident, uniquely enough a Dr. James H. Horne, whose attending physicians were W. T. Horne and John S. Ford. Relatively unconfined by his practice, Ford engaged himself in community affairs. As befitting a former teacher in the city's Union Sunday School,[26] he became active in the Austin chapter of the Sons of Temperance, accepting on its behalf in July a banner presented in a public ceremony by the ladies of Austin. Although over-

[25] "Report of Dr. Ford."
[26] Brown, "Annals," Ch. XIII, 38. Brown's date, however, is exactly one year too late.

shadowed by A. J. Fannin's oration of the day, Ford's brief speech of acceptance was well received.[27] But the prosaic incidents of prescription packet and platform were unstimulating; John Ford resumed the search for adventure.

[27] *Texas Democrat* (Austin), July 21, 1849.

4

Border Battles, 1849–51

JOHN FORD'S NEXT OPPORTUNITY also stemmed from the Treaty of Guadalupe Hidalgo. By its terms, both republics were obligated to control the Indian tribes of their respective lands, and neither nation was equal to the commitment. Profiting from the confusion created by frequent Indian raids, Mexican bandits added their operations to the burdens already imposed on the inadequate army detachments. The result was a deluge of petitions from harassed and grumbling border citizenry demanding that the state take action. Typical was a petition of June 12, 1849, to Governor George T. Wood from William W. Nelson, T. W. Tanner, and other Brownsville residents, asking that a Ranger company be organized to protect their region since the military garrison at Fort Brown consisted of only sixty infantrymen unable to cope with the situation.[1] However, Brevet Major General George M. Brooke, commanding the Department of Texas, assured Wood that there was no need to muster Ranger companies into federal service, since there were enough United States troops in the department to defend the frontier.[2]

But when depredations continued along the border during the summer, General Brooke reconsidered. On August 9 he asked the Governor for information concerning the number of men Texas had placed in the field. It was his opinion that a company

[1] Governors Letters File, Governor George T. Wood, Archives Division, Texas State Library, Austin. Hereafter cited as G. L.

[2] Brooke to Wood, July 11, 1849, G. L.

of seventy-five men might be organized and mustered into federal service to operate between Corpus Christi and the Río Grande. New raids near Corpus Christi forced a decision, and, on August 11, Brooke asked the Governor for three Ranger companies for six months' service. The companies, seventy-eight strong and patterned after United States cavalry units, were to have a general depot at Corpus Christi and were to operate throughout the Southwest Texas frontier from Goliad to Corpus Christi and thence to the Río Grande.[3] Recruits were to furnish their horses, saddles, bridles, halters, and lariats; the federal government would provide percussion rifles, pistols, holsters, and ammunition.[4]

Governor Wood agreed to General Brooke's request, but left Austin without designating officers to form the companies. The duty devolved on Adjutant General John D. Pitts, who by August 18 had selected his friend John S. Ford, the experienced Ranger John G. Grumbles, and Henry Smock.[5] Ford's recruits assembled in Austin on August 23 and chose Ford to be their captain; Thomas M. Woolridge, first lieutenant; and Jerry Robinson, second lieutenant.[6] The company then was mustered into federal service, and a day or two later Captain John Ford mounted "Old Higgins" and led his Rangers out on the San Antonio road.

Ford's commissioning displeased Governor Wood, who seems to have promised a command, without informing Pitts, to another aspirant. Upon his return to Austin, Wood appealed to General Brooke for Ford's dismissal, but the latter, after conferring with legislator-lawyer Volney E. Howard, informed the executive that Ford could be dismissed only by court-martial or by the expiration of his commission. The Governor thereupon ceased to object.[7]

From San Antonio, Ford's company, unarmed except for a few personal weapons, marched through Indian-infested country to

[3] A. A. G. Major George Deas to Wood, August 9, 1849, G. L.
[4] Order No. 53, August 11, 1849, G. L.; Brooke to Wood, August 11, 1849, G. L.
[5] Brown, "Annals," Ch. XIII, 61; Ford, "Memoirs," III, 529.
[6] *Texas Democrat* (Austin), August 16, 1849.
[7] Ford, "Memoirs," III, 529–30. Ford does not name his rival, but it may have been a Captain Johnson of Goliad, *Democratic Telegraph and Texas Register* (Houston), September 27, 1849.

Corpus Christi. The command arrived at the depot on September 5, having passed en route near the scene of a Comanche defeat by a citizens' party led by the region's foremost Indian fighter, Andrew J. Walker. Ford was relieved when the march ended; he believed that "a dozen determined Indians could have defeated the whole command with heavy loss." At Corpus Christi the Rangers received weapons and Ford employed Andy Walker as company guide. Then the Captain took his men into camp at H. L. Kinney's ranch on the Cajo del Oso, about eight miles south of the town.

Of the companies called up by Pitts, Ford's was stationed nearest the frontier, and throughout the fall and winter of 1849 and 1850 his Rangers found themselves in for hard, unrewarding work. Patrol after patrol was dispatched from the Oso camp and, later, from their relocated camp on the Santa Gertrudis, about half a mile above the spot where Richard King was one day to erect his ranch headquarters. The Rangers consistently failed to encounter raiders, usually because the frequent, heavy rains blotted out all tracks. However, Ford kept the region under constant surveillance, scouting on one occasion up the river to Laredo, then crossing to the Nueces and back to the Santa Gertrudis, a march of some four hundred miles.

One episode of this reconnaissance nearly involved the Captain in an international incident. Leaving his detachment on the Texas side of the Río Grande, Ford crossed to Mier with Andy Walker to acquire information about the activities of the Seminoles, accused by border settlers of being among the principal offenders. The two spent a night of singing and dancing in the home of "the Pearl of Mier," Margarita García. That night a party of Americans (including some of Ford's Rangers) raided the customs house and seized goods which the Mexican authorities had confiscated for having been brought across the river illegally. The Mexican consul at Mier implicated Captain Ford, lodging a complaint against him with the United States Department of State. Secretary of War G. W. Crawford, without investigating the affair, ordered Ford's arrest. Fortunately for him, Ford had reported to Brooke previously, and the General so ably defended the accused Ranger that the matter was dropped.[8]

In his report, Ford outlined to Brooke the condition of affairs along the Río Grande, pointing out that a "large number of Texas citizens, of Mexican origin, and paying State taxes upon their lands, were living on the west bank of the Rio Grande in consequence of the inadequate protection given them." So extensive were the Indian raids, particularly against the ranches between Roma and Laredo, that it was "almost impossible to procure Mexican laborers to work in the fields on the east banks of the Rio Grande. . . . A general dread prevailed everywhere." Ford learned also of the operations on Texas soil of the bandit gang of Ramón Falcon, whose men, on April 21, 1846, had murdered Colonel Truman Cross of the United States Army near Brownsville. In a grandiloquent report, Ford wrote: "Should the villain who bathed his hands in the blood of one of the best officers of the army, fall into my hands, I shall hang him to the first convenient tree, as an act of retributive justice for his crimes."[9]

When on February 23, 1850, the six months' enlistment of Ford's command expired, the company was reorganized and remustered for another half-year's duty.[10] Some of the original command, possibly disgusted with much riding through rain and knee-deep mud but no fighting, returned home. Their places were filled by others who were to help make the company the compact, hard-hitting force that border dwellers long remembered. When the reorganized company rode southwest toward a new base, Captain Ford had at his back a new set of company officers. Andy Walker, border guide and scout and a veteran of at least one Mexican revolution, was now the first lieutenant. A few years younger than Ford, he was more experienced as an Indian fighter.[11] The new second lieutenant was Malcijah (Kige) Highsmith, a tested Ranger veteran of six years' service, most of it with his father, Captain

[8] Ford, "Memoirs," III, 530, 532–33.
[9] *State Gazette* (Austin), December 12, 1857.
[10] Records Group No. 94.
[11] Ford, "Memoirs," III, 538; Walter Prescott Webb, *et al.* (eds.), *Handbook of Texas*, II, 853.

Samuel Highsmith. Company routine was in the capable hands of a determined fighter, Orderly Sergeant David M. Level. Dr. Philip M. Luckett, who had come from Austin with the original command, still rode as surgeon, a busy future awaiting him.[12]

Marching in the ranks came the seventy-odd Rangers, young men for the most part, but old in the ways of frontier warfare. The inimitable prankster "Doc" Sullivan rode beside his bosom friend, Alpheus D. Neal; long-nosed Voltaire Rountree filled his accustomed place in the column; John F. (Black Tan) Wilson, sunburned Henderson Miller, David Steele, and Alf Tom responded to the brazen signals of youthful Bugler Matt Nolan, hardly more than a boy, who rode proudly with Ed Burleson, John Wilbarger, and William Gillespie, campaign veterans only slightly older than himself. Bob Adams, Milt May, and Ashmore Edwards, familiar names along the border, were there, as were Jack Spencer, Sam Duncan, and Jack Sharpe, whose unheralded names ere long would be well known.

Half-Comanche, half-Mexican Roque Maugricio, one-time Comanche war captain and the border's most reliable trailer, rode ahead pointing out the way.[13] At the tail of the column, responsible for the Captain's baggage, trotted Ford's personal servant, Francisco de la Garza Falcon, self-styled hero of the Mexican War battle of Monterrey. Because of his colorful boasting and unpredictable antics, he had been dubbed "Don Monkey" by Ford, who had the knack of bestowing appropriate designations. In fact, nearly every man in the command bore a nickname personally assigned by the Captain in accordance with some trait or characteristic.[14] These men formed the company which always was remembered by both captain and men as "Ford's Old Rangers." Not all its members, however, were destined to serve out their enlistments. Sullivan and Wilbarger were to die quickly in a lonely fight west of the Santa Gertrudis, while Gillespie, Baker

---

[12] Ford, "Memoirs," III, 538–39; Webb, *Handbook of Texas*, II, 809.

[13] Ford, "Memoirs," III, 538.

[14] Charles L. Martin, "The Last of the Ranger Chieftains," *Texas Magazine*, Vol. IV (1898), 40. Hereafter cited as Martin, "Last of the Ranger Chieftains."

Barton, and William Lackey were marked to be mustered out by savage weapons. No foreseeable ill fortune darkened the future now, as they marched toward the Río Grande, nor were they of the ilk who borrow trouble. "They belonged to that class of men who lived without fear, and died without reproach," wrote Ford many years later.[15]

Very likely it was this company which fixed on John S. Ford the sobriquet by which he was to be known thenceforward— "Old Rip." The appellation, already in common use to describe individuals always involved in one affair after another, was admirably suited to Ford. It is not known who first applied the term to Ford, but it is entirely possible that the tow-headed Sullivan was responsible. "Doc," while he obeyed orders readily, stood in awe of no man, and was known to be quick with a nickname. In any event, John Ford was "Rip" to his Rangers by the early 1850's.[16]

Department headquarters had decided that the company could serve more effectively from a base nearer the Río Grande. Soon after the remuster, Ford was ordered to move toward the river and select a permanent base. He chose a site near the ruins of San Antonio Viejo (Old San Antonio), a hacienda abandoned by its owner because of Indian raids. The remains stood where the Laredo road emerged from the southern edge of the sand belt, about forty-five miles north of Río Grande City. Here were several good wells and stone watering-troughs. By early March, the company had pitched its tents in a clump of oaks about half a mile south of the wells, the tents forming three sides of a square open to the west. Across the opening the troopers erected a rude building to house Lieutenant Highsmith's quartermaster and commissary stores. This done, the command turned to its regular routine of drill, detail, and patrol.[17]

[15] Ford, "Memoirs," III, 599.

[16] Martin, "Last of the Ranger Chieftains," 40. Martin, who served under Ford at Fort Brown in 1862, may have learned the source of the name then, or from his parents, who were old friends of Ford. Walter Prescott Webb, *The Texas Rangers*, 124n., presents what has been the accepted source of the nickname.

[17] Ford, "Memoirs," III, 439.

In one respect, "Rip" Ford was an unusual Ranger officer; he believed in drill. Characteristically his men were proficient in the manual of arms and were particularly adept in performing the simple mounted maneuvers which enabled them to present their most effective strength toward an enemy. Daily drill was standard procedure for troopers not on patrol, and Ford's discipline guaranteed little evasion of the onerous duty. With Ford, discipline "had little that savored of that enforced in the regular army. It appealed to the pride and sense of honor of the men." A Ranger derelict in duty was punished in ways most keenly felt by proud frontier spirits. He was

> not allowed to go on a scout, to be detailed as an escort, or to enjoy the privileges accorded to honorable soldiers. They were on duty as camp guards, and other services, which are generally distasteful to men of energy and enterprise. This punishment . . . carried with it a loss of the respect and the confidence of the whole command. It caused fellows apparently hardened to the ordinary ideas of propriety to beg, and even cry, when told they could not leave camp. Should the captain place a man under ban, his example would be followed by all down to the fourth corporal. It required no order to bring about such a result.

Small wonder, then, that Ford recorded little shirking.[18]

Early in May, Ford sent William Gillespie and small squad to the Corpus Christi depot to exchange the command's unserviceable pistols for single-shot dragoon models. Ford planned to scout above Laredo, working gradually toward the depot, where he would pick up the supply detail. With Lieutenant Walker and about forty men, Ford rode to Fort McIntosh, just outside Laredo, for supplies. Then the command turned inland, advancing slowly and cautiously through timbered country behind the scouts of Roque and Sergeant Level. The air carried a feeling that Indians were near, a feeling confirmed when the carcass of a recently killed deer yielded a Comanche arrowhead. Ford thereupon divided the command, sending half southeast with Lieutenant Walker while he himself led the rest north toward the Nueces. "Old

18 *Ibid.*, 534.

Rip" reasoned that the Indians would soon discover one of the detachments and, trying to evade it, might be driven into the arms of the other. Events proved his logic valid.

Ford halted for a day on San Roque Creek, a small tributary of the Nueces, while Roque's scouts carefully worked the area. On the same day, Walker's men went into action. During the morning, Indians ran one of the mule drivers into camp, and the Rangers immediately began a pursuit. Failing after half a day's effort to throw the astute Walker off their trail, the Indians turned and drove hard for the Nueces. By changing mounts frequently they maintained their lead, and at dusk Walker abandoned the trail. His disappointment would have been less had he known he had driven the raiders into Ford's hands.

On the following morning, May 12, Ford moved down the Nueces toward a crossing frequently used by the Comanches. A few miles from the ford he struck the trail of the fleeing Indians. Leaving two men to guard the pack train, he and the other sixteen, including Don Monkey, crossed the stream by swimming their horses and supporting themselves by convenient driftwood. On the north bank, Ford put the command into column and led it along a trail which showed that the Indians were riding slowly, confident that they had escaped. After tracking through thick timber for eight miles, Ford suddenly emerged into open prairie in time to see the heads of the hostile stragglers disappear beyond a small knoll. Shouting back a command to hurry, he spurred forward to within fifty yards of the enemy.

Roque and Sergeant Level hurried to Ford's side, but the rest of the detachment, mistaking Ford's shout for an order to halt, impatiently reined in at the timber's edge. The Comanche war chief, seeing only three pursuers, turned his band to attack. The other Rangers joined "Old Rip" just in time. Sixteen Rangers, armed with muzzle-loading "Tennessee" rifles, faced an equal number of Comanche braves equipped with lances and bows and arrows, weapons which for close fighting were as effective as the six-shooters which only Ford and Level carried. The Comanche chief rode back and forth behind his slowly retiring warriors, about thirty yards in advance of the Rangers, trying to draw their fire so that his men could wheel and strike before the Texans could reload. Ford frustrated the design by commanding his men to keep together and fire alternately. His order was punctuated by the crack of a pistol, and he turned to see the Comanche chief swerve away, one arm dripping blood where Sergeant Level's shot had penetrated. The Captain's "Charge!" was echoed by the Texas yell as the Rangers spurred forward.

Ford, leading the assault, chose a particular victim and maneuvered to a position several yards behind him. The Indian squirmed frantically in his saddle in an attempt to loose an arrow at Ford, but in the midst of his acrobatic gyrations his saddle girth broke, dropping him on the prairie. He bounced to his feet with his bow fully drawn, but before he could release the string, "Old Rip" shot him through the head as he swept by. Both Indians and Rangers, who momentarily had paused to watch the encounter, now resumed the running combat, the savages seeking to reach the safety of the woods several miles away. When the surviving Comanches gained the timber, Ford ordered a halt. A quick examination revealed only one casualty in the detachment; Ranger David Steele had been slightly wounded by a dropping arrow. Ford dismissed as inconsequential a slight arrow scratch across the back of his own right hand;[19] he was much more concerned for his mount, wounded deeply by a poisoned arrow. The animal was to die three days later, to be regretted by the departmental quartermaster as a $150 loss.[20] Ford believed that enemy casualties were substantial: the Comanches, contrary to custom, had left one of their dead on the prairie; others, including the war chief, were known to have been hit. Oddly enough, it was with these same Comanches that Ford and his companions had camped on the El Paso journey of the preceding year. In the thick of the fight, a brave had recognized Sullivan and had called to him, asking if he would shoot his friends. Sullivan's answer was a rifle ball through a warrior's body. Two weeks later, Ford learned the extent of enemy losses—four dead and eleven wounded in a

19 *Ibid.*, 543–45.   20 Records Group No. 94.

party of seventeen. In addition, the Rangers captured about a dozen horses and many weapons.

The Rangers laughed over one incident of the fray. When the firing began, Ford's servant, Don Monkey, set out for the rear at full speed, but met Bugler Nolan, who insisted that he return to the fight. The Don faced about and rode forward until the shots and yells of the combatants again inspired him to seek safety toward the rear in spite of the threats of the Rangers to shoot him if he abandoned the fight. Until the skirmish ended, Don Monkey oscillated from front to rear at high speed. Some days later, in describing the fight to a Ranger who had not been along, the handyman recounted his own role in the battle thus:

"Notwithstanding the *capitan* was on a fine horse, and I on a pony we were side by side—'parejitos'—all the time. I fired all my cartridges, and went into them with my knife." "What," said the man, "with nothing but your knife?" "*Con nada solo mi puro belduque*—with nothing but my naked knife."

Captain Ford rejoined his pack train a short distance south of the Nueces, picketed the crossing, and went into camp. Morning revealed that two mounts had strayed, and the command spread to search for them. Roque soon came to report that the horses had taken the back trail and had been picked up by Indians not far from the Ranger camp. After collecting his men, Ford followed Roque at a brisk gallop along the Indian tracks through intermittent timber, occasionally pressing hard when a laggard brave came briefly into view. All day the Rangers tried vainly to close with the savages, whose fresher horses kept them well in advance. At sunset, Ford found that he had been riding in a great circle. That night he camped in thick timber at a water hole where the pack train had that morning been directed to halt.

Ford awoke on the morning of May 14 to find his position dangerous. The survivors of the band defeated two days earlier had fallen in with a war party of about seventy-five Comanches and had returned on the night of May 12 to attempt a surprise attack. Finding the ford picketed, they crossed the Nueces the next morning but were unable to find the Rangers. During that night they had discovered and surrounded the Ranger camp. The meat ration of the Rangers had been used up, and the hunters were not able to search more than one hundred yards from their bivouac. Even the experienced Sullivan was almost deceived by the turkey-like gobbling of a Comanche scout. In this ticklish situation, moving by short, careful marches, "Rip" Ford led his detachment through the timber down the Nueces toward Fort Merrill, the Comanches keeping pace all around the Rangers. Time after time the Comanches threatened to attack, but the hours of drill proved their worth. Invariably the Indians sheered away from the strong defensive formation of Ford's riders. At night the command camped in a circle; horses, pack mules, and equipment were secured in the center of the ring, and sentinels took post outside the camp area.

For more than three days and nights the command moved and bivouacked in this fashion. Meanwhile, rations had almost vanished. Cooks for each mess were ordered to report to Ford, who still had a small supply of coffee. Don Monkey watched anxiously as the Captain prepared to dole out shares of his own store to the cooks. Finally he mustered courage to inquire, "Is it possible you are going to divide *our* coffee among the men?"

"Yes, sir, that is just what I am going to do."

There came the Don's frantic rejoinder: "My God, who can expect me to fight Indians the way I have been doing without coffee?"

When the last of the coffee disappeared, the Rangers resorted to making a tea by boiling mesquite wood and saturating the brew heavily with sugar.[21] Fortunately, the command was by then near Fort Merrill, on the Nueces near the site of the now-vanished hamlet of Gussettville, and the Comanches abandoned their efforts at an ambush. Ford's weary riders went into camp near the fort, and the post commander, Captain Samuel Plummer, quickly provided both rations and forage for the Ranger detachment.[22]

21 Ford, "Memoirs," III, 544–49.
22 *Democratic Telegraph and Texas Register* (Houston), June 13, 1850.

At Fort Merrill, Ford granted furloughs to John Wilbarger to visit his family and to "Doc" Sullivan and Alpheus Neal, who had been subpoenaed as witnesses in pending legal suits. After cautioning them to make the return journey in company with others, he bade them a farewell more final than any suspected and turned to further business. Leaving his Rangers camped about half a mile below the fort, Ford rode to Corpus Christi. He wished to learn if the squad he had sent for pistols had made the exchange, and he needed better medical attention than either the post surgeon at Fort Merrill or he himself could provide. The scratch received in the skirmish of May 12 was causing extreme pain in his right arm, and he suspected that rattlesnake venom had been applied to the arrowhead. No successful treatment was discovered, however; the next five or six years brought almost complete paralysis to the arm, and for the next quarter of a century a skin eruption appeared annually on the hand.

With his Ranger squad and pistols, Captain Ford returned to camp on the evening of May 25. He arrived just in time for another action against Indians. Shortly after his arrival, Ashmore Edwards, who had been on guard the previous night, reported hearing on all sides the intermittent hooting of owls. Ford's rule was "to prepare for the worst and hope for the best." He ordered each trooper to tether his horse within the bivouac area. Sentinels were carefully posted, the main guard was alerted for prompt action, and guns were painstakingly loaded and placed beneath the blankets. A sharp rifle volley at three o'clock in the morning proved the worth of "Old Rip's" precautions. The Rangers sprang up, guns in hands, to find the Captain already issuing commands. A detail mounted guard over the camp while the troopers who had gentle horses rode bareback to relieve the outpost line, where brisk firing, gradually becoming more distant, indicated that the sentinels were driving back the Comanches. Amid the firing an Indian voice arose, pleading for amnesty, Roque said, but the language was unknown to the Rangers. When Ford and Roque reached the spot from which the shout had come, they found a Comanche warrior writhing in a death agony.

Ford recalled his Rangers, including young Matt Nolan, who had hopped barefoot among the prickly pear excitedly seeking a shot at the raiders. Ed Burleson was dispatched to Fort Merrill to report the incident to Captain Plummer. That surprised officer, who had maintained that Comanche raids were but talk, blurted, "What! Indians so near my post!!! I thought it was you Texians fighting among yourselves." A daylight scout located no Indians, and on the next morning Ford broke camp to begin a leisurely ride toward San Antonio Viejo.

For two days the march was without incident, but at midmorning on May 29, the command cut fresh Indian sign. While Roque trotted forward to study the tracks, Ford strengthened his rear guard and put the detachment in fighting order. Several miles farther on, the Rangers sighted the Indians encamped in a mesquite clump atop a small hill. They swept at a gallop toward the Comanches, who mounted and fled, signaling as they crossed each hillock. Roque explained that they were requesting aid from comrades in the vicinity and suggested that the rear guard might be endangered.

Unknown to Ford, Ranger Bill Gillespie was already lying behind, mortally wounded. An enemy, twice shot and left for dead during the charge, had revived just as Gillespie passed. The latter, pistol in hand, turned to finish the brave, but his mount for the day, the treacherous "Old Higgins," swerved and the shot went wide. The Comanche's arrow buried itself in Gillespie's side, penetrating his left lung. Companions helped him to the shade of a mesquite and then followed the pursuit. Ford, seeing a threat to his rear guard, ordered a headlong charge, but the Rangers, fearing that the Comanches would circle to get Gillespie's scalp and horse, stood fast. Ford had ridden some thirty yards before he realized that he was alone. When he turned to see his men lingering and shouting unintelligibly, he assumed that they had become frightened, and completely lost his temper. Turning his back on the enemy, "Old Rip" "swore at the men, calling them cowards, and other bad names," until Roque rode forward to explain. Immediately Ford had Gillespie carried to the safety of the ranks.

Now Ford halted until the rear guard began to advance. Then, marching diagonally to join it, his Rangers opened a long-range, deliberate fire which killed some of the Comanche horses and wounded several braves. Flank and rear the two groups struck the war party. The Comanche leader, Otto Cuero, gave his horse to a wounded comrade and began a rear guard action against the Rangers on foot. The Indian horsemen maneuvered to screen their footmen, who were trying to reach the brushy bank of the Agua Dulce, about a mile away. A Ranger charge broke up the movement, and the entire war band broke for the timber. Ford sent a pistol shot after the dismounted chief at a range of 125 yards, but the warrior continued on the run. At Ford's order, David Steele dismounted and lined his rifle sights on the chief, who at that instant paused to look back. Steele's shot sent the Comanche sprawling.

Ford ended the pursuit at the timber's edge, and the command turned back across the prairie. Ford and Steele halted to collect the dead chief's weapons and equipment.[23] Ford's shot had bored through the Comanche's left arm; Steele's bullet had pierced the skull. Three other Indians were dead and at least seven wounded. One of the latter, with several injuries, had secreted himself in a mesquite thicket, where he was discovered by Roque. When promised his life if he would surrender, the wounded Comanche tossed aside his weapons. This eighteen-year-old prisoner, called Carne Muerto (Dead Meat), was reputed to be the son of the famous war chief, Santa Anna.

Ford's casualties were two wounded men, Gillespie and Orderly Sergeant Level, whose enraged expression during the fight had caught the Captain's attention. Subsequently Ford learned that the Sergeant was so irate over the wounding of his horse that he considered his own musket wound above an ankle merely incidental. Painful as the wound was, Level still could ride, but Gillespie was unable to sit his saddle, and the men constructed a litter for him. Meanwhile, Ford openly praised the valor of Bob

[23] Ford, "Memoirs," III, 545–57; *State Gazette* (Austin), December 12, 1857. Steele sent the chief's arms and trappings to Governor Peter H. Bell.

Adams and apologized for accusing him of inefficiency in the clash of May 12. When the litter was ready, the command marched through the late afternoon down the Agua Dulce toward a spot about a dozen miles away, where an advanced patrol of Grumbles' company was camped. Gillespie's suffering forced a halt before the destination was reached. He died that night, and the next morning his body was carried to the bivouac of Grumbles' men and buried with military honors. When the Rangers, with drawn weapons, formed two ranks beside the grave, the Comanche captive glumly supposed the preparations were for his execution.[24]

From San Antonio Viejo, Ford submitted his report of the battle, designating it the Amargosa fight. The action brought a departmental order from Brooke expressing his "decided commendation for the activity, zeal, and success which have characterized your operations since you have been under his orders. A continuance of such efficient service . . . will have a most happy effect in carrying out the objects for which the Texas volunteers were called into the field."[25]

Early in June an outbreak of depredations drove most of the ranch population of Webb County into Laredo. Ford sent Walker and twenty men to a point from which they could defend the town, intercept marauders, and get information from the few *vaqueros* and sheepherders who had remained with their stock. Walker soon was on the downriver trail of a Comanche horse-stealing band. At Basilio Benavides' ranch, about twenty miles below Laredo, he was told that the Indians were rounding up Benavides' horse herd. Walker permitted his men to unsaddle to rest their mounts before cutting across country to intercept the band. The Comanches, however, drove the herd back to Benavides' corral to cut out the best stock. Confusion was equally divided. After a few shots, the Indians fled on the weary ponies they had ridden southward. Walker's men quickly overtook them, killing all seven raiders in a brief skirmish. One brave, Bad Finger, did not die immediately, but was put to death by a Mexican muleteer

24 Ford, "Memoirs," III, 557–58.
25 *State Gazette* (Austin), December 12, 1857.

to spare him needless suffering. He was a cousin of Ford's prisoner, Carne Muerto and, before he died, imparted information of value to the Rangers. Walker's only casualty, Ed Stevens, had a painful but otherwise negligible arrow furrow in his scalp.

The fight had several beneficial results: Walker's already substantial stock as an Indian fighter went even higher; again the Rangers had demonstrated their ability to cope with raiders; and the recapture of Benavides' herd restored feelings of confidence and security to the Mexican-American border residents.[26]

The dying Bad Finger had revealed Comanche plans for a major raid in the near future. Angered by unaccustomed losses, the capture of Carne Muerto, and white encroachment on what they considered their private mustang preserve, the war bands were gathering to punish the Rangers, whom they considered the source of their troubles. Ford believed Bad Finger's story and reported it to Brooke. Leaving Highsmith with some twenty Rangers and civilian employees at San Antonio Viejo, he took about sixty men southward to join Walker at Laredo, thus to create a force capable of blocking a Comanche incursion. This time Don Monkey, discredited by his actions at the Amargosa fight, remained behind. He had been guilty of discarding most of Ford's equipment, as impediments to rapid withdrawal, and later had demanded, on threat of a strike, a full Ranger salary of $23.50 monthly, insisting that he no longer could fight Indians for a paltry $10.00 each month. He struck to no avail.

At Laredo, Ford turned Carne Muerto over to Captain Sidney Burbank, commanding at Fort McIntosh. There the entire command was enraged by an inspection order, stemming from a malicious report to department headquarters that the men had traded their horses for inferior Mexican ponies and were no longer fit to operate. A perfunctory inspection by the sympathetic Burbank eased the situation, brought about, so Ford was told, by Captain Gabriel Armstrong, of unimpressive Mexican War memory.[27] But before the Ranger wrath had cooled, it had another object. A lathered courier from Río Grande City came in to

[26] Ford, "Memoirs," III, 560–62.   [27] *Ibid.*, 564–65.

report that Highsmith was in serious trouble. A Carrizo scout, on Ashmore Edwards' fast horse, had burst through a Comanche siege line around San Antonio Viejo, outrunning the besiegers to Río Grande City with Highsmith's call for aid.

The Indians had been gone for two days when Ford arrived after a seventy-five-mile forced march.[28] From Highsmith he learned that Don Monkey had hastily returned from hunting to report many people at the wells. Close behind him came a Comanche war party of about two hundred braves. Several Rangers delayed the attack long enough for the garrison to drive in most of the stock. The Indians, after losing a man to the first shot from the camp, retired out of range and settled down for a two-day siege. Fortunately Highsmith's men had an abundance of provisions and had just finished hauling a water supply. The steadiness of their fire discouraged any direct assault. Neither side apparently suffered much in the affair, although tempers ran high, especially the Don's.

> The Don allowed his angry passions to rise unmeasurably. He menaced the enemy, pistol in hand; shut his eyes, turned his head aside, and banged away. The balls hit the ground within ten feet of his noble self. At each discharge he would ask—"Did I kill one?" A negative reply caused his weapon to get a terrible cursing. The cooped up Rangers, disregarding the danger, amused themselves at the above recited demonstration.

Don Monkey was not alone in profane comment. August Harmuth, a conscientious mule driver, swore indignantly as he watched the Comanches butcher one of his fat charges for an impromptu feast. He pulled off his coat, strode to the edge of the camp, and in colorful language invited the banqueters to come and feel his fists. His challenge went unheeded. Toward the close of the second day the Comanches, suspecting the arrival of a rescue force, drew off. They took with them several head of stock,

---

[28] *Democratic Telegraph and Texas Register* (Houston), August 7, 1850; *State Gazette* (Austin), December 12, 1857.

including "Old Higgins." Ford's irritation at the theft may have been assuaged when he considered the surprises in store for the unsuspecting brave who acquired that irresponsible animal.

Hoping to afford better protection to the Webb County residents and to traders freighting over the Laredo–San Antonio road, Ford shifted his camp from San Antonio Viejo to Los Ojuelos (the Little Springs), about forty miles east of Laredo on the Laredo–Corpus Christi road. It was now late summer, almost time for enlistments to expire. Knowing that some men would not re-enlist, he wished to reorganize the company before relocating his headquarters; consequently, he first marched the command to San Antonio, acquired recruits, filled his wagons with arms, ammunition, and rations, and turned back toward Los Ojuelos. At the Frío, he met an unexpected obstacle: the stream, fed by recent rains, was running bank full under a cloudy sky, and a cold norther was blowing. The ford was deep beneath the muddy, hurrying waters, impossible to cross with loaded wagons. Immediately Ford ordered the stores unloaded. Next, he had the wagons dragged by ropes through the flood. Working shoulder to shoulder beside his men in the chill stream, he saw the last of the wagons across and turned to the problem of moving the supplies. The Rangers hit upon an ingenious scheme. Threading a strong rope through a stirrup, they tied it securely to trees on either bank. Short ropes then were tied to the stirrup, as well as two long ropes, each as long as the river was wide. The items of supply were tied to the short ropes; Rangers on the south bank pulled the loaded stirrup across by one long rope, and others on the north bank pulled on the other long rope to haul the stirrup back for another load. It was cold, slow, careful work, but by dusk the transfer had been made without loss. Ford and some of his men spent almost the entire day in the river, chilled by cold water and cold wind and suffering "considerably." It was a real ordeal for the Captain, whose system already was weak from the effects of the poisoned arrow; the exposure was soon to tell upon him.[29]

<hr />

[29] Ford, "Memoirs," III, 565–70; *State Gazette* (Austin), December 12, 1857.

The company remustered at Laredo on September 24,[30] with the energetic Ed Burleson as second lieutenant, replacing the departed Highsmith. Still it was the efficient fighting machine that experience and leadership had made it, but "Old Rip" surveyed his ranks with some sadness. They were full, but three loyal faces were missing: Sullivan, Wilbarger, and Neal. Even before the march into San Antonio, news of the three had brought gloom to the command. The trio had met at San Antonio after furlough to return to San Antonio Viejo. Having already overstayed their time, they disregarded their captain's parting warning in their anxiety to be off. They rode by San Patricio, and by their old camp on the Santa Gertrudis. On August 20, some twenty miles southwest of the latter point, they stopped to "noon" in the shade of a lone mesquite. As they were mounting to ride on, thirty Comanches appeared. The Rangers were well mounted and well armed; they could run or fight. They chose to fight.

Their error became immediately apparent. A long-range shot curled Sullivan over the pommel of his saddle, struck through the body. Dismounting, Neal lifted his comrade down while Wilbarger tied the horse to the mesquite. "Doc," aware he was hit mortally, demanded that Neal and Wilbarger ride out. Before they could demur, a second bullet crunched through Sullivan's skull, and he fell back dead. Neal swung into his saddle, but his horse bolted beneath the rope tethering Sullivan's mount, and the ranger was swept to the ground. His horse, with his weapons tied to the saddle, galloped away. It was quickly caught by the Indians who took the weapons and rode shooting around the vainly dodging Ranger. At length Neal fell unconscious with at least eight wounds, several of which probably would have been fatal to another man. Consciousness returned to him as the Comanches were preparing to leave. Feigning death, he lay motionless while one warrior made a final inspection of the supposed corpse. When the victors rode away, Neal crawled painfully to the water hole.

For more than an hour he huddled by the pool, scarcely aware in his pain that Sullivan's body no longer lay beneath the mes-

[30] Records Group No. 94.

quite. Neal had been stripped, and five or six arrows protruded from his naked body like pins from a cushion, shot there by the triumphant braves in their usual treatment of dead foes. Neal managed to work several arrows from his flesh, but his clumsy, painful efforts only resulted in the snapping off of the shafts of the rest. Finally he dragged himself to his feet, set his face grimly toward San Patricio sixty-five miles away, and staggered north beneath the blazing rays of a South Texas August sun.

The reeling, naked figure which several days later tottered into the little village at first was taken by the San Patricians for an Indian. Blistered and burned from sole to crown, feverish from his festering wounds, his tongue swollen almost past use, Neal was momentarily in danger of being shot by his own countrymen. When finally he could identify himself, some citizens immediately provided medical attention while others rode to the scene of the fight. There they found what remained of the bodies of Sullivan and Wilbarger. The latter had carried a six-shooter, and blood splotches on the prairie indicated that he had used it effectively. Sullivan's body apparently had been recognized by the Comanches, perhaps by some who had been the objects of his pin-sticking the previous year; it had been dragged aimlessly over the prairie and in other ways mutilated until identification was difficult.[31]

The attack on Highsmith's men was the last Comanche activity of the year near Laredo. Ford suspected that the party had come to liberate Carne Muerto and that the Comanches now would avoid the region as long as the young brave was a prisoner. It was fortunate for "Old Rip" that the raids ceased temporarily, since his exposure to the chill of the Frío and the norther brought on an illness which kept him confined to Los Ojuelos and Fort McIntosh for most of the following winter.[32] Walker and Burleson, however, kept the company actively patrolling.

The new year brought Ford's men a change from uneventful

[31] Ford, "Memoirs," III, 570–74; J. W. Wilbarger, *Indian Depredations in Texas*, 614–16. Neal survived and, according to Ford, carried one of the arrowheads extracted from him for years as a pocket piece.

[32] Ford, "Memoirs," III, 570; *State Gazette* (Austin), December 12, 1857.

routine scouting. Early in January, 1851, came an order to send Carne Muerto to department headquarters at San Antonio. Ford sent Burleson with about twenty men to escort the prisoner. He rightly believed that the transfer of the Comanche from Fort McIntosh would bring trouble to the Laredo area. Within a fortnight a Mexican hunter was killed only a few miles from town. Ford, at Fort McIntosh for medical treatment, at once took the trail with a small party of Rangers and citizens, although he was almost too ill to ride, but the Comanche assassin had too great a start to be caught. Then, in late January, news reached the still ailing Ford at Los Ojuelos of a bitter engagement involving most of Walker's detachment. "Old Rip" rode immediately for Laredo, where he found Walker and Burleson and learned that both had been in action.

On January 19, scouting northeast of Laredo, Walker and twenty men had found a Comanche campsite. The trail thence indicated that the band was heading for Mexico, bypassing the Ranger camp at Los Ojuelos. Confident that the raiders would return by the same route, Walker chose a position on high, brushy ground affording the patrol full cover. Two miles from his camp, at a high point on the trail, he stationed a picket, and placed another a mile nearer camp. For six days, despite Ranger impatience, Walker maintained a strict camp discipline respecting concealment and prohibition of fire and smoke. On the sixth day his patience was rewarded when his pickets signaled that the Indians were approaching.

Two warriors scouting ahead were permitted to pass the Ranger guards unmolested. Soon the main band came in sight, about seventeen braves driving a mixed herd of some two hundred mules and horses. Busy with their herding, the Comanches became aware of the Rangers only when Walker's charge was almost upon them. After attempting to rally, they fled into the chaparral, where pursuit was virtually impossible. After rounding up the stolen herd and taking charge of a Mexican lad captured by the marauders, the detachment returned to Laredo, where the boy was returned to his parents and the stock turned over to the Mexican owners by the Fort McIntosh quartermaster. The Rangers had killed four Comanches and wounded about six more; their only mishaps were David Level's dead horse and Level's wound, where an arrow had pinned his hand to his saddle bow. Walker's men were somewhat disconcerted by Mexican complaints that less stock was returned than had been stolen. Complaints became inaudible when "Old Rip" irritably suggested that perhaps the Rangers had been fighting the wrong people.[33]

Walker's skirmish was a pale thing beside that reported by Ed Burleson, who had just emerged from what Ford was to describe to frontier artist Frederic Remington as "the most desperate fight" of which he knew.[34] On January 27, returning from their escort mission, his detachment sighted three Comanches. Burleson chose eight men to accompany him, ordered the rest on to Laredo, and gave chase. As he closed on the Indians, they faced about to fight and were joined by eleven dismounted Comanches who had been lying in ambush for a train of traders' carts. Mistaking Burleson's orders, the Rangers also dismounted, and the Comanches hastened to attack.

The fight took place on a barren plain devoid of all vegetation; consequently, both foes attempted to use the Ranger horses for cover. It was hand-to-hand work, lances, bows and arrows against the recently issued Colt revolvers and a few Colt carbines, with the combatants trading shots and blows beneath the bellies of the frantic mounts. Warren Lyons, translating rapidly for Burleson between shots, reported that the Comanches were yelling back and forth that they were defeated but did not know how to break off the combat. Suddenly they ceased to fight and fled to the nearest thickets. Sam Duncan, riding back from the main party, came up as the fight ended to behold a veritable shambles. Of the nine Rangers engaged, only two were unmarked. Baker Barton had died on his feet from three mortal wounds, his desperate grip

[33] Ford, "Memoirs," III, 575–78; *State Gazette* (Austin), December 12, 1857.
[34] Frederic Remington, "How the Law Got into the Chaparral," *Harper's New Monthly Magazine*, Vol. XCIV (December, 1896–May, 1897), 62. Hereafter cited as Remington, "How the Law Got into the Chaparral."

on his saddle horn holding him erect a few moments after death. William Lackey, down with three severe wounds, would die at Fort McIntosh in about a week of an arrow in his lung. Burleson presented a gory head, bleeding from a furrow from which he had snatched an arrow. Jim Carr, whose four painful wounds included a perforated trigger finger, was explaining, "It was like clock work—every time I raised my Colt's carbine, they stuck an arrow in me." Alf Tom, Jim Wilkinson, and Jack Spencer, each with several wounds, were still belligerent. Only cool, deliberate Ranger Leach and interpreter Lyons were unhurt. The latter had reverted to the fighting tactics learned as a Comanche warrior and had escaped unscathed because of his bobbing, bounding, and weaving maneuvers during the fight, complaining all the while that his heavy boots were a handicap.

The Comanches fared no better. Four lay dead on the plain, and another eight had dragged themselves away bleeding from Ranger bullets. The fact that they had left their dead was the best indication of their demoralized condition and the final proof that they had been hit hard.

Burleson sent Duncan riding hard for a water hole twenty miles toward Laredo, carrying the drained water gourds of the detachment. Burleson's shattered party then set out for Laredo, with Barton's body lashed on a baggage mule. A few miles from the scene of the fight, the Rangers stopped to bury Barton and then moved on until early afternoon, when Duncan returned with water. In the January dusk the command struggled up to the water hole from which Duncan had ridden and made camp. Burleson sent a courier to Fort McIntosh to report his plight to Captain Burbank, who immediately dispatched a surgeon and an ambulance to the Rangers. Burleson's men reached the post on the evening of January 28.[35]

Soon after Burleson's fight, Ford and seventeen men rode to San Antonio on company business. Returning by the Laredo road, they struck the recent trail of a large band. Past the Nueces the Rangers made a forced night march for water, Roque and Lyons

[35] Ford, "Memoirs," III, 582–86; *State Gazette* (Austin), December 12, 1857.

leading them toward a water hole in a dry ravine. As they neared the ravine, they saw the reflected light of a large fire. The Rangers now carried six-shooters and some had Colt revolving carbines, giving the party a firepower of over one hundred shots without reloading. Confident that his detachment could handle whatever a reconnaissance might disclose, Ford sent Roque, Lyons, and Rountree forward to investigate while he brought the rest up slowly. The scouts reported a large party encamped at the spring. Just as Ford was about to order an attack, a Ranger accidentally discharged his pistol. There was a frantic stirring around the spring, and an agitated American voice shouted, "Do not shoot, you will make those Indians run off." The shouting voice was recognized as that of Lieutenant S. F. Holabird of the Fort McIntosh garrison.

Dismounting, Ford descended into the ravine. The first Indian he saw as he neared the fire was a shell-decorated brave with whom he had exchanged shots on May 12, 1850. When the leader of the band came forward, Ford recognized him as an acquaintance he had made on the El Paso journey of 1849. The chief bore the name "Fusil Recortado," a cognomen the Rangers translated "Short Shot Gun." He explained that he was visiting Fort McIntosh in the interests of peace and had notified the commander of his coming. Holabird and several soldiers had been sent to escort the band to the post. Ford and his men spent a wary night with the Comanches and marched with them to Laredo on the next day, where the visitors were quartered in vacant cabins.

During the visit, the Rangers maintained a careful around-the-clock watch over the self-invited guests. In spite of the tension, relations became cordial enough for "Old Rip" to gain a new relative.

The captain made an acquisition to his family circle. Mr. *Pi-na-hoach-man,* by interpretation Mr. Saddle Blanket, was famishing for another brother, upon whom to lavish his pent up affections. He conferred that distinguished honor on the Ranger captain, and they became a modern edition of Jonathan and David. . . . When too late, Warren Lyons notified his superior officer that the assumed relationship might give him trouble in the future. It meant a sort of alliance which obligated the parties not to fight each other, to render mutual assistance in case of peril, etc. To the honor of the Comanche let it be stated that, in 1858, and 1859, he remained true to his pledge.

The peaceful visit ended abruptly. Lyons burst into Ford's quarters one night to say that the brave who wore the shell belt was drunk and loading his gun to kill Roque, believing him responsible for the death of a brother killed in the fight the preceding May. Quickly and unobtrusively Ford called his men together and moved cautiously on the Comanche cabins. All was quiet there; an inspection revealed that the guests had speedily and secretly decamped. Since they had come in peace, they were permitted to depart unmolested. Several days later the Rangers followed their trail and learned that Short Shot Gun's band had joined the homeward-bound war party whose trail Ford had seen on his march from San Antonio.[36]

March 23, 1851, brought the end of the Ranger enlistment, but the company remustered on the same day for its fourth, and last, term of service.[37] Their last "hitch" was to be another time for them of much riding and patrolling but of no combat. Comanche expeditions ceased for a time; those far-riding warriors were weary of incursions too frequently resulting in disaster. Seminoles occasionally raided across the river, escaping before the Rangers could come up with them, but incidents now became so few that the border residents took heart. Stockmen returned to their ranges and the traders' carts again rumbled confidently over the lonely roads. Believing that Brooke would not much longer consider the Rangers necessary, Ford and his men decided not to remuster when their time should expire.[38] In September, Ford received notice to march his company to Laredo. There, on September 23, the frontiersmen were officially severed from federal service.[39] It was a solemn occasion for these fighting comrades of two years'

36 Ford, "Memoirs," III, 588–92.
37 Records Group No. 94.
38 Ford, "Memoirs," III, 596–97.
39 Records Group No. 94.

association as they stood in ranks for the last time and listened to Ford's farewell remarks.

"Old Rip"'s final words dwelled on the ties which had bound the company together and on the pain which separation brought. His appeal to his men for an orderly return to society sheds light on the character of this frontier captain.

> In the transition from Rangers to Citizens we should strive to render ourselves as useful in the one sphere as, I hope, we have been bold and efficient in the other. Ours has been a wild life. We have had the utmost latitude of conduct that could be allowed within the pale of law and propriety. Let us remember that we are about to return to the place of abode, where we shall mingle with relatives and friends, who have a right to circumscribe our actions within the bounds of civil life.
>
> We must not forget our responsibility to the laws and usages of society. A brave man generally makes a good, peaceable citizen. When the test is applied to us it is to be hoped that we will not be found wanting.[40]

It was a gloomy parting on the Laredo plaza as the company broke ranks for the last time and each Ranger sought the hand of his neighbor. That feeling of despondency was not, however, confined to the little border town. Mixed with apprehension, it crept across lower Texas and was finally expressed by the *San Antonio Ledger* in an editorial which mixed praise of Ranger accomplishments with a warning of trials to come.

> Now that the company is disbanded, the Indians who have so much dreaded its presence as to abandon their visits altogether to the country through which it ranged, can again carry devastation and death, with little dread of molestation, from the Nueces to the Rio Grande. . . . The property and lives of the citizens of Laredo, in particular, fell a daily prey to marauding bands of Indians until Capt. Ford's company of Rangers was stationed within striking distance of the town, and a short period afterward—a very brief one indeed, as in a rapid succession of bloody and victorious encounters with the Indians, soon taught them that Rangers could ride, shoot,

[40] Ford, "Memoirs," III, 597; *State Gazette* (Austin), October 11, 1851.

and maneuver rather differently from mounted infantry. . . . The ranging companies have done good service; the abandoned farms and ranches have been re-settled during their service; and the roads have been freed from danger to the traveller and the merchant. We hope Gov. Bell will recall them immediately to protect the frontier, or it will be again devastated and destroyed.[41]

Even as the Ranger enlistment period waned, below the Río Grande a situation was developing which was to involve Ford and certain of his veterans. Texas-born, Virginia-educated José María Carbajal, supported by the newly organized Liberal party and several northeastern Mexican towns, had proclaimed against the central government. Carbajal's object was the establishment of a separate republic along the river, to be governed under the democratic Plan of La Loba, promulgated at the time the revolt was announced.[42] Carbajal, known well and favorably to most of the leading citizens in South Texas, received from some of them —notably the wealthy and influential Brownsville merchant, Charles Stillman—assurances of financial and military support.[43] John Salmon Ford was among those who promised armed aid.

Sympathetic as the Texans were toward the anticlerical, republican aims of Carbajal, their offers were extended in no altruistic spirit. In return they demanded that the Mexican border should cease to provide a sanctuary for runaway slaves, an estimated three thousand of whom had escaped across the Río Grande from Texan bondage.[44] Furthermore, South Texas merchants insisted that the high tariff duties and other legal obstacles placed in the way of Texas border trade should be removed. Carbajal agreed not only to return all escaped slaves and to close the border to further runaways, but also to urge additional legislation to re-

41 Ford, "Memoirs," III, 599–600.

42 Ford, "Memoirs," IV, 627–28; Webb, *Handbook of Texas*, I, 294.

43 *Reports of the Committee of Investigation Sent in 1873 by the Mexican Government to the Frontier of Texas*, 189. Hereafter cited as *Reports of the Committee of Investigation.*

44 Ford, "Memoirs," IV, 628. Since slavery was illegal in Mexico, runaways were not extradited. Border residents referred to Mexico as "the land of the free and the home of the slave."

move the harassing commercial barriers. Satisfied by those guarantees, Texans advanced him funds for a war chest, and recruits from Texas and Louisiana began to seek the *Liberalista* standard.

At Río Grande City, Carbajal assembled his troops, including a number of Texans whose presence distressed his Mexican supporters.[45] In mid-September, the *Liberalistas* crossed the river and captured Camargo, about six miles inland on the Salado. The victorious force then went into camp to await the coming of its second-in-command, "Rip" Ford.[46]

Meanwhile, "Old Rip" was riding to keep his promise to Carbajal. Immediately after the discharge of his company at Laredo, he had set out on the hundred-mile journey to Camargo, accompanied by Andy Walker and twenty-eight other former Rangers, armed and equipped at his own expense. About October 1 the little troop rode into Carbajal's camp, where Ford promptly was commissioned a *Liberalista* colonel and placed in command of all American volunteers, designated the Auxiliary Troops, most of whom still were at Brownsville, where they had mustered under Captain Edward Hord. At Camargo, former Ranger Ford found kindred spirits in the aggregation of adventurous Americans. Commanding the *Liberalista* artillery, with rank of major, was the buoyant, six-foot Virginia lawyer and soldier-of-fortune, Roberdeau Chatham Wheat, who had seen service as a cavalry commander in the Mexican War. "Rob" Wheat afterwards would fight with William Walker in Nicaragua, again in Mexico with General Juan Alvarez, with Garibaldi in Italy, and finally under Stonewall Jackson, before death would catch him at Gaines's Mill on a hot June day eleven years away.[47] A towering Mississippian, Captain Joseph D. Howell, brother-in-law to planter-politician Jefferson Davis, headed sixty sturdy New Orleans volunteers.[48]

[45] *Reports of the Committee of Investigation*, 188. Carbajal then promised the Mexicans to enlist no more Americans.

[46] ". . . whose conduct during the whole course of his life has ever been absolutely hostile to Mexico." *Ibid.*, 189.

[47] Ford, "Memoirs," IV, 629; Douglas Southall Freeman, *Lee's Lieutenants, A Study in Command*, I, 87–88, 525.

[48] Ford, "Memoirs," IV, 640.

Also at hand were Major James Taylor, Ford's immediate subordinate, and Colonel John L. Haynes of Brownsville; both the latter and Ford would command Texas cavalrymen in the Civil War, but Haynes's men would wear Union blue.[49] These were fighting men of "Rip" Ford's pattern, and he looked forward to campaigning with them.

On October 9, Carbajal's army marched out confidently toward Matamoros, ninety-odd miles downstream, where General Francisco Avalos commanded the main body of government frontier troops—*Centralistas*, Ford called them. Only token resistance was offered by the small villages en route.[50] Carbajal arrived at the outskirts of Matamoros on or about October 21 and proceeded to expel the *Centralistas* from Fort Paredes, a defensive work on the northwest edge of the city. The elated troops of the "youthful general" (so "Rob" Wheat facetiously styled Carbajal) were played into the fort by the triumphant braying of the *Liberalista* band, and they soon welcomed Captain Hord and between three and four hundred Americans of the Brownsville muster (some of whom continued to live in Brownsville, crossing the river each evening to fight and returning home in the early morning to sleep in security and to attend to personal affairs).[51]

On the next morning, Ford initiated the attempt to seize the city. In brisk house-to-house fighting, he led the Auxiliary Troops as far as the northwest corner of Matamoros' main plaza before they were halted by heavy artillery fire. At that point Ford demanded reinforcements to prevent being flanked by the *Centralistas*. Carbajal responded with an order to withdraw, which Ford thought unwise and ignored, even a second and a third time. Finally he obeyed, after some difficulty in convincing the enraged Americans that a revolutionary army could achieve success only if it observed discipline. His men retired slowly to Fort Paredes at dusk and spent an uneasy night outside the earthworks, attempting to sleep in a pouring rain that dampened their gunpowder beyond use. Ford believed that his attack had inflicted

49 *Ibid.*, 632.   50 *Ibid.*, 629–30.
51 *Reports of the Committee of Investigation*, 189.

heavy losses on the enemy; his own casualty list numbered one killed and two wounded, one of the latter probably being John E. Wilson of the "Old Ranger" contingent.[52]

Ford renewed the attack in the morning. Again the Americans fought their way to the edge of the plaza, and once more the concentrated artillery and musket fire of the defenders pinned down the invaders. Attempting to locate the source of the small-arms fire, Ford thrust his head through the door of his command post. A musket ball penetrated his hat and plowed a deep gash in his scalp, producing a concussion not immediately apparent. Soon, however, Colonel Ford found that he could no longer remember words. Command then devolved upon Major Taylor, and Ford was taken across the river to the home of Judge William W. Dunlap, in Brownsville, where an army surgeon from Fort Brown dressed the wound. Here he remained until the siege of Matamoros dragged to its dismal conclusion.[53]

At the end of the month, Ford heard that Carbajal had withdrawn from Matamoros upon learning that government reinforcements under General Antonio Canales were on the way.[54] Although his wound was not healed, Ford immediately called for his horse and set out to join the *Liberalistas*. Failing to locate the command after a ride of a dozen miles upstream, he returned to Brownsville for more information. It soon was reported that the army had fallen back to Reynosa, about sixty miles above Matamoros. Ford promptly booked passage on the next upstream King and Kenedy steamboat and shortly thereafter disembarked at the *Liberalista* camp.

At Reynosa, Ford learned that Carbajal had decided to suspend operations until he could add to his forces. Both Texan and Mexican troops had deserted in substantial numbers, the Texans seeing little likelihood of receiving the promised $25 per month pay,[55]

[52] Ford, "Memoirs," IV, 631–32; A. J. Sowell, *Early Settlers and Indian Fighters of Southwest Texas*, 826.

[53] Ford, "Memoirs," IV, 633–34.

[54] *Ibid.*, 636–37. Canales' son was on Carbajal's staff.

[55] The Americans were also to be permitted to loot. Hubert Howe Bancroft, *History of Mexico*, V, 603.

and the Mexicans believing that American participation had perverted the revolution into a mere filibustering expedition.[56] Ford, however, had work to do. He was promoted to the command of a brigade, but until the campaign should be resumed he was to attempt to recruit other Texans. In late November or early December, 1851, with a three-man escort and $64 in expense money, Brigadier Ford arrived in Austin, where, with a wary eye cocked toward United States neutrality laws, he began his unfruitful efforts to swell Carbajal's ranks.[57]

A Texas political development soon interrupted Ford's recruiting program. The death in Austin on December 26 of State Senator Edward Burleson of the Sixteenth District created a vacancy to be filled by a special election in Travis, Hays, and Gillespie counties. At the solicitation of Austin friends, Ford stood for the senatorship and on January 12, 1852, was elected over Major Clem R. Johns on the strength of the Travis County returns.[58] Senator Ford immediately took his seat and participated diligently until the legislature adjourned on February 16. Then he prepared to rejoin Carbajal, apparently seeing nothing incongruous about a situation which permitted a brigadier general of a Mexican revolutionary army to function as a Texas state senator.

Carbajal, meanwhile, had attempted unsuccessfully to revive the flame of revolution. Late in November, 1851, he had been repulsed at Cerralvo. At Camargo in February, 1852, he again had been repelled and had withdrawn to Río Grande City, where Ford reported to him the impossibility of procuring additional Texan recruits. Lack of funds, it appeared, had spelled failure for the mission. Ford

> was apprised that the class of men likely to engage in such a service are seldom blessed with a superfluity of the good things of this world, particularly soul-endangering gold and silver. Recruits would have been numerous had there been funds on hand to pur-

[56] *Reports of the Committee of Investigation*, 189.

[57] Ford, "Memoirs," IV, 638.

[58] *Ibid.*, 640–43; *State Gazette* (Austin), January 17, 1852.

chase outfits in advance. As matters stood there were few who could furnish means to purchase the articles needed.

Lack of money may have been a major reason for the failure of the La Loba movement, but there were other important factors. Carbajal, in the minds of his Mexican adherents, was "*muy Agringado*" (much Americanized) and not to be trusted fully.[59] Furthermore, the political sagacity shown by General Avalos in obtaining lower tariff duties after the siege of Matamoros had removed from Carbajal's hands a good cause for Texan support.[60] Ford's own opinion was that Carbajal's failure to use his army *in toto* at Matamoros, and his wasting its strength by employing small, unsupported detachments, were the basic causes of failure.[61]

A final effort to obtain funds for Carbajal's revolt was made when a number of prominent Texans met in Corpus Christi in May, 1852, at what was termed the "Corpus Christi Fair." Carbajal and Ford were present and, according to the latter, Colonel H. L. Kinney, Ashbel Smith, B. F. Terry, General Hugh McLeod, General H. Clay Davis, Major James H. Durst, William Maltby, and W. M. Mann also attended. Many of them already had supplied money to little purpose, and the "Fair" ended with no provision for further support for the ambitious General.[62]

"Rip" Ford's participation in the revolution brought him criticism from some of his friends. He felt, however, that they had misunderstood his motives. "They did not know he was endeavoring to give additional support to an institution of the South. They overlooked the fact that a man has [a] right to assist a people who are resisting tyranny and battling for the exercise of their privileges as free men."[63]

---

[59] Ford, "Memoirs," IV, 640–42; *Reports of the Committee of Investigation*, 189–90.

[60] Bancroft, *History of Mexico*, V, 604.

[61] Ford, "Memoirs," IV, 633–34.

[62] *Ibid.*, 644. Ford heard that Richard King and Miflin Kenedy offered to finance the revolt if an American should have military command.

[63] *Ibid.*, 639.

5

Printer's Ink and Politics

In 1852, the acrid odor of black powder smoke faded from John S. Ford's nostrils, to be replaced by the familiar, pungent smell of printer's ink. In October he negotiated with Phineas de Cordova, publisher of the *South-Western American* in Austin, and the *American* masthead for November 5 revealed that Ford was now the publisher.[1] Directly across Congress Avenue from Ford's office was the plant of the *Texas State Gazette*, owned by William R. Scurry and Wade Hampton. In welcoming the former Ranger to the capital's newspaper fraternity, they commented that he had "the reputation of being a good writer and a courteous gentleman; he is, besides, an old Texian, thoroughly acquainted with the history and resources of the state, and will be able to make his paper a very interesting sheet. We welcome him to the ranks editorial right cordially."[2]

Hampton, the *Gazette* editor, soon grew less cordial. Largely because the two editors spoke for Democratic party factions, "the usual rivalry sprang up. Two newspaper firms seldom preserve harmonious relations when divided by a street only, and it is hard for either of the editors to do anything the other does not find out."[3] Certainly they differed concerning the aims of Carbajal's revolt, and former Brigadier Ford used the columns of his news-

[1] De Cordova was the father of Samuel Delgado de Cordova, who married Ford's daughter Addie in 1882.
[2] *Texas State Gazette* (Austin), November 13, 1852.
[3] Ford, "Memoirs," IV, 645.

paper to defend the motives of his former chief. In the *American* of November 17, 1852, the first issue to bear Ford's name as editor, appeared Carbajal's agreement to the return of fugitive slaves. News from the Río Grande made Ford aware that he was well out of the insurrection. The *Gazette* of June 26 had carried an account of the execution in Matamoros on June 14 of four captured *Liberalistas*, one of whom, Robert McDonald, was one of Ford's "Old Rangers." On November 27, another *Gazette* item related the capture and hanging of W. T. Cake, county clerk of Starr County, after a Carbajal defeat at Camargo.

Scarcely had Ford acquired the *American* when he had another journalistic opportunity. On November 24, the *Texas Ranger* at Washington was destroyed by fire. Its publisher, Joseph Lancaster, stated his determination to re-establish the paper with John S. Ford as its editor.[4] Although the *Ranger* soon reappeared, it did not do so under Ford's guidance, for he went his own way with the *American* for another year. Meanwhile, Ford plunged energetically into Democratic party activities. At an organization meeting in the capital in June, 1853, he was placed on the Democratic State Central Committee, to serve until December 8, 1854.[5] A few days later, Ford editorially committed the *American* to support Colonel M. T. Johnson's candidacy for governor.[6]

When in July a rumor that Ford was preparing to depart for the Río Grande reached the *Gazette* office, that Pease-for-Governor organ promptly accused Ford of launching a leaflet-spreading campaign to influence the uninformed Mexican-American vote in Johnson's favor. Ford answered that he went to obtain affidavits testifying to his Ranger service so that he might collect a year's arrears of pay. He would take, he wrote, his horse, a pack mule, two pistols, and, perhaps, a couple of saddlebags filled with leaflets bearing information about a worthy candidate. Hampton retorted that it made little difference what Ford took, inasmuch as he was "*non compos*" as a result of a head wound received at

[4] *Texas State Gazette* (Austin), December 11, 1852.
[5] *Ibid.*, June 25, 1853.
[6] *South-Western American* (Austin), June 25, 1853.

Matamoros, which very probably had permitted his "not overly plentiful supply of brains to leak out." In his next issue, however, Hampton did what was rare in that era of personal journalism: he admitted that perhaps his language toward his contemporary had been too harsh. With this admission Ford succinctly agreed.[7]

Editor Ford's popularity in Austin was made evident when the young men of the city, meeting on the night of August 30, 1852, to form a volunteer infantry company to be called the Travis Guards, elected the former Ranger to be their captain.[8] His prestige and influence further were shown by the fact that his friends, during the fall of 1853, prevailed upon him to stand for mayor in the December city elections. Votes of the younger citizens might be attracted by his colorful Ranger exploits, but the majority of Austin residents remembered his legislative efforts to promote the welfare of the thriving frontier town. During his short term in the state senate in 1852, Ford had introduced and carried to passage a bill amending the several acts for the incorporation of the city. Ford's bill had defined the city limits, had specified a method of establishing and collecting ad valorem taxes, and had provided an additional license fee of ten dollars on businesses serving liquor.[9] That these changes were approved by a majority of Austin voters became evident on December 31, when they elected their versatile townsman mayor for 1854.[10]

Mayor Ford's administration brought no significant changes to the city. It is true that he was primarily responsible for the passage of an ordinance prohibiting Sunday liquor sales,[11] a regulation strongly reflecting his personal attitude. Years later, however, an Austin resident, W. C. Walsh, remembered Ford's administrative platform as being, "That city is governed best which is least governed," and he also recalled that Mayor Ford "spent much time in trying to convince himself that a board of aldermen was not

7 *Ibid.*, August 6, 1853. The quarrel began in the *Gazette* issue of July 11 and ended with that of August 6.

8 *Texas State Gazette* (Austin), September 4, 1852.

9 H. P. N. Gammel (compiler), *The Laws of Texas*, III, 151–52.

10 *Texas State Times* (Austin), January 7, 1854.

11 *Ibid.*, April 24, 1854.

necessary." The habit of command apparently was not easily laid aside.

Nor did Mayor Ford squander municipal funds on the employment of a city marshal. He promised to fulfill that function himself, and soon demonstrated his method. Early one morning, a self-styled "bad man," gaudily attired and splendidly mounted, rode into town "and proceeded to 'tank up.' By noon he was noisy and trying to convince the public that he was the most dangerous of living animals by shooting off his pistol." Attracted by the shots, the mayor hurried to the saloon, where he calmly announced that the disturbance must cease at once. Momentarily aghast at the temerity of the quiet, unimposing person before him, the tippler recovered his equanimity and loosed a withering blast of profane invective about Ford's ears. When he paused briefly for breath, he heard the mayor's ultimatum: "We do not want your sort of people in our town and I give you an hour to get beyond the city limits."

As Ford turned to depart, the stranger assured him that he would not leave within an hour or any other time until he was ready. Mildly the mayor answered, "That is a question for you to settle as you see fit, but, if you are determined not to go, just leave with the bar keeper what disposition you want made of your horse and outfit." Then he strolled placidly from the saloon.

The stranger lapsed into comparative sobriety. He queried the bartender thoughtfully, "Who is that bluffer?"

Bluntly came the reply, "That is Old Rip Ford, our mayor. He is a doctor and if I wanted to enjoy long life I would rather take his advice than that of any man I know."

The subdued wayfarer gulped a final drink. "Pardner," he said, "you please tell your mayor I wouldn't stay in his d——m town if he made me a present of the whole she-bang. A pretty mayor who doesn't encourage new comers to settle in his town—Adios."[12]

During 1854, Ford's civic duties received less attention than his

[12] W. C. Walsh, "Austin in the Making," *Austin Statesman*, February 24, 1924. Walsh's article ran serially in the Sunday issues of the *Statesmen* from January 27 to April 27 inclusive.

other projects. By the beginning of the year, he had ceased to publish the *South-Western American*, had acquired Captain Joe Walker and Wilson Davidson as partners, and had begun to use the former *American* office and equipment to issue the *Texas State Times*,[13] which, according to its editor, became "the largest weekly in the state, except the *Galveston News*, and contained quite as much reading matter as the *News*."[14] To the *Times* columns Austin's politically conscious population turned for most of its information. Sensitive to the shifting winds of politics, Ford had begun to keep watch on the growth of the upstart Native American, or Know-Nothing, party, and on March 24, 1854, in a paternally admonishing editorial, he warned the old-line Democrats of the state to beware a coalition of Whigs and Native Americans.

But not all *Times* editorials in the spring of 1854 were concerned with matters political. Like his editorial contemporaries, Ford voiced opinion and sprinkled advice concerning a multitude of topics. The editorial page of a single issue (such as that of April 24) might include such varied items as "Old Rip"'s diatribe against Phineas T. Barnum's projected baby show in New York and a short admonition on the importance of proper installation of lightning rods. When a gleaning of exchange papers failed to produce matter for comment, there were always letters to the editor from subscribers who wished to make a point or take issue with an editorial opinion. If the editor were fortunate, his mail might yield a communication contentious enough to draw answering fire from other readers, and the matter would be fought out on the neutral ground of the *Times* pages.

In June, editorial pyrotechnics in Austin received additional impetus when John Marshall, former editor of the Jackson *Mississippian*, purchased Wade Hampton's interest in the *State Gazette*.[15] Marshall, experienced in the rough-and-tumble of Mississippi political journalism, was a worthy foe for Ford to cross

13 Brown, "Annals," Ch. XI, 46.
14 Ford, "Memoirs," IV, 645.
15 *Texas State Times* (Austin), March 24, 1854.

pens with.[16] His journal was to emerge as the voice of Texas Democracy when Ford left the party to promote the interests of the Know-Nothing movement in the state, a movement which resulted in state party organization in the fall of 1854.

"Of all the states in the South, Texas presented specially favorable conditions for the entrance of the American party." Not only did she border on Louisiana, where nativism was a stronger political factor than it was in any other southern state, but Texas also was the only state in the South to have a foreign country as a neighbor. In addition, her relatively numerous foreign population was not centered in the large cities as in other states, but was diffused among agrarian and frontier residents.[17] Her German settlements, which the inquisitive Frederick Law Olmsted found to be almost foreign worlds in themselves,[18] were suspect to South Texas Americans who resented German disapproval of slavery. Her Mexican population, while politically significant in relatively few counties, was thick in the southern half of the state.

The principal of unionism, contributed to the Native American program by its former Whig adherents, was a major reason for Ford's supporting the Know-Nothings.[19] The introduction into Congress of the Kansas-Nebraska Bill had produced a wave of acrimonious debate not in Washington alone but all through the country. Secession sentiment became articulate among Democrats in the southern states, and Ford, who in 1854 believed strongly in both unionism and slavery, hoped to help check its rising tide in his state. Of the purely nativistic doctrines of the Know-Nothings, Ford favored especially their proposal to lengthen to twenty-one years the period of residence necessary before a foreign-born citizen might vote.

[16] W. S. Oldham, "Colonel John Marshall," *Southwestern Historical Quarterly*, Vol. XX (July, 1916–April, 1917), 132–38.

[17] W. Darrell Overdyke, *The Know-Nothing Party in the South*, 27–30. Hereafter cited as Overdyke, *Know-Nothing Party*.

[18] Frederick Law Olmsted, *A Journey Through Texas*, 143.

[19] Overdyke, *Know-Nothing Party*, 116.

One tenet of Native Americanism, however, Ford never was able to adopt: the anti-Catholicism which was a fundamental principle of the order. Although a strongly religious Protestant adherent, he was a member of no church and entertained no ill feeling toward anyone because of a difference of religious opinion. It was only in his old age that he affiliated with the Presbyterians; until then, a self-selected moral code shaped his conduct and attitudes. As a result, the avowedly Know-Nothing *Times* carried very few anti-Catholic editorials. Those which did appear were written by the associate editor, James A. Beveridge, and were printed only in Ford's absence from Austin.

Ford supported general Texas opinion that the employing of Mexican labor alongside slaves was an unsound practice, since the free Mexicans stimulated dissatisfaction among the Negroes and encouraged many to run away.[20] The problem moved Austin residents to call a citizens' meeting on October 7, 1854, with Ford in the chair. Resolutions calling for the expulsion of transient Mexicans from the city and for curtailment of Negro activities were approved at the meeting. Negroes were not to be permitted to "hire their own time" (to work for pay for others when their masters had no tasks for them), to live away from white supervision, or to congregate for religious or social purposes without a responsible white person present. The resolutions were in accord with general practice in the South. The citizens also resolved on economic ostracism for any white who was lax in supervising his slaves.[21] On October 14, Ford was named chairman of a committee to discourage Austin residents from employing Mexican labor.[22]

The committee, however, began functioning without its chairman, for Ford left Austin almost immediately on state business. Since the mustering out of his "Old Rangers," Comanche raids into southern Texas had resumed, and Governor Elisha M. Pease had called out six Ranger companies for three months' service.

20 Ford, "Memoirs," IV, 647–49, 655–56.
21 *Texas State Times* (Austin), October 14, 1854.
22 Brown, "Annals," Ch. XVI, 35.

One was to assemble at Goliad, under Captain William R. Henry, and Ford was dispatched to muster the company into state service, should its organization and equipment pass his inspection.[23] James A. Beveridge, who had become Ford's assistant, was left in charge of the *Times*.[24] On October 28, Beveridge published a letter from Ford, in which the latter reported the mustering of Henry's company. With an eye to the interests of his rural subscribers, Ford wrote also that an epidemic of "black tongue" had broken out at Camargo and Río Grande City, but that crops were flourishing because of the extremely rainy weather.

The visit to Goliad also provided Ford with an opportunity to collect data concerning Texas history, a project in which he had become greatly interested. From a Mexican War comrade living in Goliad, Henry Scott, Ford obtained an eyewitness account of the massacre of Fannin's command in 1836 as the then six-year-old Scott remembered seeing it. The notes taken in the interview went into Ford's expanding file of Texiana, eventually to be reproduced in the *Times*.[25]

In December, Ford again took brief leave of his editorial duties, going this time to San Antonio on business of an unspecified nature. Apparently he returned within the month, for at a temperance meeting on December 29 he was named to a committee charged with raising the fee of a visiting temperance lecturer. On January 2, 1855, Ford himself was the principal speaker at a temperance gathering. Although for the most part he spoke extemporaneously, on short notice, his address was received with enthusiasm; he was unable to fulfill the many requests for copies.[26]

No doubt Mayor Ford had returned quickly to be on hand during the closing weeks of the mayoralty campaign. The vote cast at the end of December would give the *Times* editor an opportunity to evaluate the reaction of Austin toward his conversion to Native Americanism. His stand had come as a surprise to many.

[23] *Texas State Times* (Austin), October 21, 1854.
[24] The *Times* masthead shows Beveridge as assistant editor in October.
[25] Ford, "Memoirs," I, 134–46.
[26] *Texas State Times* (Austin), December 9, 1854; January 6, 1855.

His sponsorship, advantageous to political aspirants in June, 1854,[27] might be shown to be less effective by the results of the December elections. Ford staunchly supported J. T. Cleveland, widely known proprietor of the Metropolitan Hotel, as his successor as mayor. If, perhaps, the editor felt any surprise at the election outcome, it was at the unanimity of sentiment in accord with him; Cleveland received all but two of the votes, a fact which Editor Ford did not let his critics at the *Gazette* office soon forget.[28] The vote probably was a testimonial of confidence in Ford rather than evidence of any unusual enthusiasm for his candidate. Nor was Ford's popularity in extra-political civic matters any less than in politics. In January, 1855, citizens of Austin and Travis County sent him to La Grange as their delegate to a railroad meeting, in an effort to secure a line into their region.[29] When he was editor of the *South-Western American* in 1852, Ford's had been almost the only newspaper voice in the state to demand state purchase of railroad company bonds to help finance construction of a trans-Texas road,[30] a fact well remembered by the citizens who selected him to represent them at La Grange.

In spite of continual demands on his time, Ford kept a watchful eye on the "pop-gun of democracy across the street," from which emanated the pronouncements of the "Bombshells," the label applied by the *Times* to the Marshall-Pease Democratic clique. Consistently Ford spoke for the Rangers and frontier residents when he flayed the policies, both state and national, which permitted continued ravages by bandits and Indians.[31] When, early in 1855, the federal government announced a change of policy to feed rather than to fight the Indians, Ford agreed that some change was necessary. "Let the feeding policy be tried," he wrote. "It cannot be more disastrous in its effects upon the fron-

27 Aaron B. Burleson to Ed Burleson, June 28, 1854, Ed Burleson Papers, Barker History Center, University of Texas.

28 *Texas State Times* (Austin), April 28, 1855.

29 Brown, "Annals," Ch. XVII, 3-4.

30 Ford, "Memoirs," IV, 654.

31 *Texas State Times* (Austin), May 19, 1855; Ed Burleson to Ford, *ibid.*, June 2, 1855.

tier than the protective policy. . . . The military management in Texas, if signallized by anything, is uncertainty—inefficiency."[32] Neither General Persifer Smith, commanding the Department of Texas, nor Governor Pease was spared the wrathful criticism of the *Times*,[33] and the *Gazette* was hard put to it for rebuttal.

Dereliction on the part of city employees also drew Ford's fire. In an editorial captioned "Where is The City Marshal?" the editor complained of the racket made one morning on Congress Avenue by five drunken fiddlers and warned miscreants that the lack of a city jail would be no deterrent to punishment.

> For the information of such gentry, it would be well to state that, Mayor Cleveland in the absence of a "lock up" has rented for the nonce, a cistern, where he proposes to deposit all unruly and noisy customers.—"Sink or swim—survive or perish," will be the question then. . . . Look out boys, or you will get more water to your grog than you bargained for.[34]

Not only were human delinquents targets for "Old Rip"'s ire; Austin's canine population also evoked from him sharp comment concerning both its size and the blatant fashion in which its members seemed to be appropriating the city. He recommended a stringent reduction of its numbers.[35]

Comment of other nature occasionally delighted Ford's subscribers. Keenly alert for the chance to capitalize on any error Marshall of the *Gazette* might make, Ford grasped a golden opportunity to point out his rival's ignorance of Texas. When the Colorado River, which rises near the edge of the Staked Plains, ran unusually low in the spring of 1855, Marshall explained to his readers that it was due to the failure of snows to melt in the mountains at the source of the stream. One can imagine the exuberant yelp with which the *Times* editor seized his pen to en-

[32] *Ibid.*, February 24, 1855.
[33] Ford, "Memoirs," IV, 659. The attacks on General Smith were written not by Ford but by Colonel Thomas F. McKinney or a Captain Givens. The latter went before a court-martial as a result.
[34] *Texas State Times* (Austin), March 17, 1855.
[35] *Ibid.*, May 5, 1855.

lighten the little major on the nature of terrain along the upper river, and to warn the public that the appalling ignorance of the Democratic party spokesman in regard to Texas geography might indicate unsoundness on other Texas matters, politics included. So long as the two were editorial competitors, Ford never permitted Marshall to forget the blunder. When the latter expressed an optimistic prediction of Democratic election successes, the *Times* responded that the *Gazette* editor was unable to see the situation clearly; perhaps he was blinded by the rays of the sun reflected from the snow on the mountains at the source of the Colorado River. Any dissension among Democratic adherents also was received with glee by the *Times*. Henry E. McCulloch embarrassed his fellow partisans by endorsing a Know-Nothing principle and consequently lost party endorsement for office. The *Times* facetiously castigated the errant Democrat, whose exploits on behalf of frontier defense were famous.

The Captain had the impudence and effrontery to come out in favor of changing "the naturalization laws from five to twenty-one years" without consulting Maj. Marshall, and that too after the Major "had occasion to speak very favorably of Capt. McCulloch when he first came out for the Senate." Was it not ungrateful! after the Maj. had the kindness to "speak favorably" of the unknown backwoodsman then for him to have the audacity not to favor foreigners, to come out for a Know Nothing principle, without first asking permission of the Solomon of the "Bomb Shells." Ah, Henry, you'll suffer for it. Who do you expect will recommend you to the people now, you uncouth specimen of a Ranger? What did the people of Texas know of you save through the kindly notice of Maj. Marshall? . . . Didn't you know you had lived a way out here on the frontier so long that you couldn't be smart like a "States" raised man? . . . Quit the canvass there is no show for you now—you're unendorsed and have angered the big gun of the piebald democracy—made up of every ism from a Missouri Secessionist, an Alabama Whig, to the mighty "shoe-stringer" who professes no particular opinion upon any subject, which he is not willing to whittle down to a point less than the little end of nothing, to suit the times and get votes. . . . Twenty-one years to become naturalized! . . . You are a "poor thing" now—ain't you. Slink back into the state of undistinguished obscurity you occupied before Maj. Marshall deigned to notice you. You ranging, Indian-killing, beef-eating, rough sample of semi-civilization how dare you treat the patronizing kindness of Major Marshall with such black ingratitude! . . .[36]

Since the style appears to be that of Beveridge, Ford may have been absent from Austin when the editorial was published,[37] or he may have wished the comment to come from a hand other than his own.

For Ford, 1855 was a busy year. Partisan politics, border troubles, the slavery issue—these and less-publicized matters called for his attention. It was a year of decision for the Know-Nothings, whose principles in part had been publicly endorsed by Sam Houston. Ford warned his temperance friends to beware of professional politicians who might participate in temperance work to secure political support.[38] Probably he realized that Know-Nothing principles generally would have no greater attraction for temperance people in Texas than in other southern states. However, if he could keep the Texas reformers from definitely identifying themselves with the Democrats, he might win their support on purely state issues for the Native American ticket. In consequence, Governor Pease's plan for a state-owned railway, the failure of his administration to provide frontier security, and his do-little attitude toward honoring fully the Texas pre-statehood debt became prime targets for *Times* editorials.

Early in June, Ford expressed the concern of slaveholding Texans over the increasing number of runaways making for Mexico. He demanded an extradition treaty, predicting that the alternative would be a popular uprising in Texas against the Mexican Republic.[39] Slavery and its problems still occupied his pen two weeks later when he wrote from San Antonio commenting on the bit-

---

[36] *Ibid.*, July 12, 1855.
[37] Ford was in San Antonio on July 30; he was there until July 7.
[38] *Texas State Times* (Austin), May 26, 1855.
[39] *Ibid.*, June 2, 1855.

terness of feeling there against the antislavery German population, sentiment engendered also by the fact that the Germans were almost unanimously Democratic in a community where Anglo-American settlers were largely Native American in sympathy. John Ford's own steadfast position on slavery was expressed in part when he wrote, "Should there be persons who have come among us, opposed to slavery, it is their duty to leave our midst and settle down with the abolition masses of the north." Ford also commented on the continued Indian depredations, predicting that a general Indian war would break out unless the federal government extended further protection to the frontier.[40] Still in San Antonio at the end of the month, Ford forecast victory in the August elections for the Know-Nothing candidates supported by the *Times*: Lieutenant Governor David C. Dickson for the governorship; G. W. Jowers for lieutenant governor; and Judge John Hancock for congressman from western Texas. To opposition charges that the code of secrecy enveloping the Native American organization made it a danger to democratic society, the *Times* retorted that "the greatest moral reforms of the age have been accomplished through the aid of secret associations."[41]

Whatever the reason for his trip to San Antonio, political or private, Ford was soon back in the thick of the Austin political melee. Tenseness generated by partisan campaigning in the torturous heat of a blazing summer sun created a situation in which tempers grew more explosive as election time drew near. That Ford did not find himself on what he termed the "mis-called field of honor," was a tribute to the cooler judgment of his friends. About the middle of August his participation in a duel was narrowly averted. A fellow physician named Lane wrote a letter to Ford objecting to that part of the Know-Nothing ritual which referred to the carrying of arms. Ford, in the *Times* of August 4, commented on Lane's misinterpretation of the ritual. The incensed Lane replied through the *Gazette* pages. Each disputant felt that the other was hurling the charge of "liar," and a resort

[40] *Ibid.*, June 23, 1855.
[41] *Ibid.*, July 7, 1855.

to pistols appeared imminent. T. Scott Anderson, R. T. Brownrigg, Ed Finnin, W. M. Swisher, J. M. Jennings, and Charles W. Weir, mutual friends of the doctors, hurried to mediate and restored amicable relations.[42]

The election demonstrated the fundamental unity of the Texas Democrats. Except for certain local victories, the Native American bid for administrative power was repulsed. Pease retained the governorship and his partisans secured all but thirty-nine seats in the legislature. The *Times*, however, could point proudly to the Travis County results, which again indicated that Ford's personal popularity and organizational efforts had been effective. In the county, Dickson, Jowers, and Hancock had gained majorities, and the election of Edward Peck as mayor of Austin gave the party another year's control of municipal affairs. In Hays County, voters elected a full slate of Know-Nothing county officers and Galveston had elected a Native American mayor, but returns from elsewhere in the state gave the party little to rejoice over. The critical San Antonio elections resulted in a virtually complete Democratic victory. The Know-Nothings blamed much of their poor showing on the last-minute defection of their candidate for commissioner of the General Land Office, Stephen F. Crosby, swept into office by an avalanche of Democratic votes after his sudden announcement that despite Native American sponsorship he was leaving the organization.[43]

Ford's political activity diminished after the election, but there still were affairs to occupy him. Early in the fall "Old Rip" journeyed to New Orleans to consult with General John A. Quitman and others who were attempting to organize a force for the liberation of Cuba. What Ford's role was to be is not clear, but in view of his efforts on Carbajal's behalf, it probably was to consist of military command. Quitman's project produced nothing concrete, and Ford suspected that "the risk of landing in Cuba,

[42] *Ibid.*, August 18, 1855. Lane probably was the former Kentuckian, Richard Newton Lane, who in 1855 married Annie Swisher, a sister of Ford's old friend, Colonel John M. Swisher.

[43] Overdyke, *Know-Nothing Party*, 117; *Texas State Times* (Austin), August 25, 1855.

being left without the means of withdrawing, and of being garroted, might have had influence."

September also brought another task to Ford. The citizenry of Austin sent him to Bastrop to a meeting called to determine the best method of preventing the escape of slaves into Mexico and of reclaiming those already across the border. Recalling the agreements between Carbajal and his Texan supporters, the Bastrop planners decided to offer aid in money and men to General Santiago Vidaurri, then controlling Nuevo León, if he would extradite fugitive slaves and close the border to future escapees. Selected as commissioners to Vidaurri were Ford and a Colonel Riddle, who had a residence in Chihuahua as well as a business and the additional asset of a Mexican wife.[44]

The agents first went to San Antonio, from which place Ford wrote on September 29 that Captain James H. Callahan's Ranger company, recently enlisted by the Governor, had a fortnight earlier crossed the Río Grande in pursuit of a Seminole raiding party. Ford criticized Pease for not having called out more Rangers much earlier. Two days later the editor informed the *Times* that Pease had come to town to confer with General Smith on frontier defense.[45] Realizing that Callahan's invasion would arouse anti-Texas sentiment in Mexico and that the road to Monterrey and Vidaurri might be dangerous for him, Ford assigned sole responsibility for the success of the mission to Riddle, whose personal situation would keep him unmolested. Then, too, Ford had reason to tarry in San Antonio. Riddle rode south to keep the appointment, but was halted at the river. Callahan's raid had resulted in the blocking of all American entrance into Mexico.

Meanwhile, disaster had overtaken Callahan. Ford reported on October 5 that the Rangers had won a battle near the village of San Fernando, but that growing hostility among the Mexicans had forced the company to retire to Piedras Negras. Callahan then penned a hurried plea to San Antonio for reinforcements and at the same time sent some of his men into Texas to recruit aid. Henry

44 Ford, "Memoirs," IV, 656–60.
45 *Texas State Times* (Austin), October 6, 1855.

McCulloch and about one hundred other frontiersmen hastened to San Antonio to organize a relief expedition.[46] Apparently John Ford joined the recruits, for a Callahan trooper, writing from San Antonio to Ed Burleson, noted that " 'Old Rip' is here and will go without fail."[47] However, before the recruits were ready to march, all northern Mexico arose in anger, and Callahan, after putting the torch to Piedras Negras, crossed to American soil with unofficial assistance from the United States garrison at Fort Duncan.[48] General Smith, irritated by the magnitude of the disturbance, looked on the Callahan party as a gang of pirates; Ford laid the initial blame on Smith for failing to defend the frontier.[49]

After Callahan's withdrawal, Ford returned to Austin and the *Times*. Although during October and November he continued his editorial sniping at Marshall for supporting Pease and his frontier policy, "Old Rip"'s real interest seems to have been the initiating of a multitude of candidates into a recently formed secret society, "The Lone Star of the West." It was established in Austin in the fall of 1855, with Ford at its head. Its stated objective was the "liberation" of Cuba, and it is quite possible that the society was an outgrowth of Ford's trip to New Orleans. The order conducted a highly ritualistic initiation ceremony, passing through one increasingly solemn step to another and finally culminating in a huge jape which the initiate never forgot. The order was regarded by most Austin residents as an elaborate practical joke. On the other hand, in view of the national administration's avowed disapproval of filibustering, the Lone Star leaders may have chosen to veil their sincerity behind the public view that an organization of such open secrets could have nothing more than a humorous motive. According to Ford, the order was popular until about 1860.[50] It may be coincidental that the life span of the ambitious southern order known as the Knights of the Golden Circle, among whose stated aims were the acquisition of Cuba and of northwest-

[46] Ford, "Memoirs," IV, 657–58.
[47] William Kyle to Ed Burleson, October 7, 1855, Ed Burleson Papers.
[48] Ford, "Memoirs," IV, 657.
[49] *Texas State Times* (Austin), October 13, 1855.
[50] Brown, "Annals," Ch. XVII, 43; Ford, "Memoirs," IV, 660.

ern Mexico as additional slaveholding territory, encompassed the years from 1854 to about 1860.[51] No documentary evidence connects the two societies, but the similarity of organization and purpose provides material for conjecture. The only other Texas chapter of the Lone Star in 1855 was in San Antonio; Ford had been in that city most of October. Although the order increased in popularity in the half-decade of its existence, Ford reflected that "nothing in the shape of a tangible benefit to the oppressed islanders ever grew out of it."[52]

November, 1855, brought changes to the *Texas State Times*. It moved from Congress Avenue to quarters around the corner on Pecan Street, and, at about the same time, Joe Walker left the partnership, the business becoming that of Ford and Davidson. This latter association was short lived; a notice dated February 1, 1856, informed readers that John T. Pruitt, foreman of the *Times* printing staff, "is authorized to settle the books of the late firm of Ford and Davidson." Davidson now vanished, and on March 1 the *Times* masthead again bore Walker's name as Ford's partner, along with that of William E. Jones, a new co-publisher and editor. The front page flag of that issue showed another change: "Texas" had been deleted from the name, making *State Times* the paper's official designation.[53]

A proposition more challenging than that of mere newspaper reorganization reached Ford early in 1856, but other than the fact that the scheme was ambitious and involved Mexico, it remains unknown. Its proponents sought the editor's aid and counsel because of his experience in Mexican affairs. "Old Rip" was liberal with his advice but chary with his participation, as he revealed in a letter to his old friend and Ranger lieutenant, Ed Burleson, then busy operating his San Marcos ranch but also evidently one of the plotters.

I have written to Perryman telling him what I thought of mat-

[51] George W. L. Bickley Papers, Records of the War Department, Office of the Judge Advocate General, National Archives, Washington, D. C. Bickley was the originator and prime mover of the Knights of the Golden Circle.

[52] Ford, "Memoirs," IV, 660.   [53] *State Times* (Austin), March 1, 1856.

ters pertaining to the Rio Grande. If you, or McCulloch or Callahan, would go upon the Brazos you could get money. I look upon the movement as a political necessity—a duty we owe to Texas and the South. It has occupied my thoughts for years. I do not wish to take a prominent part in getting up the thing, because I have said and written so much on the subject I begin to think people don't believe me. Houston and Burleson and a host of other chivalrous spirits redeemed and annexed Texas—why may not others of less note secure another slice from the grasp of anarchy and place it under American control? There is no government in Mexico— everything is in confusion. The people are oppressed, ground down by taxation, debased by ignorance and paralyzed by the influence of the priests. She is a dangerous and harmful neighbor. Her people aid in taking off our property, in fact they rob us. They allow hostile expeditions to be fitted out against us upon their territory. We have the right by the laws of nations, by the right of self-preservation and self-defense which we acquired from God himself to demand "indemnity for the past and security for the future." These can only be obtained by placing the country between the Rio Grande and the Sierra Madre under the control of Americans and by giving protection to slave property in Texas and the South. I conscientiously believe we would be right and that Heaven would bless the enterprise with success.[54]

Politically speaking, Ford during 1856 found himself in a position becoming increasingly untenable. Although the Know-Nothing Party in Texas dropped its veil of secrecy, many of its quondam adherents drifted back to former Democratic affiliation. Joe Walker again, by mid-summer, withdrew from the *Times*, perhaps through a loss of interest in Native Americanism. Ford's own enthusiasm gradually waned, although his journal remained the Know-Nothing state organ and duly supported Millard Fillmore and Andrew J. Donelson in the general elections. Never in sympathy with the party's anti-Catholicism, it may have been that plank in the Native American platform of 1856 which determined the *Times* editor to break with the organization. Ford's remaining partner, W. E. Jones, began to show dissatisfaction with

[54] Ford to Ed Burleson, February 15, 1856, Ed Burleson Papers.

the publishing business, and as early as July 25 the eventual disso-
lution of the partnership was presaged by a *Times* announcement
that "Mr. Joel Miner is authorized to receive and receipt for
money due this office."[55] With Jones's departure from the firm in
the late fall, the newspaper resumed its former title, *Texas State
Times*, and Ford acquired a new co-publisher, Ed Finnin, a young
Austin auctioneer who had been one of those to patch up the
quarrel between "Old Rip" and Dr. Lane.[56]

The new association was greeted by a temporarily calamitous
newsprint shortage, making *Times* publication impossible between
the middle of November, 1856, and mid-January, 1857.[57] Ford
took advantage of the slack period to make another visit to San
Antonio, leaving office affairs in the hands of the inexperienced
Finnin and the compositor Pruitt. The editor's frequent excursions
southward had made him for some time the object of sly chaf-
fing on the part of his intimates, who suspected that romance as
much as politics drew him periodically away. When the *Times*
resumed publication, the editor on February 7 justified the sus-
picions of his cronies.

A great deal has been said in relation to the supposed exit of the
editor of this sheet from the state of single blessedness.—For the
information of friends, who are of course, suffering from an undue
amount of intense solicitude, it may be necessary to state, that
nothing prevented the aforesaid *hombre* from sliding gently off the
"log of celibacy into the pool of matrimony" but an *obstinate disposition* on the part of the lady.

After this disappointing visit, John Ford dropped from the ken
of Alamo Plaza and reappeared on his regular rounds of news-
and-opinion gathering along Congress Avenue and Pecan Street.

Ford's editorials during the spring of 1857 were noticeably silent
about the Know-Nothings, since he was in the process of deliberately divesting himself of Native American ties. Instead, his articles
dealt with other local and national issues. The obvious failure of

55 *State Times* (Austin), August 9, 1856.
56 *Texas State Times* (Austin), December 6, 1856.
57 *Ibid.*, January 17, 1857.

the slavery movement in Kansas Territory and the rising abolitionist storm drew from Ford a flat statement of his views on the "peculiar institution." "Slavery is right. It is an institution founded by God. . . . The Bible is the strong-hold of the slave owner. . . . If slavery is wrong the Bible is wrong. They must stand or fall together. There can be no middle ground."[58] Ford's opinions, as well as the load of writing, were shared after the middle of March by a new associate, the Reverend F. M. Gibson, formerly an editor at Richmond, Texas, who purchased Finnin's interest. He was listed as co-editor, but the firm name was John S. Ford and Company. It was not commonly known for some time that in the reorganization X. B. DeBray, a translator in the General Land Office and a political schemer, had actually become the "Company."

The *Times* and the *Gazette* continued to exchange sporadic shots. Although Marshall was aware that Ford had lost interest in the Know-Nothings, he occasionally exasperated "Old Rip" by referring to the latter's association with the declining political group. In early April, Ford publicly announced his break with the Know-Nothings, maintained that never had he been wholly in sympathy with their program, and objected to being further attacked as a Native American partisan. His stand was emphasized a little later by Gibson, who declared that the *Times* no longer would be a party organ but an independent home newspaper. These declarations removed the basis for political controversy, but bickering nevertheless continued as Ford accused the *Gazette*, which held the public printing contract, of doing a poor professional job.[59] Marshall retorted that the "old coon" at the *Times* had no just cause to complain of the *Gazette's* monopoly, since Ford had held the monopoly in 1846 and 1847; the little Mississippian, however, was wise enough not to take issue over the quality of his printing.

In May Ford openly returned to the Democratic party. The state Democratic convention was held in Waco early in the month, and Ford attended, ostensibly to report the proceedings for the *Times*. On the motion of John P. Border of Leon County, Ford

[58] *Ibid.*, February 21, 1857.   [59] *Ibid.*, March 21, 28, April 4, 11, 1857.

was officially invited to a seat in the convention, and in company with F. E. Williams of Cherokee, another reconverted Democrat, he marched through a storm of good-natured guying to the speaker's platform. Marshall briefly described the incident in the *Gazette* of May 6.

> Both the gentlemen entertained the Convention by giving their tortuous windings through the mazes of Know Nothingism, in the way of "Experience." They thanked the Democratic party, and congratulated themselves on being again admitted within the folds. Col. Ford assured the convention that in future he was with the Democratic party, and concluded by observing that hereafter, "Your Country shall be my County, and your God my God."

Aware that he had lost considerable political prestige, Ford became active in the party as an indication of his good faith. When the Georgia Democrat Robert Toombs came to Austin, it was as a staunch partisan that Ford joined in petitioning the fiery southerner to address the community on public affairs. Toombs gladly consented and spoke that night, to a packed house, sentiments which Editor Ford highly praised. In the same issue in which he lauded Toombs's address, he publicly announced his reaffiliation with the Democratic party and explained his deviation to Native Americanism. "The act . . . was performed after due deliberation, and from a firm conviction that patriotism, a desire to perpetuate the Union and to preserve inviolate the 'peculiar institutions' of the South, demanded its consummation."[60] However, the editorial left little doubt of Ford's regret for having adopted Know-Nothingism. Much later he wrote in his memoirs: "The act of joining was one of those inconsiderate things men do sometimes."[61]

On the same day that the *Times* stated Ford's political recursion (May 23), Marshall, in the *Gazette*, hailed Ford's return in complimentary style.

> Our cotemporary [*sic*] of the State *Times*, Col. FORD, being voluntarily returned to the Democratic Church, and being rein-

[60] *Ibid.*, May 16, 1857.   [61] Ford, "Memoirs," IV, 647.

stated by the Waco Convention, it gives us pleasure to salute him as a member of our great party. He is a gentleman of talents, and a good writer. He is also known to a large portion of our people. He may yet, therefore, render the Democracy much and efficient service in preserving its organization and advancing its principles. We can truly say, after all our battles, that no one will more heartily rejoice than ourselves to see our cotemporary hereafter striking his blows with effect against the enemies of the Democracy.[62]

The little Major never wrote more sincerely than when he penned the above comment. He now could hope that he no longer would be the main target for "Old Rip"'s editorial shafts. Furthermore, he had seen clear and repeated demonstrations of Ford's influence in Travis County and Austin.

On May 30, at the organization meeting of the Young Men's Democratic Association of Travis County, Ford was assigned membership on the Committee on Invitations, charged with recruiting young party members. Judge Williamson S. Oldham and William Byrd, the Democratic nominee for representative from Travis County, addressed the association, as did Ford, who "reiterated his sentiments of attachment to the party, in a happy manner."[63] As further testimony to his political value, Ford was elected on June 13 to the group's finance committee.[64]

If Major Marshall, the recognized Democratic spokesman in Texas, hoped to see Ford's facile pen employed in the party's cause, he was disappointed. June brought "Rip" Ford's withdrawal from capital journalism, although rumor was to associate him with the *Gazette*. The *Texas State Times* suspended publication. From its offices soon appeared a new journal, the *Texas Sentinel*, owned by Ford's former silent partner, DeBray, William G. O'Brien, and A. G. Compton, and issued under the name of William G. O'Brien and Company. Pruitt, the printer, weathered this reorganization also, and Gibson became the editor. Although it had been he who had announced that the *Times* would forego partisan political activity, the *Sentinel* immediately proclaimed

---

[62] *State Gazette* (Austin), May 23, 1857.
[63] *Ibid.*, June 6, 1857.   [64] Brown, "Annals," Ch. XVIII, 14.

its sponsorship of Sam Houston for governor in 1857.[65] DeBray's joining the *Times* firm apparently was a deliberate step of Houston's adherents toward gaining an editorial voice in Austin.

For the first time in five years, John S. Ford found himself free from press deadlines and inter-columnar dissension. Now, in this summer of 1857, his thoughts swung outward to the frontier, where the busy and destructive Comanches provided opportunities for men of action.

[65] *Texas Sentinel* (Austin), June 27, July 11, 1857.

6

The Canadian River Campaign

THE INDIAN THREAT in 1857 provided an opportunity which John S. Ford turned into one of his most spectacular services to the state. Throughout 1856, Indian depredations had been curtailed greatly in the exposed portions of Texas, but the gradual withdrawal of Regular Army units during 1857 encouraged the wild tribes to resume their raiding; not one successful punitive expedition was carried out against them that year.[1] Also the location on two northwest reservations of part of the Penateka (Honey Eater) Comanches and the remnants of other tribes irritated the Texans. Frontiersmen felt that the situation had been aggravated by the establishment of the reservations, at least that of the Comanches, at Camp Cooper on the Clear Fork of the Brazos.[2]

To repair the situation, Brevet Major General David E. Twiggs, commanding the Eighth Military Department (the Department of Texas), suggested to Secretary of War John B. Floyd that Congress be urged to authorize the creation of a regiment of Texas Mounted Volunteers for federal service. His suggestion included the recommendation that the command of such a force should go to John S. Ford.[3] A bill embodying Twiggs's suggestion

[1] Ford, "Memoirs," IV, 679; Rupert Norval Richardson, *The Comanche Barrier to South Plains Settlement*, 231. Hereafter cited as Richardson, *Comanche Barrier*.

[2] Richardson, *Comanche Barrier*, 231–32; Ernest Wallace and E. Adamson Hoebel, *The Comanches: Lords of the South Plains*, 301–302.

[3] Ford, "Memoirs," IV, 667.

was introduced into Congress, and Texans turned an anxious and hopeful ear toward Washington.

While Congress vacillated, the frontier situation became an issue in the Texas gubernatorial campaign of 1857. Sam Houston, running as an independent and apparently reluctant to commit himself to any positive stand against the Indians, "was accused . . . of blaming the frontier settlers for the Indian outrages."[4] His Democratic opponent, Hardin R. Runnels, was successful at the polls after campaigning vigorously for increased frontier security measures.

When Runnels took office, it was plain that there would be no quick Congressional action on the "Ranger Regiment Bill." The frontier situation, however, could not wait on far-off discussion. While congressmen debated in Washington, men, women, and children died beneath Comanche lances in Bosque, Erath, Brown, and other counties on the fringe settlement, and the Governor's file of incoming correspondence bulged with irate petitions for aid over the signatures of fortunate survivors. Honoring his campaign commitments, Governor Runnels, in his first annual message to the legislature, urged immediate action to relieve the frontier. Largely because of the efforts of frontier state Senator George B. Erath, the legislature responded by passing a bill entitled "An act for the better protection of the frontier," which Runnels signed on January 27, 1858.

The executive was thus authorized to call into state service an additional one hundred men and to place them, along with Ranger companies already in the field, under a single commander whose rank would be that of senior captain. While the period of enlistment was set at six months, the act provided that the men might be discharged sooner or continued longer in service, as the commanding officer might see fit. To equip, pay, and subsist the command, the act appropriated $70,000 from the state treasury.[5]

Late in 1857, when the proposal to create a state force was

---

[4] Anna Irene Sandbo, "Beginnings of the Secession Movement in Texas," *Southwestern Historical Quarterly*, Vol. XVIII (July, 1914–April, 1915), 57.

[5] Gammel, *The Laws of Texas*, IV, 949–50.

being widely discussed in Austin, Marshall of the *State Gazette*, on December 12, had recommended Ford's appointment as a field-grade officer, describing "Old Rip"'s traits as those of "order, watchfulness, coolness in danger and intrepedity without foolhardiness." The editorial was sufficient suggestion for Runnels; the day after he approved the frontier bill, he sent Ford his commission as senior captain.

The choice was logical. Ford's operations in South Texas from 1849 to 1851 had established his prestige as an aggressive, highly competent Indian fighter, and the knowledge of Comanche character he had acquired there and on the El Paso journey with Neighbors could be usefully employed in the projected campaign, in which "the intention was, from the very beginning, to carry the war into the hunting grounds of the Comanches." Then, too, Ford's situation fitted the urgency of the project: he was in Austin, serving on a federal grand jury, and he was fully acquainted with the problems involved and could begin preparations without delay. An additional reason for his appointment suggests itself: good-naturedly forgiven for his temporary aberration in favor of Know-Nothingism, Ford had returned to the Democratic ranks to work earnestly for the party's candidates during the campaign of 1857. Here, then, was an opportunity to reward political service by an appointment which would command general approbation.

On January 30, 1858, the *Gazette* applauded the Governor's act.

It is an excellent appointment. The Captain had been previously recommended by the President, by members of both branches of the Legislature, by the Supreme and Federal Courts, and by many private citizens, for a field office in the new regiment expected to be created at the present Congress. He is an old Indian fighter, and we predict that he will rid the frontier of all annoyance in the first campaign.

"Old Rip," however, privately was less assured than the optimistic editor. Ford's appreciation of the factors involved, as much as innate modesty, made him feel that "these expressions were complimentary, but were calculated to lead the public to expect a great deal,—perhaps too much, from the officer mentioned."[6]

In making the appointment, Runnels informed Ford that he was "clothed in the full and complete command of all the State Troops now in the field and of all to be called out in contemplation of the Law of January 28th, 1858." He ordered the Senior Captain to co-operate with Indian agents and with officers of the Regular Army "if expedient, convenient or practicable."[7] He authorized Ford to contract for supplies and, in closing, stressed the necessity for action and energy.

With energetic action Ford responded. In less than a month, recruiting, organization, and most supply procurement had been accomplished. Recruiting, although rapid, was deliberate, for "the intention was to get good men." When most of the company had been enlisted, Ford ordered an election for company officers. The results placed him in a dual capacity: by election he was a company commander; by Runnels' commission, he was, in effect, a battalion commander. To fill the remaining offices, the men elected as first lieutenant Edward Burleson, Jr., son of a vice-president of the Republic of Texas, and as second lieutenant, William A. Pitts. Dr. Powhatan Jordan was employed as contract surgeon.

Ford was fortunate in the choice of his officers. Able Ed Burleson had served under Ben McCulloch on the northwest frontier during the Mexican War, as well as with Ford's "Old Ranger" company of 1850–51. Billy Pitts also had Ranger experience, with Henry E. McCulloch and in Callahan's debacle. Ford's ranking noncommissioned officer, English-born Robert Cotter, youthful and observant, had left his clerking job in George Hancock's Austin dry goods store to enlist. Although ranked as orderly sergeant, he actually functioned as battalion sergeant major.

[6] Ford, "Memoirs," IV, 680–81.

[7] At the time, Major Robert S. Neighbors was Supervising Agent, Texas Indians, charged with the administration of the two Reserves. Resident agents were Captain Shapley P. Ross at the Brazos reservation and Colonel Matthew Leepers at the Camp Cooper, or Clear Fork, Reserve. The latter, in Ford's opinion, was purely a political appointee and a singularly inexperienced and incompetent official. But then, Ford was suspected by Neighbors of wanting the position for himself.

Ford found it necessary to devote some attention to the Rangers already in the field. Lieutenant James H. Tankersley was scouting with his company in Comanche County, and to the eastward in Bosque County, Lieutenant Allison Nelson was active with a command. Ford had confidence in both officers, particularly in Nelson, who had organized and led a company during the Mexican War, but he decided to muster out a company commanded by Captain John S. Connor and a small detachment under Lieutenant T. C. Frost, both patrolling in the Pecan Bayou region northwest of Austin.[8] Ford may have lacked confidence in the two latter officers; it is equally possible that his decision was influenced by the fact that both held commissions from a political foe, former Governor Pease. To replace these units, Captain Henry E. McCulloch, at Ford's request, agreed to raise a company and to join the main command on the frontier.

To arm Ford's men, Governor Runnels asked General Twiggs for a supply of Colt revolvers, but Twiggs refused, saying that he could not issue the arms unless the Rangers were in federal service. Nevertheless, the command was able to ride out armed after the usual Ranger fashion; most of the men, like Ford, owned two Colt pistols, and every man carried at least one, as well as the familiar muzzle-loading rifle. The firepower of the company was estimated at fifteen hundred rounds without reloading, a volume impressive enough to draw newspaper comment.[9] By obtaining waterproof leather panniers, "*cayaques*," which the baggage mules could not dislodge, Ford assured his Rangers of dry ammunition and blankets. Finally, he acquired two light wagons to carry supplies and, perhaps, sick or wounded.

At last Ford gave the order to break camp. Eager for a change from "Old Rip"'s inflexible garrison discipline, the Rangers marched at daybreak on a chilly February morning. One can visualize the column of riders as it wound through the shallow passes and past the low hogbacks of the rolling hills north of the capital. Nondescript, casual men in nondescript, casual clothing, each wore the garments he felt would serve him best during an

[8] Ford, "Memoirs," IV, 683.   [9] *State Gazette* (Austin), May 22, 1858.

arduous campaign, but a certain uniformity was lent the column by the cap-and-ball rifles, walnut butts protruding forward from scabbards near the left legs of the horsemen. Coat skirts bulged at almost every hip where rode the heavy six-shooters, additionally protected from dew or dust by voluminous holsters. Screening the head of the column, and within eyeshot of it, spread a thin fringe of scouts, alert but not anxious, since the route for the first few days lay through relatively peaceful country. Leading the column at a swinging walk rode the quiet captain, and at his elbow, like a shadow, bobbed his personal orderly Falcon, Don Monkey, whose service with Ford on the Río Grande had kept his master alternating between fits of smoldering irritability and high good humor. Trailing the fighting force came the phlegmatic baggage mules and hired muleteers. Closing the files, except for Ford's usual rear guard, the light wagons rattled and chattered protestingly at the stony trail.

Ford and Pitts led the column up the Colorado to Pecan Bayou and the Chandler settlement, now Brownwood. There they halted to await Burleson, who had traveled by way of San Antonio to procure supplies unavailable in Austin. On March 15, the main command moved north under Burleson, who had orders to establish a base camp on Hubbard Creek, in what is today northern Stephens County. Ford wanted a camp approximately twenty miles from each of the two agencies and about equally distant from Fort Belknap. From such a location he could keep watch on the reservation bands, particularly the Comanches, to learn whether they were giving clandestine aid to hostile Indians.

To be sure that no Indians lurked in the rear of the command, Ford and Pitts, with a small detachment, followed the main body, reconnoitering the valleys of the Colorado, Pecan Bayou, and Jim Ned Creek. When they overtook Burleson, they learned that by mistaking his orders he had marched several miles past the intended camp location and had gone into camp on the Clear Fork of the Brazos just above its junction with Hubbard Creek, about twelve miles above present-day Breckenridge. The location, however, met Ford's requirements: it was convenient to the reservations and to Fort Belknap, and wood, grass, and water were plentiful. Ford therefore approved the site and called it Camp Runnels.[10]

"Old Rip" felt that his command was too small to begin a campaign before McCulloch's company arrived. While he waited, he conducted a training program consisting primarily of mounted drill and target practice, the latter exercise including firing both on foot and from horseback, at various gaits. Meanwhile, the detachments of Nelson and Tankersley rode in to join in the drill and in the patrols which Ford regularly maintained between the reservations, patrols that convinced the Rangers of the duplicity of the Comanches on the Clear Fork reservation.[11] As March waned, Ford became increasingly impatient for McCulloch's arrival. Finally word came that McCulloch had not enlisted a company. Immediately Ford called upon William Preston and William N. P. Marlin to raise small units of twenty-five or thirty men, and both promptly complied.

Ford believed that his command still was not strong enough to guarantee success. However, an effort to raise twenty more men was frustrated by the selfishly motivated interference of John R. Baylor, who in 1857 had been discharged as agent at Camp Cooper. By mid-April of 1858, even the frontier had heard that the volunteer regiment bill had passed Congress and was awaiting presidential action. Baylor hoped to raise a company for the regiment and wanted to be sure that sufficient men would be on the frontier to form his company if the regiment should be activated in Ford's absence. If all the frontier fighting men went with Ford, Baylor's hopes might be disappointed. The news concerning the regiment may account for McCulloch's failure to come to Ford's support.[12] According to the *State Gazette* of May 22, Baylor's

[10] Ford, "Memoirs," IV, 686.

[11] A. Nelson to Ford, April 20, 1858, G. L.

[12] Ford to Runnels, April 26, 1858, G. L. McCulloch may have had other reasons. He may have felt that he, not Ford, should have been appointed Senior Captain. Anyway, Ford wrote to Runnels on May 23, 1858, "You know the arrangement between Captain McC. and myself and how signally he failed to comply. I am thankful, that I had a little success without his assistance."

hopes were vain anyway. An item in that issue stated that Governor Runnels would appoint Ford, H. E. McCulloch, William G. Tobin, E. A. Palmer, E. R. Hord, A. Nelson, A. M. Truett, E. A. Carroll, J. H. Rogers, and Sam Bogart "to command companies in the Texas Ranger Regiment." One may conjecture what would have happened along the frontier if a full regiment of veteran Rangers, led by that hard-bitten corps of commanders, had ever been permitted to take the field.

While the Rangers drilled and scouted, Ford spent much time with Captain Shapley P. Ross, agent at the Brazos reservation, where the Caddoes, Tonkawas, and other tribal remnants were being trained in the white man's way, hoping that volunteers from these tribes would provide him with a scouting and auxiliary force. Major Neighbors came out from Waco to assist Agent Ross in recruiting such a group. Some delay occurred in obtaining scouts. Casa María, the able Caddo leader, was reluctant to participate because of a tripartite treaty among the Caddo, Creek, and Comanche nations, an agreement providing that if one member of the trio attacked another, the third member must be previously notified, else it would join against the aggressors. With Ross's permission, the Caddo chief sent notification to the Creeks. After a few days, the Caddo courier returned with Creek acknowledgment of the message, and the way was open to organize the Indian complement.

The mounting war spirit on the reservation infected Agent Ross, that doughty veteran of Indian campaigns under Jack Hays and Peter H. Bell, who indicated his willingness to lead the Indian contingent if at least one hundred of his charges would agree to go. At his suggestion, the chiefs announced a feast and a war dance for April 9, after which Ross would know how many braves the war party would number. Ford and several of his men rode in to observe the activities. The dance, judging by the Senior Captain's description, must have been a memorable spectacle.

The war-dance was "grand, gloomy, and peculiar." Every participant had his own way in the matter; some sounded the fear-inspiring warhoop; others crept along, cat-like, to pounce upon their astonished and demoralized foes; a squad would move up and attack an imaginary band of Comanches, and a shout of triumph would go up, loud enough to set a donkey's ears to ringing. Many sang in a style which would have crazed an old maiden school teacher. Every face had a daubing of rueful colors, intended to strike terror into the beholder. The sight of one was enough to stampede a regiment of dudes, and a battalion of school-marms. The impression made upon a civilized spectator may be illustrated thusly: An immense paint pot, hundreds of miles in depth and circumference, filled with colors of every conceivable hue and shade has been overturned, the contents have deluged the infernal regions; hell has taken an emetic, and cast up devils upon earth, and here they are.

At the end of the dance, more than Ross's requisite one hundred signified their determination to march with the Rangers, thus assuring Ford of the agent's valuable experience. This was fortunate for Ford, since business was to summon Lieutenant Burleson home at the last minute, and the reluctance with which Captain Ford granted leave to his battle-tested subordinate was somewhat tempered by the acquisition of the veteran Ross.[13]

By early April, Captain Ford already knew the location of the Comanche village he planned to surprise. His target was the Nokoni band, camped along the Canadian River near the Antelope Hills, whom frontiersmen blamed for most of the winter's depredations. There was a rumor in the settlements that Ford had sent a spy to the camp, who returned bearing the Nokoni challenge to the Rangers to come after them.[14] By mid-April the Rangers were almost ready to move in response to the Nokoni defiance. Powder, cartridges, and percussion caps for pistols and rifles were packed for easy access and distribution; Surgeon Jordan had overhauled and arranged his instruments and drugs; picket ropes, one for each animal, were distributed among the men. But no forage was packed, for the mounts and baggage mules must subsist on grass. For the men, Ford apportioned extra rations, particularly of coffee and sugar. On the campaign, bacon would give way to

[13] Ford, "Memoirs," IV, 686–88; Ford to Runnels, April 7, 1858, G. L.
[14] *State Gazette* (Austin), May 22, 1858.

buffalo meat and bread would not be missed, but coffee, all the better for sweetening, was an item few Rangers ever patiently did without.

Captain William Ford, seventy-three-year-old father of the Senior Captain unexpectedly provided an ambulance. In this vehicle the elder Ford had jolted into the middle of Camp Runnels' busy preparations, announcing that he intended to accompany the expedition. John Ford was glad to get the ambulance and approved the intention, since the old gentleman "possessed strong will—[was] a good rider, and capable of enduring considerable fatigue."[15]

Reveille and the order to saddle up came in rapid succession on the morning of April 22. With good-natured jibes at Lieutenant Marlin's small complement remaining to guard the camp and to patrol along the Clear Fork, the eager command tossed bedrolls into the wagons, ate a hasty breakfast, and formed the marching column of twos. Then, with 102 Rangers, his pack train, and his vehicles at his back, "Old Rip" Ford rode north looking for trouble.[16]

For two days the company rode slowly, waiting for the Indian auxiliaries. On the night of June 24 it camped at old Fort Belknap, on the main Brazos about twenty miles above its confluence with the Clear Fork. A second short march brought the men to the Cottonwood Springs, approximately six miles below the present town of Olney. On April 26, Shapley Ross and 113 of his colorful wards straggled into camp, and, late in the afternoon when the laggards had come up, the march continued.

Tribesmen of at least half a dozen nations came with Ross. Casa María and Jim Pock Mark led the Caddo-Anadarko group; tough old Placido and his war chief, O'Quinn, marched with their Tonkawa braves; a mixed party of Shawnees and Delawares followed Jim Linney; Ah-qua-quash (Shot Arm) brought his Wacos, and the Tahuanacos were there under Nid-o-wats. In addition there came Caddo John, Jem Logan, Chul-e-quah, and the Indian lin-

15 Ford, "Memoirs," IV, 689.

16 Ford to Runnels, May 22, 1858. This communication was Ford's official report of the campaign published in the *State Gazette* of May 29, 1858.

guist Keechi, who had lived among the Comanches and who may have been the spy sent to the Nokonis, if that story is true. Young Bob Cotter, from his seat atop "Old Woolly," beheld "a very imposing scene—Indian and white man together hunting one common enemy, the wily Comanche, the terror of mothers and children on this frontier." Not all of Placido's people had horses, but the Tonkawa footmen marched well and the column was not thereby delayed. In the late afternoon of April 27 the force reached the lush pastures and thick timber along the Little Wichita River and camped on its bank. It evidently was a favorite camping ground; Sergeant Cotter counted 140 fires twinkling in the dusk along the stream and presumed that they indicated a large party of Indians.[17]

On the Little Wichita the Tonkawas decided upon a ceremonial rattlesnake feast and soon accumulated a squirming pile of reptiles. The irresponsible orderly, Falcon, precipitated a crisis by innocently contributing a blacksnake to the menu. There was prompt Tonkawa reaction. Had not Ford quickly intervened, it "appeared probable from the demonstrations of the incensed snake eaters that . . . the Don would have come to grief" at their hands for his sacrilege.[18]

Next day the expedition passed the Big Wichita, at a point where Cotter thought the land good, although insufficiently timbered. Ford's older eyes, however, saw the area otherwise. To him the locality of the ford was "a dreary one. The sand, the apparent sterility of the soil, the abhorrent taste of the salty water, combined to produce a gloomy feeling. Some of us spoke of the Dead Sea, and Sodom and Gomorrah." By continued hard marching on that day, April 29, Ford reached Red River, crossing to camp on its north bank. After the main body had trotted across, Lieutenant Tankersley, officer of the day, unloaded the wagons, distributed their burdens among his rear guard, and urged vehicles and baggage men at a run through the quicksands of the

[17] Robert Cotter to John Marshall, *State Gazette* (Austin), May 20, 1858. Hereafter cited as Cotter to Marshall.
[18] Ford, "Memoirs," IV, 689–90.

treacherous stream, while the anxious Rangers and Indians cheered the operation.

Here they entered the buffalo pastures and spent several days traversing the thirty-odd westward miles to Otter Creek, at the base of the Wichita Mountains. The force moved slowly to permit hunting, and now buffalo meat replaced bacon in the rations. So many ravines impeded the column in this area that it was repeatedly necessary to unload the wagons, unhitch the mules, and lower the vehicles by ropes down the precipitous bluffs. Even so, Ford was satisfied at the speed of his progress under the circumstances.

The command spent two days at Otter Creek hunting buffalo and feasting on the succulent meat which later called forth a panegyric from "Old Rip." Between hunts the Rangers climbed to the crests of the mountains, returning laden with currants, grapes, strawberries, and other wild fruits which Sergeant Cotter found growing profusely. Then, the commissary replenished, Captain Ford led the mixed command north by west up the North Fork of the Red. He was now in Indian Territory, outside the boundaries in which he could legally operate. This he may have known; it is doubtful that he would have been much concerned.

Now Ford moved cautiously, with scouting parties from fifteen to twenty miles out in all directions. For several days he followed the river. On May 7, having seen no Indian sign, he swung to the right, away from the North Fork and its "gyp" waters, crossing on the next day to the upper Washita, where scouts discovered the recent trail of a large warrior band, estimated on the basis of the remnants of their campfires to number about four hundred. Confident that it was a Comanche trail, Ford warily followed it for two days. On the evening of the second day, the scouts came in with a Comanche arrowhead, cut from a wounded buffalo which they had killed. On the following morning, May 11, a hurrying scout reported that he had seen a Comanche killing buffalo, and that the direction in which the hostile had led his meat-laden horse indicated the way to the Comanche camp.

Hastily, "Rip" Ford prepared to attack before a wandering

enemy hunter should stumble across the command. William Ford, a couple of Rangers, and the muleteers were detailed to guard the pack train and vehicles, blankets and rations were lashed behind saddles, and early in the afternoon the Senior Captain led his combat force carefully in the direction shown by the scout. As the afternoon waned, Ford halted on the Fort Smith–Santa Fe "bull-wagon" road, slightly southeast of the gap through which the greater frontier commercial artery emerged from the Antelope Hills. Down a valley to the north he could see Comanches moving about in the distance. At his orders, the Rangers and their allies disappeared into ravines flanking the road. Dismounting, Ford and Ross strode to a point where the road topped the Washita-Canadian watershed and from there gazed speculatively at the enemy.[19]

The curious Rangers, eyeing their captain, beheld a lithe, erect man of average stature, his broad hat pushed back to avoid interference with his spyglass. From beneath his hatbrim, light hair curled above a high, clear forehead. Intent blue eyes peered over high, weathered cheek bones, past the bridge of an aquiline nose.[20] As he changed position to watch the hostiles, unconsciously he may have favored his right arm, weak from an old Comanche wound; perhaps by this time he had received the undescribed injury which caused old Rangers to remember him as "three-fingered Rip."[21] At forty-three, already he was an old man to many youngsters in the Ranger ranks. Few of the men realized that the officer they watched was becoming a legendary figure. Every night, at home or in the field, he studied his Bible, in accordance with a youthful promise to his mother, and when in Austin he taught Sunday School classes in his quietly humorous way; yet in 1858 he was a member of no church. Ordinarily soft-spoken, he could roar pointedly and bluntly—on occasion profanely so. Among those who lived by the gun, he was a peer who "reckoned to be able to hit a man every time with a six-shooter

[19] *Ibid.*, 690–92; Cotter to Marshall; Ford to Runnels, May 22, 1858, G. L.
[20] Martin, "Last of the Ranger Chieftains," 38.
[21] *Frontier Times*, Vol. XV (October, 1937–September, 1938), 471–76.

at one hundred and twenty-five yards."[22] He always had full knowledge of the capabilities and competence of each officer in his command, and almost every trooper bore a nickname he had aptly bestowed. He never slept, so his guards maintained. The quiet confidence of jobs well done, radiating from his bearing, was reflected by the high morale in the ranks.

Oblivious to the intent eyes of his men, John Ford looked north, a battle plan taking shape behind the cool, blue stare.

When the Comanches drifted out of sight, Rangers and painted auxiliaries mounted and reformed the column. Then they moved slowly and quietly northward through lengthening shadows, concealed by the broken land. When late evening twilight had covered the Canadian and its tributary valleys, the invaders drew rein and made camp. Guards rimmed the bivouac area, and Ford sent a squad of Indians forward to find Keechi, earlier ordered ahead to locate the Comanche camp.

The empty-handed return of the scouts altered Ford's plan. He intended to move up near the Comanche village during the night. Just before dawn he would have the Indian allies stampede the Comanche horse herd, and, in the confusion, the Ranger attack would smash into the village. But now the opportune time had passed—the column must move in daylight, and Ford could only hope to find and strike the Nokonis before they should discover him. The latter possibility probably did not alarm "Rip" Ford as he prowled his outpost perimeter; it was an occupational hazard of frontier command.

As daylight of May 12 came to the Canadian, the officer of the day passed from one blanket-shrouded figure to another, waking the sleepers. The guard returned. Dusky faces blossomed with fresh war paint. Bronzed hands fixed white cloth badges to bizarre headdresses so that friends might be distinguished from hostiles in the dusty tumult of battle. Red man and white methodically checked caps and loads. An order passed through camp; Rangers swung into their saddles, and the swarthy reservation tribesmen

22 Remington, "How the Law Got into the Chaparral," 61.

scrambled on their ponies. Quickly the column moved out of the hills and down the quiet valley below.

After a brisk advance of about six miles, action came swiftly at seven o'clock. Across the Ranger route appeared five Comanche lodges, about which Indians were in motion. The Texas yell and a variety of tribal war whoops rent the still morning air as the command descended upon the small camp. Two Comanche braves leaped for their ponies and galloped hard for the rising ground three miles north across the valley. Ford's riders thundered through the camp in pursuit, except for the Tonks, who stayed to loot and to get horses for their footmen.

From the crest of the rise, the pursuers saw the snowy lodges of the Tenawa Comanche camp spread before them, about three miles distant on the north bank of the Canadian—a big camp, thought Ranger William Mathews, of "fully 350 warriors." In their haste to warn the camp, the fleeing Comanches unintentionally betrayed a safe ford through the swampy banks and across the sandy channel of the river. Ross and his Indians, followed by the Rangers, splashed across at a run to firm ground on the north bank. There the Texans pulled up, grinning at the drenched orderly sergeant who belatedly joined them. "Old Woolly" had stumbled over an unseen rock, catapulting Cotter head foremost into the shallow stream.

Over the drum of hoofbeats and the ululation of battle cries, Ford shouted to Ross to take the reservation Indians forward and to open the fight. Their advance would give Ford time to form the Ranger ranks and, he hoped, would deceive the Comanches temporarily into thinking that they had only Indians, armed no better than themselves, to meet. Ross beckoned to his chiefs and the painted partisans swung into position on the right front. Ford turned to his impatient Rangers. "Steady, boys, until I give the word," he called.

Into the two hundred yards of open ground between Ross's Indians and the Tenawa lodges, a single, armored figure rode to bar the way. It was Po-bish-e-quash-o (Iron Jacket), head chief of the band, possessor of a powerful medicine which enabled him to blow aside the arrows of his foes. An ancient coat of scaled mail, looted perhaps by some long-dead ancestor from an unfortunate conquistador, covered him from throat to thigh. Riding assuredly before his hereditary enemies, he described small circles, then advanced, swelling his cheeks and expelling his breath vigorously toward the surprised command. Confident of his invulnerability, he rode deliberately forward and leveled his rifle at the invaders. Then the trance-like tension was shattered by Billy Pitts's stentorian shout: "Kill the son-of-a-bitch!"

Abruptly Iron Jacket's medicine failed. Most of his foes bore firearms rather than bows and arrows. A ragged volley brought his horse crashing to the ground. As he sprang clear and straightened to face his attackers, a second, crisper blast crumpled him forward, and a lagging shot finished him. A wail of startled anguish arose from the dead chief's warriors, and "Rip" Ford, taking advantage of the Tenawa consternation, hurled his yelling ranks upon the village.

Despairingly the Comanches broke and fled. Ford and Pitts, leading the right wing of the Ranger formation, burst through the encampment in pursuit, while Nelson, supported by Preston and Tankersley, drove with the left wing to cut off the warriors running for the hills behind the camp. The Rangers broke ranks to pursue the scattering Comanches; the battle became a series of duels spread over eighteen square miles of broken ground, "and it appeared like every man picked his Indian and took after him, man to man." "The din of battle . . . rolled back from the river— the groans of the dying, the cries of frightened women and children mingled with the reports of fire-arms, and the shouts of men as they rose from hill top, from thicket, and from ravine," and Bob Cotter saw that "Captain Ford . . . was everywhere, directing and controlling the movements of his men."[23]

[23] Cotter to Marshall; Ford, "Memoirs," IV, 696; *Frontier Times*, Vol. XV, 50–52; Remington, "How the Law Got into the Chaparral," 64; Ford to Runnels, May 22, 1858, G. L. After the battle, the Rangers removed Iron Jacket's armor and divided it as souvenirs, according to Sergeant Cotter who sent a scrap of it in a letter to the Governor. Cotter to Runnels (n. d.), G. L.

As the mounts grew jaded and the Comanches drew out of range, the firing dwindled away and the Rangers and their allies turned back toward the village. When Ford and the irrepressible Pitts rejoined the main body, they found that Nelson and Ross had assembled the Indians and the returning troopers.

Ford reined in beside Ross. "What time in the morning is it?" he asked.

Ross stared at the Senior Captain. "Morning, hell!" he blurted. "It's one o'clock."

It was Ford's turn to stare. He had been totally unconscious of time during the six crowded hours of combat.[24]

The sound of the battle and the stream of fugitives had brought other Comanches hurrying from several miles upstream, where lay the large Nokoni camp, Ford's intended goal. The appearance of the Nokonis swarming on the hills above the stricken village had caused Nelson, at Ross's suggestion, to call the command together. For a brief time the Rangers stood quietly, resting their winded steeds, while their Indian allies and the Comanches exchanged insulting badinage across the valley. Then the reservation warriors cantered out on the flat to challenge the newcomers, who swept from the hills to join battle. The Rangers witnessed a unique sight.

A scene was now enacted beggaring description. It reminded one of the rude and chivalrous days of Knight-errantry. Shields and lances, and bows and head dresses—prancing steed and many minutias were not wanting to compile the resemblance. And when the combatants rushed at each other with defiant shouts, nothing save the piercing report of the rifle varied the affair from a battle field of the middle ages. A detachment of Rangers was advanced to reinforce the friendly Indians, and the Comanches quited the field, and the imposing pageant vanished from view like a mimic battle upon the stage.[25]

Ford's second maneuver went awry. Ross's Indians had hoped to lure the Comanches into an ambush, but when Nelson led the

[24] Remington, "How the Law Got into the Chaparral," 60.
[25] Ford to Runnels, May 22, 1858, G. L.

Ranger left wing sweeping around the base of a small hill to hit the flank of the unsuspecting enemy, Placido's screaming Tonka-was sprung the trap prematurely and the Comanches fled to the bluffs. The Rangers followed as rapidly as they could push their weary horses, but were unable to come to grips with the enemy. Furthermore, most of the reservation Indians had removed the white badges from their headdresses, claiming that the insignia made them easy targets for the Comanches. Since at long range it was impossible for the Rangers to recognize friendly from enemy warriors, they headed back after a run of several miles. It was difficult for Ford to persuade the raging Pitts and the equally agitated Placido to retire. "They wanted more blood."[26]

As the Rangers again rode back through the debris of Iron Jacket's camp, commenting on the piles of gorgeously beaded buffalo robes, the bales of dried meat, and the heaped containers of cornmeal, salt, and coffee obtained from the *Comancheros*,[27] Ford was astonished to see that among the bodies of Comanche warriors there were some which lacked hands and feet. The reason became clear when he rejoined Ross. The missing extremities dangled from Tonk saddle bows; those voracious and cannibal people were planning a victory feast.

Between maledictions called down by a captive crone, Ford learned that Buffalo Hump and his band were hunting about a dozen miles down the Canadian. It was now two o'clock, and fugitives had had ample time to tell Buffalo Hump of the assault. Possibly in no hurry to resume an old acquaintanceship and certainly concerned lest his camp be exposed to attack, Ford marched to join the supply train. It was dusk before the entire command, slowed by the winded horses and impeded by prisoners and the captured pony herd, went into camp a dozen miles south of the Canadian.

That night, while the Tonk allies squatted above their grisly

[26] Wilbarger, *Indian Depredations in Texas*, 325; Ford, "Memoirs," IV, 698.

[27] *Comancheros* were traders who dealt with the Comanches for horses. Texans believed that such trade encouraged the horse-stealing raids into Texas, and were bitter against the traders. A party of Mexican *Comancheros* left Iron Jacket's village only two days before Ford's raid. Ford to Runnels, June 2, 1858, G. L.

feast, Ford silently debated his situation. Angry voices suddenly rising high in the starlight sent him hurrying to the Tonkawa fires. There he found Bugler Billy Holzinger, pistol drawn, loudly berating the astonished and indignant war chief, O'Quinn. Sharp questioning revealed the cause. O'Quinn, as an authority on human flesh, had been asked by a Ranger what nationality the Tonk considered the best eating, and the gourmet instantly recalled the flavor of "a big, fat Dutchman he and his men had killed on the Guadalupe river in 1849." Holzinger immediately challenged O'Quinn for ridiculing his countrymen. It was some time after Ford restored order that the bugler realized that he himself narrowly had escaped scalping in the affair mentioned by O'Quinn.

"Rip" Ford realized that the time had come to return to Camp Runnels. His horses were too fatigued for further combat operations, and his meat supply had been exhausted for several days. Then, too, Ross's Indians felt it was time to go.

> Capt. Ross expressed the opinion that the friendly Indians were satisfied with what they had done, were quite elated at the number of horses captured, and thought, perhaps, it would be wise to let well enough alone. . . . They were already badly stirred up; there was no hope of getting another fight out of them; . . . These were among the reasons, indeed the main reason, for the return.

At sunup on May 13 the command broke camp to retrace its route to the Clear Fork base. As one vehicle after another broke down and was abandoned, the column increased its speed and the eighteen-day outward march from Cottonwood Springs was accomplished in eight days. At the springs the Rangers parted from their red allies. The tribesmen had sent word ahead to the agency of their coming, and the colorful welcome and exuberant praise for the trophies, horses, and captives by those who had remained behind reminded Ford of the "reception of Saul and David from the field of Sohoceh [Shochoh]." On the evening of May 20, the Texans unsaddled their leg-weary mounts in the Camp Runnels compound, just less than a month after their departure.

Two days later Ford sent off his official report of the campaign to Governor Runnels. In it he praised the wise counsel and able co-operation of Shapley P. Ross; he recommended to Runnels' attention the prompt, cheerful, and efficient conduct of Nelson, Tankersley, and Preston; finally, he commended the men for "obedience, patience, and perseverance" and for their "gallant and soldier like manner under fire," concluding that "they have fully vindicated their right to be recognized as Texas Rangers of the old stamp." Also he remembered that his Indian allies "deserve well of Texas and are entitled to the gratitude of the frontier people."[28]

On his campaign, Ford had marched about five hundred miles over unfamiliar country, had fought almost continuously for seven hours, and had led his command back safely from the heart of a hostile land. The sole Ranger loss had been Robert Nickles of Nelson's company, who when cut off from his command had attempted to outrun the enemy instead of taking cover until aid could come. In the second fight, a Waco Indian had been lanced to death, and two other Indians and one Ranger had been wounded, George W. Paschal, Jr., having acquired three lance wounds. In contrast, Ford had counted seventy-six dead Comanches but was sure the total must be higher, since he had seen many enemy wounded helped from the field. The Rangers had captured eighteen women and children, among them a lad said to be the son of Iron Jacket. More than three hundred Comanche horses had been taken, most of which were turned over to the reservation Indians. Possibly the expedition had forestalled a major raid; a captured Mexican lad told Ford that the Comanches were drying and packing meat to use on a campaign against the settlers and the reservation tribes, and the bales of dried meat that both Ford and Cotter had seen in the village gave credence to the boy's story.

Ford believed that the true value of the campaign lay not so

28 Ford to Runnels, May 22, 1858, G. L.; Ford, "Memoirs," IV, 528–29, 699, 702. Ford apparently accompanied Ross to the Brazos agency before returning to Camp Runnels.

Robert S. Neighbors, U.S. Indian agent in Texas,
whom Ford accompanied to lay out
an El Paso–San Antonio wagon route.

From Walter Prescott Webb, *The Texas Rangers*

Ford's attack on the Comanche village on the Canadian,
from his description to Frederic Remington.

From *Harper's Monthly* (December, 1896)

much in the tactical as in the strategic aspect of his success, however much the former might be applauded.

This expedition has decided several questions—Indians can be pursued and caught in the buffalo region—the country beyond Red River can be penetrated and held by white men, and the Comanches can be followed, overtaken, and beaten, provided the pursuers will be laborious, vigilant, and are willing to undergo privations.[29]

In a private letter to Runnels, Ford expressed the hope that "the fight will satisfy the people, vindicate you from the assaults of your enemies, and be of permanent value to the frontier." He emphasized that the Brazos portion of the frontier was "dreadfully exposed" and referred to depredations—in this instance horse-stealing—which had occurred while his command was absent. "I have reason to believe the Agency Comanches are the [guilty] parties, and if I fix it upon them I shall give them hell and trust to the people to sustain me." Frontier families, he added, were "forting"; some had been "forted up" since the departure of the command in April.

Referring to the matter of the Ranger regiment, Ford commented,

If not too late I shall run for Colonel. I suppose I should be the Runnels candidate as McCulloch has pulled against you, or at least it would be put up so, as they couple me with you in abuse. . . . If you can consistently with your duty and your feelings give me a fair show for the Colonelcy I ask you to do so. The election may be over—or the cards may be stacked. If the game is not too far advanced I should like to shuffle and have a hand dealt me. I think there is a combination to beat me, and under the circumstances it is equivalent to beating you.

The tone of the letter makes one wonder if McCulloch, perhaps, had not lost more by his partial break with the Democratic leaders

[29] Cotter to Marshall; Ford, "Memoirs," IV, 697, 702; Ford to Marshall, May 22, 1858, G. L. Ford does not explain why he officially reported eighteen prisoners instead of the sixty he actually took, nor what became of them. Three, including the Mexican boy, escaped the night of May 12.

than had Ford by a complete, prolonged separation. "Old Rip," however, had more political value to John Marshall—which possibly accounted for his appointment as senior captain and McCulloch's resentment.

The Governor, on May 28, acknowledged receipt of Ford's report and enclosed an address of commendation to the Rangers, expressing the thanks of the people of Texas. He congratulated Ford upon his successful campaign and authorized him to enlist more Rangers if he thought it necessary.[30] Evidently he could tell "Old Rip" nothing of the status of the regiment proposal, for on the day he wrote to Ford, he wrote also to the Texas delegation in Congress that he had given Ford permission to recruit for the frontier emergency until he should learn what had been done about the bill. Runnels asked the Texas congressmen to "confer with the President and Sec. of War and urge them to action with the least possible delay," and to insist upon the removal of the agent at Camp Cooper, "to whose inefficiency much of the trouble is to be attributed from the Indians of that reserve." For their benefit, Runnels enclosed a *Gazette* account of Ford's expedition.[31]

The Governor then called upon Ford for a detailed description of frontier conditions and for suggestions regarding the most effective means of protecting the region. Ford's reply of June 2 discussed the extent of the frontier, the paucity of federal troops, the contemptuous disregard of the general government of Texan pleas for aid, and the additional indignity of the state's being depredated by tribes drawing annuities from Washington. Rhetorically he asked when Texas might expect peace, under the conditions, and answered himself, saying, "Never so long as we have a horse left, or as long as there is an Indian left to steal him." The true solution, Ford believed, lay with Runnels:

> You have the remedy in your own hands. Call out the Regiment immediately—let a campaign be made against the Comanches and their confederates—carry the war into Africa—and, if practicable,

30 Runnels to Ford, May 28, 1858, G. L.
31 Runnels to the Texas Delegation in Congress, May 28, 1858, G. L.

let the gentlemen who have traded with the enemy come in for a share of the punishment—wipe them out altogther. . . . Call the regiment into the service, and the people of Texas would be amply compensated, if the United States should refuse to reimburse the expenses, by the rapid ingress of emigrants—the prompt development of the mighty natural resources of the country, and her onward march to prosperity, wealth and power. Call out the Regiment and every frontiersman from Red River to the Rio Grande will bless you; and your name will go down with the worthies whose patriotism and actions have become the common property of a mighty people.[32]

Writing from the Brazos Reserve on July 5, he reiterated to the Governor the need for a larger frontier force, saying that he had just learned that the Comanches were negotiating treaties with tribes east of Red River, preparing for a fall or winter raid against the frontier. By July, however, Runnels, had decided against additional recruiting, since Congress had failed to appropriate funds to sustain a Ranger regiment. On July 6, he ordered Ford to disband the company at the end of the enlistment period. "Old Rip" was disappointed, but he knew that his Canadian River campaign had cost almost $35,000, about half of the defense appropriation, and, as he put it, the Governor "had been bitten by the economic bug."[33]

In mid-August, their enlistments having expired, Ford's Rangers left Camp Runnels. Nelson's company marched to Stephenville for mustering out, where the grateful citizens entertained them with a barbecue. Ford, Pitts, and Burleson (who had returned to Camp Runnels), took the rest down country to Lampasas Springs, now Lampasas, for discharge.

At Lampasas Springs, about sixty miles northwest of Austin, Ford's men, too, enjoyed a barbecue. Old Placido, for more than two decades a fighting ally of the whites, accompanied Ford and met at the springs old comrades-in-arms he had not seen for many

[32] Ford to Runnels, June 2, 1858, G. L.
[33] Ford, "Memoirs," IV, 755.

years. The reunion called for a prolonged celebration, but Placido was distressed at being the only Tonkawa present, for their wise custom dictated that when warriors got drunk, one must always remain sober to keep the rest out of trouble. The presence of Billy Pitts, whom the Indians had come to admire greatly, provided the solution to the old chief's dilemma. Placido sought out the Ranger and placed in his care "medals and badges he prized highly, saying 'You must be chief for a while . . .' For three days Pitts sported the badges before Placido resumed them. . . . In the absence of a Toncahua brave, Pitts played the role of sober Indian."[34]

Feeling that the campaign had resulted, at best, in only a temporary check to the Comanches, Runnels continued to bombard Secretary Floyd with pleas for federal assistance. Finally, disgusted with Floyd's noncommittal attitude, he appealed directly to the White House, complaining that Floyd had returned no satisfactory answer, stressing the "insufficiency of the military force in Texas to give that prompt and adequate protection required," and warning of the Indian desire for revenge for Ford's raid.[35] The President offered no more satisfaction than had his Secretary of War, but Buchanan seems to have been characteristically disinclined to take positive action.

The Comanches soon began to validate Runnels' pessimism, and his mail in September and October was full of petitions for protection. On October 4, Gainesville residents called for John Ford and a company.[36] Possibly at Ford's suggestion, Runnels commissioned James Bourland, who raised a command which patrolled the Gainesville frontier until the following spring.[37] By mid-autumn, Comanche incursions and the consequent petitions for relief had become so frequent that the executive again turned to "Rip"

[34] *Ibid.*, 700, 747.

[35] Executive Record Book No. 277, Governor Hardin R. Runnels, Archives Division, Texas State Library, Austin, 153–54, 253–59, 379–80. Hereafter cited as Exec. Rec. Bk. These contain official copies of correspondence and documents emitting from the executive office.

[36] E. C. Palmer to Runnels, October 4, 1858, G. L. Other examples are those from San Saba, Decatur, Wise, and Lampasas Counties in September, and from Lampasas in October, 1858.

[37] Runnels to Bourland, October 4, 1858, and March 19, 1859, G. L.

Ford. On November 2, 1858, Runnels authorized Ford to enlist a company for the usual six months' service. Runnels informed Floyd of Ford's muster, calling again for federal assistance against "the threatening storm which is now beginning to burst with all its fury on the suffering frontier." He also observed indignantly that Indians recently had raided about sixty miles from Austin, on the Belton Road, killing two men and stealing three hundred horses.[38]

Acting with his usual energy, Ford soon had his company together. The *State Gazette* commented that most of the recruits were young, but were "good riders and excellent marksmen," and that because of their commander it could be expected that they would "destroy or scatter the savage enemies."[39] The company was mustered in on November 10, and immediately elected Ford captain and first and second lieutenants, respectively, John R. Gibbons and Aaron B. Burleson, the latter a cousin of Ed Burleson. Young Matthew Nolan of the "Old Rangers" turned up in the ranks, again to serve as Ford's bugler.

On November 23 and 24, in two sections, the company left for the frontier, armed with the customary Colts and long, heavy muzzle-loaders of a type called "Minié" rifles, somewhat unwieldy for mounted service but considered by Ford to be reasonably accurate at ranges up to half a mile. The Captain led his troopers into northern Comanche County and there, near the junction of Mercer Creek and the South Leon River, erected the stockade and permanent buildings of Camp Leon.[40] Then he began to drill his eager but inexperienced Rangers in the tricks of the Indian-fighting trade.

During the winter, Ford unintentionally became involved in the unpleasant Garland controversy in Palo Pinto County. A band of seventeen Indians, mostly women and children, traveling beyond the borders of the Brazos Reserve with Agent Ross's permission, were attacked early on the morning of December 27

[38] Exec. Rec. Bk. No. 277, 219–21.
[39] *Ibid.*, 222–23; *State Gazette* (Austin), November 13 and 27, 1858.
[40] Ford, "Memoirs," IV, 757.

by a party of frontiersmen allegedly led by one Peter Garland. Seven adult Indians were killed while they slept and a number of women and children wounded. Some details of the attack reached Ford, who promptly forwarded them to the Governor.[41] Ford went to Austin about the middle of January, probably to confer with Runnels about the position to be taken by the Rangers during the uproar over the incident, possibly to discuss a reconnaissance to the Colorado and Concho rivers. He also consulted with Major Neighbors, assuring the agent of his co-operation should civil authorities request Ranger assistance.[42] Upon returning to Camp Leon, Ford found awaiting him a deputation from Judge N. W. Battle of the Nineteenth Judicial District, ordering him to arrest Garland and seventeen other men. "Old Rip" immediately informed E. J. Gurley, prosecuting attorney in the affair, that he refused to recognize the deputation, since he had been addressed as a military officer in what was a civil matter, and that the Governor alone had authority to command him under the circumstances. Gurley complained to Governor Runnels of Ford's rationalization, and the executive ordered Ford to assist the civil authorities at their request.[43]

Captain Ford replied promptly to the order, privately informing Runnels that he had refused the deputation because he was sure that action on his part would bring on a clash between Rangers and citizens, to the embarrassment of Runnels' administration; that, while he had promised Neighbors to assist the civil authorities, he had not agreed to substitute for them in making arrests; that he had heard he was to be dismissed from the service for his refusal; and that "if anything in the shape of a sacrifice of position should be demanded [he would] make it most willingly." He stated his intention of making a scout to find Indians and warned the Governor that the recall of the Rangers might create a situation resulting in additional expense to the state. Ford feared, on

41 Ford to Runnels (n. d.), G. L.

42 Ford, "Memoirs," IV, 765.

43 Ford to E. J. Gurley, January 22, 1859, *State Gazette* (Austin), March 5, 1859; Gurley to Runnels, February 3, 1859, G. L.; Runnels to Ford, February 11, 1859, G. L.

the ground of earlier information from Runnels, that the company might be discharged before its enlistment term was up—perhaps before a new campaign might be launched.

Doubtless Ford welcomed the circumstances which called him from the region of the Garland incident. On February 22, 1859, he was at Camp Cooper to muster out Lieutenant Marlin's small company, which had been retained past its enlistment period, probably at Neighbors' suggestion. While there, Ross summoned him to the Brazos Reserve, where a crisis had arisen. A band of hostiles had taken some Caddo mounts in a daylight raid on the Reserve pastures. Quickly, Ford and the agent organized a force to take the trail of the raiders.

Ford left the Brazos Agency on February 24, with a command composed of twenty-three of his own company, ten of Marlin's men, enlisted for the expedition, and about twenty-five Indian scouts, including Chul-e-quah, Jim Linney, and others of the May, 1858, raid. He followed the trail of Jim Pock Mark and a band already tracking the marauders. Near the head of the West Fork of the Trinity, Ford struck the camp of the reservation party. There he learned that Pock Mark and a few men had continued after the thieves. Not fully understanding the situation and uncertain of his control over his Indian scouts, Ford finally decided to abandon the trail and march on to Camp Radziminski, established in September as a Regular Army depot on Otter Creek, near the Ranger camp of the previous May. Major Earl Van Dorn and a Second Cavalry contingent were based there, and Ford hoped to merge his men with Van Dorn's troopers in a joint expedition against the hostiles high up on the North Fork of Red River.

On the way to Radziminski, Ford was dismayed to hear that Van Dorn was absent on a scout. Since it was now too late to turn back to the trail of the horse thieves, Ford pushed forward, camping on the bitter cold night of February 28 on Otter Creek, about eight miles below the depot. The next day the Captain and a few Rangers rode to Radziminski for supplies, arriving just before a blizzard which drove the cavalry patrol back to camp. The two commanders discussed the possibility of a joint operation, but heavy snow on March 6 and 7 chilled Van Dorn's enthusiasm for the project, and the suffering of the horses from both severe cold and lack of forage made the plan, in his opinion, impracticable.[44]

"Rip" Ford, however, had come to hunt Indians, and prepared to move out as soon as the weather would permit. He shifted his camp several miles nearer the depot and waited for the grass to turn green and his mounts to recuperate. Meanwhile, the Rangers hunted buffalo and Ford whiled away pleasant hours at Radziminski with Lieutenant Fitzhugh Lee and other amiable Second Cavalry officers. After about a week the Rangers broke camp. Some of the Indians returned home, but the remainder of the command followed "Old Rip" westward. For several days they filed along Red River before angling across country to the Pease. After skirting the brushy banks of this stream for about two days, they turned south on the open plains where buffalo grazed by the thousands, the Rangers estimating (too highly, Ford thought) that they occasionally had thirty thousand beasts in view at a time. Where buffalo were numerous, so also might Indians be, and the group marched with extreme caution, Chul-e-quah and a few companions scouting ahead. They rode southward until Chul-e-quah's abrupt signal brought the short column to a halt. In solemn sign language, he imparted to Jim Linney, riding beside Ford, that no water lay in the direction they were taking and the course thereafter must be southeast. Ford suspected that the scout had changed the line of march deliberately to avoid hostile Indians and that the reservation allies would prove undependable if commanded to continue southward. Since their defection would leave him with too few followers to engage a large enemy band, he reluctantly turned his party in the direction indicated by Chul-e-quah, and on March 30, behind their disconsolate Captain, the frustrated Rangers rode into Camp Cooper. From that point the

[44] Runnels to Ford, February 7, 1859, G. L.; Exec. Rec. Bk. No. 277, 246–47; Ford to Runnels, February 16, 24, April 12, 1859, G. L.; Sergeant L. G. Fidler to Runnels, March 21, 1859. G. L. Van Dorn may not have been anxious to share a campaign with the Rangers. Regular Army officers seem to have felt some jealousy over the success of Ford's raid in 1858.

command marched for Camp Leon, traveling by way of Ross's agency to discharge the Indian scouts and Marlin's men.[45]

The march from the Brazos Reserve to Camp Leon was un-eventful, except for momentary excitement among the Palo Pinto County citizens, who feared that the Rangers had come to arrest the Garland party and thus revive the trouble which, in spite of Major Neighbors' protests, was being permitted to subside with the offenders going unpunished.[46] On April 11, the patrol arrived at Camp Leon after a scout of seven hundred miles, and on the next day Ford sent Sergeant F. A. Kirk galloping for Austin with his official report, which summed up the expedition by saying, "We did not meet the enemy, but we did all we could to find him."[47] The enemy, however, had found the Rangers; during Ford's absence, an Indian paid a nocturnal visit to the Camp Leon corral and removed two horses from beneath the nose of a dumb-founded and inexperienced sentry, to Lieutenant Gibbons' cha-grin and Ford's disgust. Ford did not blame Gibbons, saying, "He could keep on a guard, be on the alert day and night, but it was beyond his power to put brains into the thick skull of a natural booby."[48]

Ford's report informed Runnels that the frontier still was fear-ful of a major Comanche invasion, and that it was harassed con-stantly by small thieving parties which entered the settlements on foot, stole horses, and vanished leaving no trail. Frontiersmen still nursed resentment against the reservation Comanches, a point upon which "Old Rip" elaborated in a separate letter to Runnels on April 14, stating his certainty that the Penatekas were acting

[45] Ford, "Memoirs," IV, 760–61. The Rangers changed direction in western Cottle or eastern Motley County. A year later, Ranger "Chicken" Morris, who had been with Chul-e-quah's scouts, confirmed Ford's suspicion about the prox-imity of hostiles.

[46] *Ibid.*, 762–63; Ford to Runnels, April 12, 1859, G. L.

[47] Ford to Runnels, April 12, 1859, G. L. Kirk's arrival in Austin disproved "The account of the company being slaughtered by Indians." Kirk made the trip in two days, perhaps a new record over the distance. If he was the Fred A. Kirk of Austin who was married at Lampasas the next week, his speed may be understandable.

[48] Ford, "Memoirs," IV, 781.

in complicity with their wild brethren and insisting that they were "doing more damage to the frontier than if they were openly hostile." Ford believed that the Reserve Comanches were waiting for a convenient opportunity to raid the settlements before absconding to their belligerent kinsmen. He presented the problem thus: "Whether it would be policy to anticipate them is the question. We have facts to justify us in attacking them."[49]

Even as Captain Ford wrote, a solution to the situation was in the making. On April 15, Runnels informed Ford that the *State Gazette* of that day reported the plan of the federal government to remove the Reserve bands from Texas. It now seemed unlikely that the executive would revoke his earlier order to disband the Ranger company upon the expiration of its enlistment. Furthermore, the defense appropriation had been exhausted, and it was obvious that the Governor would not request more money for the purpose. Runnels suggested that, pending action by the federal government, the citizens in the exposed settlements organize for defense, presenting an idea which certain of his Llano constituents seemed to have anticipated.[50]

Ford's failure to engage the hostiles did not, however, cause the settlers to discredit Ranger operations. An anonymous correspondent who disclaimed holding any brief for Ford defended the Rangers in the *State Gazette* of April 30, 1859:

> I have had repeated conversations with the settlers in the vicinity of Camp Leon (Capt. Ford's Station) and they speak in high terms of the energy and activity of Ford's command. If any of those gentlemen who, with Argus eyes, have feigned to discover his derelictions, will address a communication to the citizens of the North Leon they can procure sufficient testimony to convince them that they are in possession of the common frailties of humanity: *verb. sat.*

With no immediate use for his pistols, Ford now took up his

[49] Ford to Runnels, April 12 and 14, 1859, G. L.

[50] Smothing [*sic*] Iron and the rest of the Denocratic [*sic*] Mountains to Runnels, March 5, 1859, G. L. The writer, who was as sincere as he was illiterate, ends: "if *you*—our next hope, fail us our last (and) (only) hope is in our own good rifles."

pen, believing that his position in the now closed Garland affair perhaps had not been understood sufficiently. Certainly he had not emerged with credit, except in the eyes of Allison Nelson and other Palo Pinto men. John Marshall threw open the *Gazette* columns to Ford and his chief critics, Judge Battle and Gurley. Side by side in the issue of April 30 appeared the judge's letter deputizing Ford and the latter's two-column defense of his refusal to accept deputation, based, he said, on his belief that a civil judge had no authority to issue orders to a military commander. Included in the defense was a letter from Gurley to Ford, which the Ranger characterized as an excellent illustration of "soft soap." Gurley, however, appears to have had the last public word. His reply in the issue of May 21 said, after commenting on "soft soap," that enough of a "lather" already had been worked up, and he believed it was now time to cease such "barbarous" correspondence.

One other matter remained for Ford's disposition. On his return from the High Plains scout, he was surprised to learn that current Austin rumor had him a possible gubernatorial candidate. He wrote quickly to Runnels, disclaiming any such aspirations, and the rumor quickly died.

Early in May, Ford ceased to patrol around Camp Leon and took his men to Austin, where they were discharged on May 10. After the muster out, Ford turned over his accounts and state weapons to Texas Secretary of State Bird Holland, the responsible official since the adjutant general's office had not functioned during most of Runnells' administration.[51] His official duties ended, "Rip" Ford again rode home to shed his frontier buckskin for the sober broadcloth of Congress Avenue and to resume the relatively quiet round of civic affairs until another Texas crisis should summon him to the saddle.

[51] Ford, "Memoirs," IV, 781. Because of a conflict of personalities, the legislature during most of Runnels' term refused to appropriate money to operate the adjutant general's office; thus routine Ranger reports and requisitions were made to the office of the Secretary of State, who carried on the adjutant general's functions. The subsequent gap in the adjutant general's records has been responsible for frustration and bad language on the part of more than one researcher.

7

Cortina and the Border War, 1859–60

UNTIL NOVEMBER OF 1859, John Ford remained in Austin, verifying the expense accounts of his late company. Until he had justified his expenditures, he could draw no pay, nor could he reimburse the bondsmen whose services he required when he accepted a commission as a financially accountable officer. This he explained to his friend and bondsman, Ed Burleson, in a letter also containing comment on the recent gubernatorial race between Runnels and Houston.

> The election has gone largely for Gen. Houston. I doubted the result, unless a change could be effected on the frontier, and I saw no prospect of that. . . .
>
> You may rest assured if Gen. Houston does not accord a very liberal degree of protection to the frontier he will get he-ll from that quarter and very soon too. Gov. Runnels ran his boat against that rock and went overboard—Gen. Houston should profit by his example.[1]

Like most Texans during the autumn of 1859, Ford followed with indignant interest the events of a disturbance along the Río Grande soon dignified as the "Cortinas [*sic*] War."[2] Juan Nepomuceno Cortina, son of a respected Mexican ranching family, was

[1] Ford to Burleson, August 11, 1859, Ed Burleson Papers.
[2] Correctly spelled Cortina. No effort has been made to call attention to its misspelling in quoted material because of the frequency with which the error therein occurs.

making life and property in the Brownsville area unsafe. In July, 1859, Cortina had shot the Brownsville marshal and fled to Matamoros, returning on September 28 with a group of friends in search of Adolphus Glavaeke and others who had attempted to form a posse to arrest him. After killing several citizens in the town, he retired up the river to his mother's ranch, where he attracted a following of Mexican outlaws and disgruntled Mexican Americans. Since General Twiggs, anticipating increased hostile Indian activity, had transferred the river garrisons to the northwestern frontier, the desperate border citizens organized for defense and sent out calls for help. Their refusal to release a captured Cortina follower brought reprisals. The bandit chieftain attempted to capture Brownsville, and subsequently issued a proclamation against the legal authorities in the area. Meanwhile, his band swelled by enthusiasts who had heard that he meant to restore Texas to Mexico, Cortina harassed the border from Brownsville up to Río Grande City. By November, Twiggs realized that the situation was critical and sent the Brownsville Expedition, under Major Samuel P. Heintzelman, First Infantry, to the border. Governor Runnels also acted. He commissioned William G. Tobin of San Antonio a major of Rangers, ordering him to organize companies and to co-operate with the federal troops.[3]

Shortly after Heintzelman left for Brownsville, "Rip" Ford unexpectedly was summoned into service. A rumor reached Austin that Cortina had invaded and burned Corpus Christi. State Senator Forbes Britton of that town, in the capital for a legislative session, was greatly perturbed. Ford sought to reassure him that the rumor probably was false. Encountering the agitated Britton on Congress Avenue, Ford had almost calmed him when Governor Runnels came along. Senator Britton passionately described the calamity which had befallen his home town to the Governor. "The General's [Britton's] eyes danced wildly in their sockets, his chin trembled, and his voice quivered with emotion." Visibly

---

[3] "Troubles on the Texas Frontier," 36 Cong., 1 sess., *House Exec. Doc. 81*, 2–14. Hereafter cited as "Troubles on the Texas Frontier."

impressed, Runnels turned to the amused Ford, who stood watching Britton's histrionics. "Ford," the Governor ordered, "you must go; you must go at once, and swiftly."[4]

Next evening, with seven companions Ford rode south without waiting for official written orders. Others joined them on the road to Goliad, where citizens raised funds to outfit a company. On November 17, Runnels sent Ford orders and authority to act, with the rank of major. Ford was to organize a company at Goliad and lead it to the river, where he would take command of all state troops in the field. The Rangers were to co-operate with the United States authorities and to go to the aid of Tobin at Brownsville. Ford's basic task was made clear: "The service required is to protect the western frontier against Cortinas and his band and to arrest them if possible."[5]

Ford reported on November 22 that Cortina's force was estimated at 600 to 700 men, and that Twiggs's withdrawal of Regular Army troops had caused the Mexicans to think that Texas had been abandoned by the federal government.[6] By that time, however, Runnels believed that the emergency was over. He instructed Ford to discharge all his recruits except one company of from 100 to 150 men and to take it to Brownsville or the seat of the disturbance. On November 23, the Governor sent additional instructions to Ford to have the Goliad men and Tobin's company elect a major to command both units as a battalion.[7]

"Old Rip," meanwhile, had moved on to Banquete, twenty-four miles west of Corpus Christi, where he procured supplies and assembled about fifty men. He left his camp about December 1, bearing south for Richard King's ranch. From there the Rangers marched to the ranch of Los Indios, about twenty-two miles north of Brownsville, where they camped on the evening of December 13, under the watchful eyes of Cortina's scouts. Here the command elected Joe Walker, Ford's erstwhile publishing part-

4 Ford, "Memoirs," IV, 789–90.
5 Runnels to Ford, November 17, 1859, G. L.
6 Ford to Runnels, November 22, 1859, *ibid.*
7 Runnels to Ford, November 22 and 23, 1859, *ibid.*

ner, as captain; William H. Fry, first lieutenant; and William Howard, second lieutenant. Next morning, soon after the Rangers had broken camp, the distant booming of cannon indicated a battle off to the west. When the galloping company rode into Brownsville, nervous residents at first mistook them for Cortina adherents. Miflin Kenedy, whose citizen company was drawn up in the street, told Ford that Heintzelman had taken a command of Regulars and Rangers upriver that morning and that the distant guns signified that he was fighting. To the cheers of the Brownsville people, Ford led his men at a run up the river road. At one o'clock, too late to get into the fight, Ford's riders reined in at Jesús León's ranch, about thirteen miles above Brownsville, where they found Heintzelman's command resting after having defeated and briefly pursued Cortina.[8]

Heintzelman gave Ford details of the affair. With 165 Regulars and 120 Rangers under Tobin, he had left Brownsville at 2:00 A.M. to surprise Cortina, who was reported to be entrenched some eight miles above town. Although the position was abandoned, the command ran into an ambush two miles farther on. After a short skirmish, Heintzelman occupied La Ebonal ranch, which had served the insurgents as a headquarters. Cortina's horsemen escaped over the river and his infantry withdrew up the road. After a pursuit of several miles to León's, Heintzelman halted, a steady rain having dampened his gunpowder sufficiently to make a further chase useless.[9] On December 15, Ford and his men returned with Heintzelman's force through the continuing downpour to Brownsville, from where "Old Rip" reported the events to Austin.[10]

At Brownsville, Ford placed himself and his men under Heintzelman's orders, as Tobin already had done. There was no chance to hold the election for a battalion major, for Heintzelman immediately sent all mounted units out to patrol. After scouting for

---

[8] Ford, "Memoirs," IV, 781–93.
[9] "Difficulties on the Southwestern Frontier," 36 Cong., 1 sess., *House Exec. Doc. 52*, 87–88. Hereafter cited as "Difficulties on the Southwestern Frontier."
[10] Ford to Runnels, December 18, 1859, G. L.

four days, the patrols returned late on December 20 without having encountered any sign of Cortina.[11] On the following morning, with 150 Regulars and 198 Rangers, Heintzelman again marched up the river in search of his quarry.[12]

Ford, with two Ranger companies, was detailed to protect Heintzelman's right flank. For two days and nights the Rangers followed an inept, timorous guide through densely thicketed country without finding more than an abandoned bandit camp. Before day on December 23, Ford's detachment joined the main command on the river road and marched with it to Las Cuevas ranch, eighteen miles below Río Grande City, where Cortina was assumed to be. On Christmas night, the federal and state officers assembled to plan the next day's operation against the town.

It was decided that Ford should immediately begin a night march around Cortina's left flank, arriving by daylight on the river road between Río Grande City and Roma, while the main command would march at midnight and be in position to open battle at daybreak. When the council broke up, Ford led out the companies of Captains Walker, Herron, and Hampton, guided by the volunteer aide, border rancher H. Clay Davis. After an hour's ride, the column halted abruptly when a challenging shot from a Cortina outpost briefly lit the gloom. Upon Davis' assurance that the thick chaparral would prevent the bandit from warning his comrades before the American attack began, Ford resumed his march. The Rangers soon reached the home, near Ringgold Barracks, of a Mexican friend of Davis. Here Ford learned that he could not flank Cortina because of the density of the chaparral, that the bandit force was larger than Heintzelman had estimated, and that Cortina had a strong picket stationed only two hundred yards away. In view of the unexpected situation, Ford decided to await Heintzelman's arrival. The weary Rangers, long accustomed to sleeping when and where they might, lay down on the trail, their bridle reins wrapped around their hands.

Shortly before daylight the rumble of gun carriages told of

11 Ford, "Memoirs," IV, 794-96.
12 "Difficulties on the Southwestern Frontier," 97-98.

Juan Nepomuceno Cortina, who for more than a decade
was a red-headed thorn in the side of South Texas
in general and Rip Ford in particular.

From Walter Prescott Webb, *The Texas Rangers*

George Stoneman, whose cavalry company rode
with Ford's Rangers after Cortina.

Heintzelman's approach. Ford hurried his command to the main road, made a hasty report which the fatigued Heintzelman only partially comprehended, and requested permission to open the attack. The Major assented, assigning the remaining Ranger companies of Tobin and "Uncle Pete" Tomlinson to Ford's complement. "Old Rip" immediately moved to the front, drove in Cortina's picket, and, at the corner of Ringgold Barracks, repulsed a bandit reconnaissance party. Then, skirting Río Grande City, he rushed a hill reported to be Cortina's command post, but the bandit had withdrawn to a position above town on the Roma road. Obscurely, through the heavy fog, Ford could see that Cortina's right flank lay between the Roma road and the river, while the bandit left wing enveloped a cemetery. Ordering Tobin to attack the cemetery, Ford advanced with his own column against the enemy's right, leaving the center open for Heintzelman to move in and employ his fieldpieces.

While crossing the Roma road, Ford was caught in the fire from Cortina's artillery, ensconced in a fence corner beside the road. He promptly sent Lieutenant Fry and a small detachment to silence the cannon. Fry's band hurried away, accompanied by tall, urbane S. A. Loughridge, a volunteer aide who had been a colonel under William Walker in Nicaragua. Moving up to the fence behind which the guns lay, Fry's riflemen opened a harassing fire on the cannoners and their protecting infantry force. Loughridge, with an empty pistol, found himself within ten yards of a Cortina rifleman who fired at him once, twice, and began reloading for a third try.

> At this critical moment George W. Morris came up. The Colonel saluted him blandly—"Good morning, Mr. Morris, will you please kill that Mexican?" pointing to his opponent. Quick as thought Morris' Sharpe was heard; the Mexican fell dead. Loughridge bowed politely—"very much obliged to you Mr. Morris."[13]

Meanwhile, with his main force, Ford swung in an arc to the right to flank the artillery. Forty yards from the guns he dis-

[13] Ford, "Memoirs," IV, 797–806.

mounted his men and moved up to reinforce Fry. In spite of a blast of grapeshot which bruised Ford and wounded fourteen other Texans,[14] the rifle fire soon drove the gunners from their pieces.

Before Ford could take the guns, Cortina opened a heavy musket fire on the Rangers from front, right flank, and rear. As Tobin's men, repulsed at the cemetery, rejoined Ford's command, "Old Rip" recognized the "Charge" sounded by a Mexican bugler. Hurriedly he dismounted his men and concealed them in the chaparral. Out of the mist came Cortina's charge, but a roaring volley from the partially hidden Rangers emptied many saddles. The remaining riders turned and disappeared in the enveloping fog. The dismounted Rangers followed in pursuit for a short distance until Ford recalled them. Heintzelman, unaware of the early action because of the muffling effect of the fog and the failure of two of Ford's couriers to reach him, came up at this point. Ford obtained permission to pursue the reluctantly withdrawing Mexicans, and the Rangers vanished up the Roma road.

About five miles up the road, Cortina rallied his hard-pressed men for a stand. Because the fog made identification uncertain at even twenty yards, Ford held his fire until a volley from the enemy muskets revealed their position. Then "Old Rip" led a shouting charge which forced his foes to abandon one of their cannon. Ranger "Big" Henry sprang upon the loaded gun and fired it, sending the enemy fleeing in panic toward Roma.[15] Fearing that they might loot the town, Ford followed closely, but Cortina and about twenty men evaded "Redhead" Thomas and a Ranger squad by swimming to safety in Mexico.[16] The rest of the bandit force dispersed before Ford's relentless pressure. He appropriated their other cannon and reached Roma with no interference. That night, "Rip"'s command marched the fifteen miles back to Ringgold Barracks. Upon Ford's recommendation, Heintzelman sent Captain George Stoneman and his "E" Company of the Second Cavalry to garrison Roma, lest Cortina attempt to take it.

[14] "Difficulties on the Southwestern Frontier," 97–98; *New Orleans Picayune*, January 22, 1860.

[15] Ford, "Memoirs," IV, 803.   [16] Ford, "Memoirs," IV, 804.

At Río Grande City, Ford found an old friend, Judge Sam Stewart, who had been Cortina's prisoner. His execution had been planned for dawn on December 27, but, he reported, "Just after daylight . . . , I heard Col. Ford shout out these words, 'O yes, you yellow sons of guns, we've got you.' I thought his was the sweetest voice I ever heard."[17] It was heard in Austin that Ford actually used a much harsher epithet.

Reporting on December 29 to Governor Houston, who had taken office at the beginning of the month, Ford advised that the Cortina War was not over. He believed that Cortina was supported by the conservative Miramón party, then in revolt against the Juárez government. Four or five hundred men, he thought, should be kept in border service.[18]

With operations temporarily suspended, Ford called the election for major. He suggested to Tobin that they both resign their commissions before standing for election, the loser to serve in the ranks. Tobin rejected the proposition. He defeated Ford by six votes, largely through the efforts of Lieutenant John Littleton, a successful aspirant for commander of Tobin's company.[19] Under no legal obligation to remain in service and not wishing to serve under Tobin, whom he regarded as inefficient, Ford decided to leave the service. Captain Walker and his company shared Ford's views and, since like Ford they had enlisted for no specific period, marched with "Old Rip" to Brownsville for discharge.

At Brownsville, Ford received a pleasant surprise. Ángel Navarro and Richard H. Taylor, commissioners acting under authority from Governor Houston, were there to make a complete investigation of the Cortina trouble and to expedite its settlement. Already they had decided to reorganize the Ranger force, excluding Tobin from the new organization. As Taylor explained to Houston, "There is nothing like *command* among the Rangers, so we have ordered 'Major' Tobin from Río Grande City . . . to be mustered for discharge. . . . The present officer [Tobin] I am

[17] *Ibid.*, 803–805; "Difficulties on the Southwestern Frontier," 97–98.
[18] Ford to Houston, December 29, 1859, G. L.
[19] Tobin to Houston, January 2, 1860, G. L.; Ford, "Memoirs," IV, 810–11.

told by good judges is utterly incompetent to command in the field."[20]

Certainly the commissioners' action was justified. Tobin's command had provided an inglorious chapter to Ranger annals. From the night of November 10, 1859, when they had entered Brownsville under fire from citizens who mistook them for Cortina's men, they had neither morale nor discipline. On the next night they removed Tomás Cabrera, a Cortina lieutenant, from jail and informally hanged him. Several days later, Littleton and a patrol fell into an ambush on Palo Alto prairie and lost four men. On November 19, the Rangers demonstrated futilely at a safe distance from an insurgent stronghold. On November 24, Tobin and about 250 Rangers and citizens were repulsed at Cortina's entrenchments above Brownsville, retreating rapidly before the fire of two cannon which Cortina had earlier seized from a joint Brownsville-Mexican National Guard force. In council next day, "it was decided imprudent to risk an attack," whereupon the command returned to Brownsville. When, on December 5, Heintzelman came to Brownsville with 122 regulars, Tobin promptly put himself under the Major's orders, but when ordered to scout Cortina's position, he failed to get close enough to the enemy to obtain any useful information. On the La Ebonal expedition of December 14–15, they were of no particular advantage, according to Heintzelman.

> I was desirous of having a reconnoisance [sic] made before proceeding further; the rangers were so thoroughly stampeded by their previous expedition that it was only after much difficulty and delay that I could get anyone to go, and then only by Judge Davis, who had been sent out with them before, volunteering to go with them; . . .

Nor were Tobin's men any less a problem when not in action. Mail-rider F. M. Campbell, whose ranch near Brownsville Tobin had used as a base, complained of their carelessness to Captain J. B. Ricketts at Ringgold Barracks: "They burnt up my pens and

[20] Taylor to Houston, January 16, 1860, G. L.

fences for firewood, and one horse by accident. They also used a few hogs and goats and fifty barrels of sweet potatoes, and for which the commander refuses to pay me." He estimated the value of property stolen by Cortina at two hundred dollars; of that destroyed by the Rangers at one thousand dollars.[21]

Navarro and Taylor worked rapidly to correct the situation among the state troops. At the same time they ordered Tobin downriver, they asked Heintzelman how many Rangers he needed to support his cavalry.[22] He estimated that two companies would be enough,[23] and the commissioners found the nucleus for a force of that size at hand. When Ford, on January 17,[24] had mustered out Walker's company, the Captain and some twenty men had gone home, but "Old Rip" and the others stayed in Brownsville to see what might develop. On January 20, the commissioners enlisted thirty of the group for twelve months, "unless sooner discharged by the Governor." The Company elected Ford captain, Matt Nolan first lieutenant, and John J. Dix and William D. Howard second lieutenants. This was "A" Company, which Ford was told to recruit to a strength of eighty-three. On February 1, Littleton's company arrived from Ringgold Barracks for discharge. He and his men volunteered for the new organization and were promptly sworn in by the commissioners, with Ford's consent, since he considered Littleton a more competent officer than his record under Tobin indicated. Littleton was elected captain of "B" Company, with John N. Paschal as his first lieutenant and Arthur Pugh and Bennett Jordan his second lieutenants.[25] Thus was formed the Río Grande Squadron, which was to be largely instrumental in bringing to a quick close the Cortina War. When news of Ford's appointment as senior captain of the squadron got to Austin, W. A. Pitts, Ford's former lieutenant, passed the word along to Ed Burleson, now a Ranger captain about to leave

[21] Ford, "Memoirs," V, 844–51; "Troubles on the Texas Frontier," 2–14.

[22] "Difficulties on the Southwestern Frontier," 117.

[23] "Troubles on the Texas Frontier," 62.

[24] Tobin to Houston, January 2, 1860, G. L.

[25] Ford, "Memoirs," IV, 812–13; Navarro to Houston, January 26, 1860, G. L.

for the Nueces frontier. Apparently Pitts considered Ford a poor risk for a bondsman at the time, either because of Ford's free dispersal of state funds or because of the hazardous nature of his new assignment. He told Burleson:

> I have made some inquiry in relation to Old Rip's a/cs [accounts] with the State. I find him charged with some $500 on a/c of his last company. I do not know how much more, he has not settled for neither of his last 2 companies. I understand that Bob Taylor has mustered him into service with 80 men, if so he will not be back for some time. I would if I were you try before you leave to get off his bond, for he may never get back—(but it is not my business[).][26]

The commissioners, in reporting to Houston, defended their arrangements. "Our action in this matter may give rise to unpleasant feelings, but it is better to have one hundred good men than one thousand inefficient or bad ones."[27]

The Río Grande Squadron was composed principally of seasoned frontiersmen. Besides Nolan, "Old Rangers" Dan Givens, John Ingram, and Voltaire Rountree were on hand, as were "Chicken" Morris, who had been Comanche hunting with Ford during the previous winter, Corporal Milton Duty, Bennett Musgrave, A. C. Hill, and at least two hard specimens, William D. "Red" Thomas and a former sailor referred to only as English Tom. Squadron surgeon was the pugnacious John T. Eldridge.

Soon after the reorganization, Heintzelman scattered his mounted units along the river from Brownsville to Río Grande City, to prevent Mexican raiders from crossing. Preceding the cavalry, Ford, on February 4, sent Corporal Duty and the Ranger advance party to prepare a camp at Zacetal Ranch, at a river bend named for the Bolsa Ranch on the Mexican side. At the Bolsa ford, Duty surprised about thirty Cortina men driving horses across the river. During the ensuing skirmish, Captain Tobin and his company, on their way to Brownsville for discharge, fortunately appeared in

[26] W. A. Pitts to Ed Burleson, January 28, 1860, Ed Burleson Papers.
[27] Navarro and Taylor to Houston, February 4, 1860, G. L.; "Difficulties on the Southwestern Frontier," 120–22.

time to assist Duty. Heavy firing, in which Fountain Woodruff of Tobin's command was mortally wounded, now broke out from Cortina's main force, occupying the Bolsa rancho. Into the fight plodded the Kenedy steamer *Ranchero*, bound down for Brownsville with goods and specie valued at $200,000. It was to intercept this rich cargo that Cortina had moved into the Bolsa.

Here was a larger mouthful than Duty could chew, and he sent a courier down the back trail to find Ford. Two hours later, during a lull in the firing, "Rip" and his Rangers galloped onto the scene. Despite his understrength command, Ford immediately prepared to attack Cortina. Tobin and "Uncle Pete" Tomlinson took ten men across to reconnoiter while Ford, after detailing a camp guard, got Captain John Martin of the *Ranchero* to carry "A" Company over the river. Most of Tobin's men, perhaps remembering the Callahan debacle, bluntly refused to cross to Mexico.

Under heavy fire, Ford joined the reconnaissance party on the south bank of the river and distributed his command in the shelter of the bank, at right angles to the enemy line. In his haste to cross, Ford forgot his personal weapons, an oversight which brought him a stern lecture on foolhardiness from "Uncle Pete" Tomlinson as they crouched behind the shelter of the bank. While twelve riflemen maintained a steady fire on Cortina's horsemen, Ford led his dismounted Texans in a charge on Cortina's footmen, protected by a palisade fence. The bandit left flank collapsed under the deadly pistol fire of the advancing Rangers, their center broke, and the force, some three hundred strong, ran for the chaparral. Cortina, after a vain effort to rally his men, made himself their rear guard and was the last to leave the field. Under a pall of smoke from the burning *jacales* of the ranch, which had been fired without authority,[28] the Rangers returned unharmed to the *Ranchero* and were ferried back to Texas. That evening Tobin resumed his march toward Brownsville, shortly before Stoneman and Lieutenant Manning Kimmel rode into camp with their cavalry units.

[28] "Troubles on the Texas Frontier," 63, 68–80; Ford, "Memoirs," IV, 816–17.

In a brief conference the commanders decided to escort the *Ranchero* down the river to safety, the cavalry companies to keep pace with it on the American side while Ford and his Rangers would protect it from the Mexican bank. A night reconnaissance revealed that Cortina had abandoned the Bolsa. In the early morning, the steamboat transported forty-eight Rangers and their horses to Mexico. Near Las Palmas Ranch, a short march down the Río Grande, Ford was halted by a strong force led by a prefect of the Matamoros police. The official, after hearing Ford's explanation of Ranger presence on Mexican soil, asked them to wait until he could communicate with his superiors in Matamoros. Ford conducted him to the *Ranchero*, where Stoneman gave consent. Ford used the delay to prepare for an attack if the Mexicans should decide to resist his advance. Late in the day came word from Matamoros approving Ford's movement. The prefect then revealed to Ford that a corps of about six hundred "rural guards" were in front of him, and that about two hundred others were close in his rear. When asked the identity of the latter group, the prefect evaded with "*Quien sabe?*" Ford was certain they were Cortina and his men.[29]

After an uneasy night, during which the Ranger picket line was menaced, Ford was assured that the militia would guard the *Ranchero* from the Mexican side, and thereupon recrossed his men to Texas. Stoneman informed Heintzelman that he and Ford would escort the vessel as far as necessary. He was disgusted with the attitude of the Mexican troops.

> There appears to be very little disposition to catch Cortinas, who is doubtless near or with the rural guard, and the guard state that their authority extends simply to guarding the steamer, but not to the apprehending or molesting Cortinas. If the steamer is again interfered with, *everybody* will probably interfere and escort her as far as Matamoros.[30]

Both Rangers and cavalrymen spent the next six weeks patrolling the river against raiders. Occasionally Ford halted at the ranch

[29] Ford, "Memoirs," IV, 822, 832.

[30] "Troubles on the Texas Frontier," 70.

of Cortina's mother, Señora María Estéfana Goascochia Cavasos de Cortina. She was "very small, not weighing more than one hundred pounds. She was very good looking—had a pretty face—bright eyes, and very white skin. She was held in high esteem by both her Mexican and American acquaintances. Her manners were those of a cultivated and polished lady." Ford treated her with great deference and permitted no conduct which might distress her or bring reflection upon his Rangers, little suspecting that her renegade son one day would show his appreciation.

Ford supplemented his scouting with his customery daily drills. About March 1, while leading a mock charge, he was painfully injured when his horse stepped in a hole and fell with him. The somersaulting steed's descending rump caught the Captain squarely between the shoulders and "flattened him out considerably." A passing Ranger shouted, "Boys, look at Uncle Rip." His men bore him, bleeding from nose and mouth, to his quarters, where he began a slow recuperation.[31]

He was still spitting blood from his injury when, on March 16, a courier arrived from Heintzelman. The Major had learned from General Guadalupe García, commanding at Matamoros, that Cortina was said to be at La Mesa rancho, four miles south of the river from Ford's Agua Negra camp. Ford's Mexican spies already had located the bandit bivouac in the chaparral near the ranch, but the Ranger hesitated to attack in spite of permission to cross the river extended to the United States officers by Ford's old friend, José M. J. Carbajal, now governor of Tamaulipas. Ford feared an ambush, knowing that García was co-operating reluctantly with the Americans. Stoneman, with two companies, rode in the next day with orders to cross the river, and was surprised to find "Old Rip" still on the Texas side. When night fell, the two captains moved. Ford, pleading his injury, got Stoneman to supervise the crossing, while he himself rode over with the advance party.

Earlier in the evening, Ford had sent a picket to a small ranch on the Mexican side, about half a mile below the crossing, to watch

[31] Ford, "Memoirs," IV, 784; V, 837, 906.

the road from the ranch to La Mesa. When he had crossed, he sent Dan Givens with a squad forward on the road to La Mesa. Givens reported that there were Mexican troops before him. Ford informed Stoneman of the ambush and suggested following a trail to the small ranch below, crossing it, and taking a little-used road thence to La Mesa. Stoneman agreed and the command began its circuitous march.

The head of the column was half a mile from La Mesa when Ford, searching the predawn gloom, saw a light off to his right. Matt Nolan investigated and reported it to mark the station of a Mexican picket, who had fled at his approach. The captains hurried their troopers forward to strike before the enemy could organize a defense. Ford's Rangers, forming the right wing, almost immediately engaged the enemy infantry, and within ten minutes had turned its flank. Stoneman, on the left, encountered Mexican cavalry who withstood one volley and then bolted precipitately. He then pivoted around the enemy right flank, and the two captains rolled up the line until the Mexicans dropped their guns and ran to shelter in the houses of the rancho.

The Rangers set about collecting prisoners and arms, taking them to a large, well-lighted house. There a noisy captive identified himself as the major commanding the defeated troops, a Mexican National Guard unit, and peremptorily demanded the return of his sword and valuables. As he spouted his complaints, Stoneman rode up. Said Ford wryly, "Well, Captain, we have played Old Scratch, whipped the *Guardia National,* wounded a woman, and killed a mule." Investigation disclosed that the woman had been shot unintentionally by Stoneman's troopers as she ran to close a door through which a *Guardia* officer was firing on the cavalry. Nolan admitted having killed the mule, which he mistook in the dark for a Mexican. Arms and captured property, including some of that of the vociferous major, who had been discovered cowering beneath a bed, were promptly restored. "The unfortunate sword of the major's was an exception. It was restored to him three times. The news in camp was that when last seen one of [the] Mexican guides was wearing it."

As they boiled their morning coffee, the Americans were interrupted by a report that a large enemy force was advancing. They hastily mounted and waited. A Mexican officer came forward to arrange a conference between "el Coronel Ford" and his own colonel, rejecting an offer to confer with Stoneman. The Mexican colonel demanded that Ford explain why United States troops had invaded Mexico and had fired on Mexican troops. In return, Ford called for an explanation of the attempted ambush on the La Mesa road. The Colonel answered ambiguously and boasted that had he and his troops been at La Mesa, results would have been reversed. Wrathfully, Ford offered to ready his Rangers for another battle, with Stoneman's cavalry pledged to neutrality. When the Colonel declined, Ford served an ultimatum: "Then, sir, you will please change your tone as to the probable results of a collision, or prepare to decide matters on the instant."

Already suspecting collusion between Cortina and the *Guardia Nacional*, Ford and Stoneman were convinced of it when they learned that the horsemen routed by Stoneman were Cortina's. Flatly rejecting the Colonel's proposal that they remain at La Mesa until he could receive orders from Matamoros, the captains led their men back to Agua Negra. Their report to Heintzelman put Mexican losses at four or five dead, and an unknown number wounded; there were no Ranger casualties.[32]

There was no time to rest after the La Mesa fight. The *Ranchero*, returning from another upriver trip, had put in at Ford's camp on March 15. On March 19 she continued toward Brownsville, with the American companies marching as guard along the Mexican bank. At the Bolsa, Ford's scouts surprised a party of Cortina's men. When Ford came up, Ranger "Red" Thomas hurried to him to report, "We have captured the Indian, Faustino."

"I do not wish to see him," came "Old Rip"'s grim reply.

Thomas vanished abruptly. Seconds later a shot informed the Captain that Cortina's murderous leader of Indian auxiliaries had finished raiding. This incident may have given rise to the widely

[32] "Troubles on the Texas Frontier," 79–81; Ford, "Memoirs," V, 836–38, 840–42.

circulated tale that one could follow Ford's trail from La Mesa to Matamoros by the Mexican bodies dangling from the mesquite; again, the story may have had other sources, for not everything that occurred found its way into the official reports (or, for that matter, into Ford's memoirs).

At a ranch a short way below the Bolsa, a spy informed Ford that Cortina was sixty miles away, at the rancho Maguey south of Matamoros. Fifty southeastward miles lay behind the column the next afternoon when the scouts flushed a Mexican rider who spurred toward the ranch. Lieutenant Kimmel and a squad were sent in pursuit. As Stoneman and Ford neared Maguey, they heard a burst of firing and, incorrectly assuming that Kimmel was fighting, rushed to his assistance. The column stormed into the rancho, scattering a Saint Joseph's Day procession in which the participants, in customary fashion, had been discharging blank loads. The only opposition came from a belligerent celebrant who fled into the chaparral and opened fire with ball on the Americans. The Rangers quickly killed him.[33]

Ford ordered bread and beef brought to feed the famished troopers, waiting meanwhile near a house before which stood three doleful women. Dix and Thomas whispered to him that the oldest was Cortina's wife and the youngest his favorite daughter. Ford pledged the two to secrecy and detailed them to keep a protective eye on the women. When the command had eaten, it moved out to where grass and water were plentiful. At twilight a spy brought word that Cortina had ridden toward Monterrey. When the dusk was thick, the troopers silently broke camp and resumed their relentless pursuit of the bandit chieftain.

Daylight found the Rangers thumping on the doors of the huts at the Cayetano Ranch, some forty miles from Maguey. Frightened inhabitants informed the grim riders that Cortina was gone,

[33] Ford, "Memoirs," V, 852–55; *Reports of the Committee of Investigation*, 196; Ford to Heintzelman, March 24, 1860, "Troubles on the Texas Frontier," 99 (This report was badly scrambled by the government printers; the signature is transposed from a communication of Tobin to Houston, and the last half of the report obviously has been exchanged with part of a report on the Bolsa fight of February 4).

warned, as at Maguey, by a swift courier. Now forty-odd miles deep in Mexico, with no definite knowledge of Cortina's whereabouts and also short of forage, the captains decided to return to Texas. About a dozen miles from the Río Grande, they rode through the camp of a startled detachment of Reynosa troops. Without pausing, the Americans exchanged cautious courtesies with the Mexicans and proceeded to the river, where they found a steamboat that included in its cargo badly needed corn. While Ford talked with Captain J. B. Ricketts and other passengers, a one-eyed Ranger rode up on the Texas bank. He came aboard to hand Ford an envelope, remarking that he had seen the smoke from the steamer and thought to find Ford there. Ford glanced quickly at the contents and then at the Ranger. "I wish the devil had found you first. Why didn't you go to camp?"

"Old Rip" showed Stoneman the note and shared with him responsibility for the "many unsanctified expressions floating around on the air." The message was Heintzelman's order for the command to return to United States soil. The two captains had hoped for authority to raid Matamoros, but now the weary horsemen recrossed the river and late that night, March 21, bedded down at Ford's Agua Negra camp. Thereafter, so he claimed, "Rip" Ford nursed a lifelong prejudice against one-eyed letter carriers.

Ford's report of the expedition brought approving comment from Heintzelmann to department headquarters: "The whole operation was carried forward with much energy. A march of one hundred miles was made in two days and nights. It is not believed that Cortinas will again attempt to concentrate a force in the vicinity of the Rio Grande." Ford had been told at Cayetano Ranch that Cortina and a few companions had sought refuge beyond Monterrey in the little mountain village of Burgos. Hounded from one camp to another, the river boundary closed to them and without further support from timid Mexican officials, Cortina's followers deserted, and their chief disappeared into the interior. He would return a year or so later, under surprising and disturbing circumstances, but for the time he was not a factor to be reckoned with. Except for a few unreconciled raiders, the Cortina War was over.[34]

A by-product of the Cortina War was to make "Rip" Ford's name familiar wherever small boys read adventure tales. Ranging up on the Nueces with Captain Burleson at the time of Ford's operations was a runaway New England youngster named Samuel Stone Hall. In the late 1870's, under the name of "Buckskin Sam," Hall began to write dime novels based on events with which he was familiar. Of the more than fifty published for him by Beadle's New York Dime Library, Half-Dime Library, and Nickel Library, four dealt specifically with the Cortina War. Through the pulp pages of *Kit Carson, Jr., the Crack Shot of the West* (1877); *Thorny Trails; or, Meanderings in Mexico* (1881); *The Rough Riders; or, Sharp Eye, the Seminole Scourge (A Tale of the Chaparral)* (1883); and *Little Lariat; or, Pecan Pete's Big Rampage* (1885), Ford and his Rangers pursued Cortina in even more spectacular fashion than they had dogged him through the mesquite. The Canadian River campaign of 1858 provided the narrative thread for another thriller, *Bow and Bowie; or, Ranging for Reds* (1882).[35]

There remained one item of unfinished business, which "Old Rip" took upon himself to settle. In Reynosa and smaller Reynosa Vieja (Old Reynosa), a dozen miles below the city, lived a number of Cortina's former infantrymen. Ford was anxious to teach the city not to harbor such citizens. Both Regulars and Rangers still were eager for a fight and remembered the Reynosa boast that the Americans could not handle her as they had La Mesa, reputedly offering to back their claim with $30,000. Both Ford and Stoneman, interpreting their authorization to cross the border after Cortina as applicable when in pursuit of any of his followers, determined "to capture these members of Cortina's marauding

---

[34] Ford, "Memoirs," V, 852–57; "Troubles on the Texas Frontier," 82–83; *Reports of the Committee of Investigation*, 197.

[35] J. D. Dykes, "Buckskin Sam, Ranger and Writer; or, The Life and Sub-Literary Labors of Samuel Stone Hall," *American Book Collector*, Vol. X, No. 7 (March, 1960), 9–14; ———, "A Bibliographical Check List of the Writing of Samuel Stone Hall," *ibid.*, 15–18.

band or drive them from the valley of the Rio Grande."[36] They decided that Ford should take the Rangers downriver to Don Francisco Garza's Babasco Ranch, cross after dark, and search Reynosa Vieja. Stoneman and Kimmel would move secretly to conceal the Regulars in the chaparral near Edinburg, across the river from Reynosa. At the sound of firing, they were to cross to Ford's assistance.

Late in the evening of April 3, Ford reached Babasco and began to cross the river. At midnight, after cautiously extending his lines around the village, he moved in for the capture. To his disgust, he learned that one of his parties had been late in filling its portion of the line and that seventeen of his quarry had bolted through the gap. When the Ranger Captain explained the purpose of his visit and purchased a quantity of supplies, the relieved residents quickly organized a fandango for their unexpected guests. At daylight, after locking the villagers in sheds to prevent their passing the alarm, "Rip" Ford led his men up toward Reynosa.[37]

Writing some twenty years later, Ford indicated that the search for Cortina adherents may have been a pretext to launch a larger project:

> Maj. Heintzelman, Capt. Stoneman, and the writer were thoroughly convinced of the complicity of the Mexican authorities on the Rio Grande in the war prosecuted by Cortina against the United States. . . . In order to put an end to this quasi-war, or to cause it to expand into actual and open hostilities, the descent was made on Reynosa. An armed collision there was, in our opinion, sure to cause the prompt inauguration of hostilities or a settlement of the matter, and ultimate peace. . . . Had a war been on our hands, it is possible the sectional quarrel might have been stilled for a season at least, wise counsels might have prevailed, and the fratricidal contest averted.

The Río Grande officers, it appears, may have anticipated Governor Sam Houston's own idea for a Mexican war which, he

[36] Ford, "Memoirs," V, 843, 858.
[37] "Troubles on the Texas Frontier," 85–87; *Reports of the Committee of Investigation*, 196.

believed, would unite American opinion and postpone or prevent civil war.

Aware that something was in the wind, Reynosa citizens were busy preparing for defense, although they seemed to expect trouble from bandits rather than from Americans. Residents able to bear arms were joined by recruits from the adjacent ranchos, some of which could supply as many as 150 men, and Colonel Juan Trevino took command of the municipal artillery, a one-pounder cannon mounted on a water cart. Four hundred men stationed themselves around the plaza; others concealed themselves on strategic rooftops. The town council sent out a patrol and waited. Shortly before noon, the scouts sighted the Ranger column and, apparently too frightened to hear Ford's shouts, raced back to give warning without attempting to identify the invaders. The Rangers followed slowly, without further effort to make themselves known, in accordance with Ford's hope that the Reynosans might mistake them for bandits and open an attack, which the Captain could then condemn as an overt act of war.

At the edge of the city the command divided into three detachments. Led by Ford, Littleton, and Nolan, the Ranger columns approached the plaza by different routes. Riflemen, their weapons trained on the horsemen, lined the rooftops along the street up which Ford's column passed. In the makeshift *lingua franca* of the border, the Texans called insults at the silent defenders on the roofs, hoping to goad one into firing a shot which would be the excuse to open battle. When these attempts failed, more than one Ranger deliberately dropped his rifle to the rocky pavement, hoping that it would discharge and precipitate a fight. When Ford reached the plaza, he was recognized by a Mexican who shouted: "It is Old Ford, he has not come to rob us." Thereupon the tension relaxed. A few minutes later, the Ranger leader agreed to an invitation to meet with the town council, and set off for the city hall.

The agreement came none too soon, for Nolan's advance was blocked by a superior force, supported by Trevino's artillery. "Halt," demanded Trevino.

"I do not take my orders from you," came Nolan's curt answer.

Again Trevino challenged: "Halt, or I shall fire on you with my cannon."

"Fire, and be blasted," retorted Nolan. "If you do I'll take the confounded thing away from you."

At that instant someone shouted that Ford was on his way to confer with the council. As the two commands broke ranks and intermingled, Ranger "English Tom" pressed close to Trevino. Knowing no Spanish, the Ranger did not understand that a truce was in effect. He requested permission to kill the Colonel, pointing out, "He has two six-shooters and a gold watch."

Perhaps something about Trevino's physiognomy prompted a companion's facetious reply: "No, no, do not kill him; we can make him prisoner—carry him to Texas, and sell him for $1,500." Trevino, who knew English, "was very mad."

Ford, meanwhile, with Littleton, Surgeon Eldridge, and Dix as interpreter, had arrived at the city hall. At the door a sentinel demanded Eldridge's rifle. The surgeon brought up its muzzle. "I will not give you my gun—I will give you its contents," he fumed. When peace was restored, the Rangers, still armed, took their seats at the council table.

Council president Francisco Zepeda began by inquiring the purpose of the Ranger visit. Ford's prompt answer chilled the hearts of the *ayuntamiento*: "To get the thirty thousand dollars you promised, if we would come to your town, and run things as we did at Las Palmas and La Mesa." The councilmen breathed more easily, however, when they learned that Ford sought Cortina henchmen. It was agreed that he would return to American soil and from there submit written demands. Ford consented because he saw no opportunity for a justified assault. Escorted by the armed and wary citizenry, the officials conducted the Texans to the public ferry, not trusting them to cross elsewhere. On the way, Trevino boasted of the victory he would have won, but subsided quickly when Ford offered to summon his men to decide the issue. That evening the disappointed Rangers camped in a field a short distance above Edinburg.

Promptly Ford sent his demand for the surrender of the Cortina bandits. The town council replied that none were in Reynosa. Ford knew it was a lie; the Reynosa council knew that Ford knew, and anticipated a fight. An elderly townsman entered the Ranger camp, volunteering information on condition that the Rangers spare his property if they attacked. Ford was sure that the visitor was a spy, but he was courteous to him, assuring him that there would be no unannounced assault. An incident of the night of April 6, however, aroused the old man's distrust. Littleton and several other officers proposed a practical joke on Reynosa. With Ford's consent they hauled brick from Edinburg and built a wall with a central embrasure like a cannon port. In the opening they placed a simulated cannon, a log on an oxcart. Next they filled an immense cow horn one-third with powder, the rest with tar and grease. This they placed over a powder-filled hole and inclined it toward Reynosa. Someone tossed a match into the hole; there was a heavy boom, followed by a long, wide streak of fire arching toward the city. Subsequently the Rangers heard distinct sounds of agitation from Reynosa. On the next morning, the old spy met Ford in Edinburg and upbraided him for violating the pledge. Littleton finally interrupted the tirade to explain the prank. The Reynosan struggled to contain himself, but at last gave way to his wrath:

> I am more than sixty years of age. I have travelled, and have seen iniquity in many shapes, but you Texians are the most consummate rascals I have ever seen. Last night no one in Reynosa slept a wink. We had a heavy guard on the river bank, above and below town, to ascertain where you would cross. The women packed rocks in their laps with which to barricade the streets. All, all on account of this infernal deviltry of you Texians.[38]

Soon after Ford's passage from Reynosa, unauthorized firing from the Texas bank had wounded several Mexicans.[39] Still later, during a saint's day celebration, paraders discharged firearms loaded with ball instead of the usual blank charges, and several

[38] Ford, "Memoirs," V, 861–67; *Reports of the Committee of Investigation,* 196; "Troubles on the Texas Frontier," 85–87.
[39] "Troubles on the Texas Frontier," 87.

bullets fell in Ford's camp. He restrained his men, but the Mexicans were surprised by the sudden appearance at the Edinburg ferry of Kimmel's cavalry, who heard the firing and supposed an attack was under way. Reynosa was shocked into realization that not Texas alone, but the United States too, was interested in the affair.[40]

"Old Rip" decided to hold his hand until the arrival on the border of the temporary department commander, Brevet Colonel Robert E. Lee. Lee came with orders to move into Mexico should Mexican officials fail to co-operate in suppressing Cortina.[41] Already, troop units were under orders to return to the Río Grande stations, and the Mexican authorities, cognizant of Lee's instructions, no longer doubted that further vacillation would bring disaster upon them. Escorted by Captain A. G. Brackett's cavalry company, Lee arrived at Edinburg on April 7. That night Ford rode to the cavalry camp, where he dined with Lee and Brackett and verbally reported the Reynosa incident. The quiet Colonel deeply impressed the Ranger, who felt himself "in the presence of a man of superior intellect, possessing the capacity to accomplish great ends, and the gift of controlling and leading men."

Except to suggest that Ford "should have sent them a courier to inform them who you were," Lee had no criticism to make of the conduct of the Reynosa operation.[42] He immediately sent a stern ultimatum to the Reynosa council. That body returned a humble answer, disclaiming that it harbored outlaws and promising faithfully to seize any who might be found. The fact that Andrés Trevino, temporarily governing Tamaulipas, had acquiesced to a similar demand showed Reynosa how matters stood.

So well had Ford and Stoneman done their work that little was left for Lee to accomplish. His presence, however, insured continued quiet. As a result, when State Commissioner George McKnight told Lee of Governor Houston's suggestion that the Rang-

---

[40] Ford, "Memoirs," V, 865-66.

[41] "Difficulties on the Southwestern Frontier," 134-35; "Troubles on the Texas Frontier," 88.

[42] Ford, "Memoirs," V, 867-68; "Troubles on the Texas Frontier," 102-103.

ers be mustered into federal service if they were to remain in the field, the Colonel replied that not only had he no authority to do so but that he now had enough Regulars at hand to keep the frontier at peace.[43] In explaining the situation to Houston, Lee added that "Major Heintzelman . . . speaks in complimentary terms of both officers and men composing the squadron, and particularly commends Major [sic] Ford and Captain Littleton commanding the two companies."[44] This correspondence foretold the end of the Río Grande Squadron. McKnight had been sent to muster Ford's command out of state service.[45] The squadron marched first to Brownsville, where citizens honored the Senior Captain with a supper and a ball. A characteristic toast at the banquet was "to the man who could always find a ford to the Rio Grande." Before Colonel Lee and the other guests, Ford responded briefly, expressing, incidentally, his "sentiments of preserving the union."

After a few days' delay in Brownsville, Ford rode on after his Rangers, accompanying Lee and Heintzelman as far as Banquete before turning toward Goliad. There, on or about May 16, McKnight assembled the companies for discharge. He was not well received by the men because of a rumor that he had been sent to keep them from stealing their state-supplied weapons. Rejecting offers of assistance from Ford and his officers, McKnight followed his own procedure. He stood at the front end of a covered wagon and called every man's name in turn. As each Ranger stepped forward, McKnight gave him a receipt for his weapons and handed them to a man in the wagon. Early in the afternoon the muster-out ended and the men took their ways homeward. Ford, Dr. Charles B. Combe, and John Ingram rode out for Austin. On the Gonzales road, passing one squad of discharged Rangers after another, "Old Rip" was astonished to see them still bearing their weapons. Finally one rider explained:

43 "Troubles on the Texas Frontier," 84–89, 101–102.

44 Lee to Houston, April 20, 1860, G. L.

45 Houston to Ford, March 24, 1860, Exec. Rec. Bk. No. 278, Governor Sam Houston, Archives Division, Texas State Library; McKnight to Houston, May 15, 1860, G. L.

Indicated are places with which Rip Ford was familiar—as well as points in between.

That man thought he was mighty smart, coming all the way down to the Rio Grande to keep the rangers from stealing. We just thought we would put up a job on him. He had a man in the fore-part of the wagon receiving the arms, and we had a man in the hind-part handing them out. Oh, no, he didn't want you officers to help him.[46]

In Austin, Ford spent a month settling his accounts with the state. On June 20, in an informative letter to Ed Burleson, out with a company on the Nueces, he commented:

I have the pleasure to inform you that my QMr & Paymaster's papers have been settled. . . . The returns for the Rio Grande campaign were passed on favorably, and I have come out all right at the Comptroller's Department. I am very glad of it, and I have no doubt my securities are. . . .

I shall leave for Brownsville tomorrow. I was due there to day, and shall catch hell, I suppose, for my non-performance of promise. I could not think of leaving before adjusting my accounts at the Comp. Dept. The apology should satisfy any reasonable person, and if it does not I can't help it.[47]

From whom he expected to "catch hell" is not explained, but it may have been a certain Addie Smith. Early in July, John Ford, with his pay in his pocket, returned to the Río Grande, free for four months to bask in the admiration of his friends before national events enmeshed him in what would be his most extensive public responsibilities.

46 Ford, "Memoirs," V, 868–71.
47 Ford to Ed Burleson, Ed Burleson Papers.

8

Secession and Strife

UNTIL AFTER the presidential elections in November, 1860, John S. Ford spent a leisurely time among his Brownsville friends, probably paying court to Addie Norton Smith, a daughter of the long-time border merchant Elihu Smith.[1] But strong as the call of romance may have been for the battle-marked widower, its voice was drowned by the increasing roar of the secession controversy emanating from Austin. Without waiting to learn the election results, Ford set out for the capital.

In Austin, he found sentiment sharply divided concerning what action the state should take. Many people, favoring the Union principle, preferred to await an overt act against southern interests before considering separation; others believed secession inevitable but felt that it would come peacefully, since they assumed that there was inherently less fighting spirit in the North. With the latter assumption, "Old Rip" could not agree. He had campaigned enough with northern men to have estimated their fighting qualities and, as compared with Texans, he "found no very great difference in them." Ford had no belief in the constitutional right of secession, but the fundamental right of revolution, which he interpreted as being upheld in the Webster-Hayne debate, offered him solace. He would exercise that right to serve Texas, should

[1] Ford's presence gave rise to a rumor that he was to lead the Knights of the Golden Circle in an invasion of Mexico. C. A. Bridges, "The Knights of the Golden Circle: A Filibustering Fantasy," *Southwestern Historical Quarterly*, Vol. XLIV (July 1940–April, 1941), 294.

she secede.[2] His view of the secession principle appears to have been inconsistent; he had defended something very like the idea two years earlier, when, in a special report to Governor Runnels, he had maintained positively that federal neglect had provided the state with legal and sufficient grounds to leave the Union.

> The Citizens of this State are entitled to protection and they ought to have it. The General Government have failed and refused to accord it. . . . There is no better principle established than, that when a Government fail [sic] or refuses to protect its citizens the ties of allegiance are dissolved, and they have a perfect right to take care of themselves. In my opinion Texas has already had ample cause to sever her connection with the Union on this very head.[3]

When the news of Lincoln's election reached Austin, a small group of secession-minded citizens took prompt action. Ford was among those who, about the middle of November, met with Attorney General George Flournoy to determine a course of action. They sent for Justice O. M. Roberts of the state Supreme Court and asked his advice. Roberts suggested three possibilities: first, they might arouse citizens to demand of Governor Houston a special session of the legislature to consider the question; second, they might build a political machine strong enough to capture the legislature in the 1861 election, and thus issue a legislative call for a convention; third, if they believed there was a majority sentiment for secession throughout the state, they might themselves call a convention. There was no suggestion that Texas remain in the Union until the Lincoln administration should by its actions make its intentions plain.

The group declared for quick action and a few days later held a public meeting at the courthouse, with about two hundred secession sympathizers attending. A stirring address by Thomas Harrison of Waco and a "rough and ready" oration by equally rough and ready George Baylor were instrumental in crystalizing secession sentiment in the audience. A Union meeting at Smith's Hotel several days later ended in a fiasco for its organizers when the

[2] Ford, "Memoirs," V, 872-73, 941-42, 968.
[3] Ford to Runnels, June 2, 1858, G. L.

crowd demanded secession speakers and gave a roaring vocal majority to sustaining "Southern rights."

When a committee from the city of Houston arrived to petition the Governor for a special legislative session, they found him hospitable but noncommittal. Soon thereafter, William P. Rogers of Houston met with Ford, Flournoy, Roberts, and several others and decided to issue a convention call, to be written by Roberts and Flournoy. At Roberts' request, Ford was designated to assist. He and Flournoy persuaded Roberts to draft the call. As the latter took up his pen, he "recollected the singular coincidence that Colonel Ford and he drew up the first annexation resolutions in Eastern Texas, which were adopted by the citizens of San Augustine."[4] Copies of the call were sent to Waco, Houston, and other cities, with a request that they be issued on December 3, 1860, simultaneously with the call in Austin. Delegates were to be elected on January 8, 1861, and were to convene in Austin on January 28, in time to vote Texas out of the Union before Lincoln's inauguration, should there be a secession majority among the delegates. Of this, Ford, Roberts, and their fellow agitators had little doubt. Ford himself estimated that Unionists were most numerous in the counties immediately around Austin; elsewhere, he believed, they were decidedly in the minority.

In mid-December it was learned that Houston intended to call the legislature into special session on January 21. The secessionists decided to follow their original convention plan, at the same time endorsing Houston's action as a concession to the will of the people. In response to a clamorous demand, Houston made a speech which the secessionists interpreted as a promise to summon the legislature but also to keep the state in the Union. Roberts believed that the Governor hoped to "kill off" the convention or, that failing, to block legislative approval of it by controlling at least one-third of the House membership and using his veto power.

Ford vigorously promoted secession sentiment in Travis Coun-

[4] Ford, "Memoirs," V, 943–45. In his memoirs, Ford quotes extensively from a journal kept by O. M. Roberts during the secession crisis. This journal is missing from the file of Roberts Papers in the Barker History Center.

ty. Years afterward he remembered that "the contest brought about by the secession movement was sharp, though not necessarily bitter. Men of different opinions remained friendly."[5] But there is testimony to the contrary, including a letter of his former Ranger lieutenant Aaron Burleson of Shoal Creek, writing to his cousin Ed Burleson at San Marcos. Aaron, a strong Union enthusiast, still smoldered as he wrote, "Me and old Rip had like to got to fighting the other night and dam him I will whip him if he does attempt to stop me from speaking my sentiments at any place or time in these States God dam him."[6]

Secession demonstrators paraded in Austin on January 5, 1861. As marshal of the parade, Ford rode at the head of the procession with his assistants, Andrew A. Hopkins, William C. Walsh, and Thomas E. Sneed. Behind them came blaring bands; ladies on horseback, each bearing a banner adorned with the coat of arms of a Southern state, that of Georgia born by Ford's daughter Fannie; a group of gentlemen pedestrians; and, finally, a train of carriages conveying secessionists of both sexes. The parade passed through the center of the buzzing city, swung westward, and halted at the intersection of Colorado and Eighth streets, several blocks southwest of the present capitol grounds, where secession sympathizers had erected a towering flagpole. At Ford's command, willing marchers sent the Lone Star flag mounting steadily until it caught the breeze 130 feet above the applauding hands and the Texas yells of the enthusiastic demonstrators.[7]

Concrete approval of Ford's stand became evident on January 8, when Texans voted in their respective counties for delegates to the Secession Convention. The border folk had come to look with admiration and affection on "Old Rip," as the results in Brownsville and Cameron County revealed. Although he was not a Cameron County resident, voters there chose him over Unionist E. J.

[5] *Ibid.*, 949–62, 967.

[6] A. B. Burleson to Ed Burleson, November 19, 1860, Ed Burleson Papers, Barker History Center. Yet the same Aaron B. Burleson, in the spring of 1861, raged at the Committee of Public Safety as being a "bunch of jackasses" for permitting Union troops to depart with their arms.

[7] Brown, "Annals," Ch. XXI, 4–5.

Davis to speak for them in the Austin convention.[8] Twenty days thereafter, the specially convened legislature meanwhile having sanctioned the convention, Ford took his place among the Texians who were to remove from the Union the state which he had diligently labored to usher into it.

From where he sat expectantly on the convention floor, Ford could recognize many old friends and "Old Texians." Because of his diversified career, he probably was acquainted with more of the delegates than any other member, but he was on most familiar ground with former Governor H. R. Runnels, down from his Red River plantation; former Rangers T. C. Frost, Allison Nelson, and John Littleton; and two who had accompanied him from Brownsville: Edward R. Hord, Carbajal supporter of a decade past, and Francis W. Latham, United States collector of customs on the lower Río Grande. These men were of the sort whose names provide only the subtitles of history; they were, nevertheless, capable, purposeful, and characteristic of the leadership in the local communities, willing to lay aside their professions and pursuits to deal with this public crisis in the manner they thought best. Of their general pattern was John S. Ford, although he was in one respect unique—of the 182 delegates who finally were entered on the convention roll, he was the single participant for whom no profession, occupation, or employment was listed.[9]

On February 1, the convention approved by a vote of 166–8 an ordinance declaring that "Texas . . . is a separate sovereign State, and that her citizens are absolved from allegiance to the United States, or the Government thereof." A referendum on the ordinance was conducted on February 23, and on March 2 the convention sat to count the votes. The tally was completed on March 4, when the convention, announcing a secession majority of 46,129 to 14,697, declared Texas out of the Union as of March 2, thus placing her on record as having seceded before Lincoln's inauguration on the fourth.

[8] Ford, "Memoirs," V, 967.
[9] Ernest William Winkler (ed.), *Journal of the Secession Convention of Texas, 1861*, 406. Hereafter cited as *Journal, Secession Convention.*

The referendum was decidedly after the fact. The convention, in its initial session, had chosen as its chairman Judge Roberts, who immediately set about forming an interim government to serve until the legislature could provide for a secession state government. For the committees authorized by the convention, Roberts had an embarrassing plethora of competence from which to choose. It was with the utmost deliberation, however, that he selected the members of the committee which in the crisis had the greatest immediate responsibility—the Committee of Public Safety. He turned to Ford, whom he considered "unquestionably the very best military man . . . in Texas at the time of the war," for advice on its composition. Ford's particular knowledge was essential, Roberts later wrote.

> Indeed, I called him to my assistance in selecting the members of that committee from the extreme west, because, first, of his general acquaintance there, and secondly, on account of his knowledge of military men upon the frontier.
>
> He was of very great advantage to that committee on account of his information of military matters within the state, as well as his general military knowledge. By these he was called to take a leading part in devising the measures for taking possession of the public property, and especially in dictating the necessary order to commissioners, officers, and agents of that Committee who were employed in that bold and hazardous enterprise.[10]

There were in Texas then more than 2,500 United States soldiers, along the Río Grande, on the western frontier, and at the Eighth Military Department headquarters in San Antonio. To remove these troops peaceably from the state and to appropriate the posts and federal property were the ends toward which Ford and Roberts now consulted. Under date of March 3, the Committee of Public Safety issued to Ford, Henry E. McCulloch, and Ben McCulloch commissions as colonels of cavalry, with orders to achieve the capitulation of the federal troops, installations, and

[10] Quoted in Ford, "Memoirs," V, 995.

property.[11] Ben McCulloch was to go at once to San Antonio to support with a show of force the state commissioners' demands on General Twiggs for the surrender of the headquarters property and personnel,[12] Henry McCulloch was to occupy the western forts, and Ford was to assume command of the Río Grande posts.

By the orders which he himself had helped to prepare, Ford was directed to enlist six hundred men, or more if necessary, and to proceed with state Commissioner E. B. Nichols, who would act in a civil capacity, to the island of Brazos Santiago, off the mouth of the Río Grande. Ford's assignment was, first, to acquire the valley posts and property (on March 2, if the federal officers offered no resistance) and, second, to protect the Río Grande line from foreign invasion.[13] The Military District of the Río Grande, created as Ford's jurisdiction by the committee,

> was defined by beginning at a point on the Rio Grande, halfway between Forts Duncan and McIntosh and including all forts on the Rio Grande below said point, and the entire district of country between the Nueces and Rio Grande, and at right angles with the general course of said river to the point of beginning.[14]

Ten United States companies were stationed within the area, five of them infantry, the others cavalry and artillery. Texans reasoned that General Twiggs, Georgia born and a known secession sympathizer, would accede to the state's demands if he could find a way to do so gracefully. The reactions of his subordinates in the river garrisons, however, could not be predicted.

Hastily firing orders to Matt Nolan, John Littleton, and John Donelson to muster mounted companies at Corpus Christi and proceed with speed to the border, "Old Rip" caught the south-bound Hempstead stage. At Hempstead he boarded a train for Houston, pausing briefly to muster in a volunteer infantry unit

[11] *The War of the Rebellion: A Compilation of the Official Records of the Union and Confederate Armies*, Series I, Vol. 53, 651. Hereafter cited as *O. R.*
[12] The commissioners were P. N. Luckett, S. A. Maverick, and T. J. Devine.
[13] *O. R.*, Ser. I, Vol. 53, 650–51.
[14] *Journal, Secession Convention*, 320–21.

before hurrying on to Galveston to organize the force for Brazos Santiago.[15] At Galveston, Ford consulted with Nichols, who almost immediately departed for New Orleans, under the committee's authorization, to raise money and arms. Ford, meanwhile, accepted recruits and began to weld them into a disciplined task force.

Nichols returned on February 17, having acquired from the Citizens Bank of New Orleans and from private sources some $24,000, part of which he had expended in New Orleans for arms to be shipped to Galveston. At Ford's suggestion, he chartered the Southern Steamship Company steamer *General Rusk* and a schooner, the *Shark*. With six companies numbering about five hundred men, Nichols, and Lieutenant Colonel Hugh McLeod as second in command, Ford cleared for the Río Grande late on the night of February 19.

Two days later, the expedition dropped anchor off Brazos Santiago, where Lieutenant James Thompson and twelve Regular Army artillerymen occupied the United States installation. Ford and Nichols hastened ashore to confer with Thompson, who after some hesitation agreed to surrender the place and property and to remove his detachment to the mainland. Disembarking his force, Ford drew it up in three ranks on the beach to watch the Stars and Stripes come slowly down the flagpole, to be supplanted by the Lone Star banner of Texas. Ford reported that "no unpleasant remark dropped from either party during the affair, and a high-toned courtesy seemed to prevail throughout."[16] He wrote later that he was deeply affected by the ceremony. "This was the first time [he] ever saw the flag of the United States lowered to an opposing force. His ancestors had fought to create and sustain it, and he had marched beneath its victorious folds. Now to see it lowered, even to men born beneath it, was a trial of no ordinary character."[17]

Less amenable than Lieutenant Thompson was Captain B. H.

---

[15] Ford, "Memoirs," V, 997.

[16] *O. R.*, Ser. I, Vol. 53, 622, 651–52, 655, 657–66.

[17] Ford, "Memoirs," V, 998–99.

Hill, commanding several companies at Fort Brown. At noon on the next day, Ford, Nichols, and McLeod arrived in Brownsville. Ford went immediately to the post to talk with the federal officers, but returned late in the afternoon with no positive knowledge of their intentions. Nichols then sent his secretary, H. B. Waller, to Hill with a request for a meeting. Waller came back with an "indefinite reply," but Nichols meanwhile had heard a rumor that Hill planned a night attack on the Texans at Brazos Santiago. At midnight, Waller again was sent with a note from Nichols, deprecating such an action and requesting a written answer. Shortly before noon on February 23, Hill consented to a conference. In a stormy interview at Fort Brown, the Captain asserted that only the advice of his officers had deterred him from arresting Ford, Nichols, and McLeod on charges of treason. After exchanging written summations of their respective demands, Nichols withdrew to confer with Ford. It was decided that the commissioner should take the *General Rusk* back to Galveston for more rifle companies to reinforce McLeod, now busy fortifying Brazos Island. Nichols sailed on the morning of February 25 while Ford was dispatching orders which would hurry forward the mounted companies marching from Corpus Christi.

"Old Rip" now sought out his former raiding companion, Captain George Stoneman of the Second Cavalry. As anxious as Ford to avert a clash between state and federal troops, Stoneman advised Hill to adopt a conciliatory attitude. Hill's receipt of Twiggs's order of February 18 directing the surrender of all troops and property in the state practically assured Ford's success. Nichols learned of Twiggs's order when he arrived at Galveston on February 26 and announced that he expected no further trouble with Hill. He had intended to notify Hill to send the women and children out of Fort Brown on March 2, preparatory to opening hostilities, "if he did not acknowledge the Texans owned Texas. We intended to whale him into a knowledge of that fact." On February 28, Nichols reported to the Committee of Public Safety that he was sending additional troops to McLeod, a battalion including a Liberty company, the Galveston Rifles, and the Fort Bend Rifles, about 325 men in all, under command of B. F. Terry, whom Nichols had commissioned a lieutenant colonel.[18] Nichols and Terry arrived with the battalion at Brazos Santiago at noon on March 1.

The situation at Brownsville was static, Nichols learned. Affairs, however, quickened suddenly with the appearance of the New York steamer *Daniel Webster* on March 3, bearing Major Fitz-John Porter of the United States Army, who had come to expedite the departure of the federal troops. Ford went to meet him, and the two left for Brownsville late in the afternoon.[19] On the next morning, McLeod's command heard from Fort Brown the regulated grumble of artillery fire. The Texans, past condoning loyalty among any but those of their own views, and believing (probably correctly) that the shots were salutes honoring Lincoln's inauguration, became excitedly wrathful at what they interpreted to be a deliberate insult to Texas and themselves. McLeod sent an officer to Brownsville to learn the cause of the firing and to report to Ford the anger of the men.

> They feel that a salute fired by the garrison at Fort Brown, on the day of Lincoln's inauguration, dishonors this command and through them the state of Texas. They know that the insult is only aggravated by the fact that their commanding general has acknowledged the authority of the State, as expressed through the Committee of Public Safety of the Convention, and issued public orders for their retirement from our territory, and they—our officers and men—express their determination with a spirit which my own feelings do not permit me to repress.[20]

Ford soothed the ruffled feelings the next day by informing McLeod that the firing was merely routine practice, in no way intended to offend the honor of Texas and her sensitive citizens.

Stoneman, whom Major Porter had assigned to supervise the federal evacuation, assured Ford that the Regulars intended to depart peaceably, despite rumors of an impending clash which

18 *O. R.*, Ser. I, Vol. 53, 619–20, 655.
19 *Ibid.*, 652–53, 657–66.
20 *Journal, Secession Convention*, 359.

Samuel Heintzelman, who as a major
was in command of operations against Cortina.

John Bankhead Magruder, who sanctioned Ford's
Río Grande Expeditionary Force.

had stirred the border population, especially the Mexican residents, who imperfectly understood the issues involved. To reassure the citizens, Ford published a proclamation on March 6 explaining the change of government and calling on the people to continue their peaceful pursuits.[21] Nichols, who had become seriously ill, turned his duties over to Secretary Waller and sailed for Galveston on March 13, taking with him for discharge about one-third of the expeditionary force, on Ford's assurance that the remaining seven hundred men, including the mounted companies, were sufficient to accomplish the remainder of the mission. The federal troops were already embarking when Nichols sailed, and by March 21 the last United States officers had departed,[22] Captain Stoneman, "upon a touching appeal from Colonel Ford," leaving behind his company weapons for use by the citizens against possible Indian attack.[23] Full responsibility on the border now devolved upon "Old Rip," who on March 19 had been confirmed in rank by the convention's electing him colonel of the Second Regiment, Texas Mounted Rifles.[24]

Colonel Ford had now completed the most delicate part of his assignment. In contrast to the excitable Nichols, he had negotiated with quiet informality, making profitable use of his friendship with the federal officers. O. M. Roberts expressed the majority opinion in Texas when he wrote: "I do believe that, but for his prudence and masterly management of the troops, and his address with the United States officers, the war would have opened there, before we had finally seceded, and very probably to our disadvantage greatly."[25]

Ford now turned his attention to the other phase of his mission: protection of the Río Grande frontier from hostile invasion. The Juárez administration in Mexico, harassed by the revolt of the powerful Miramón conservative faction, offered no threat. Know-

[21] Ford, "Memoirs," V, 1000.
[22] *O. R.*, Ser. I, Vol. 53, 653–54.
[23] *Ibid.*, Vol. I, 600–601.
[24] *Journal, Secession Convention*, 200–205.
[25] Quoted in Ford, "Memoirs," V, 996.

ing well that Mexican border commanders, however, could be practically independent of the central government, Ford set out to gain their good will toward the Confederacy. His suave diplomacy and his record of the previous year along the river had their effect; both General García and Colonel Macedonio Capistrán in Matamoros promised to maintain friendly relations with Texas.[26] Consequently, Ford anticipated that, unless an American civil war broke out, his chief problem would be that of suppressing Indian and bandit depredations. Already he had sent his mounted units to strategic bases up the river to forestall the inevitable disturbances, retaining the infantry companies at his Fort Brown headquarters. With Mexican official co-operation and with more men on the border than Heintzelman had had, "Old Rip" could expect guarding the frontier to be a relatively simple task.

His task, however, became almost immediately complex. On April 18, 1861, he received word that Fort Sumter had been fired upon. Promptly relegating Indian and bandit activities to the position of routine local affairs, he began preparations to defend his district against possible federal invasion. Union forces could most easily threaten Texas by way of the lower Río Grande. They must be repelled, for, with a naval blockade established by Lincoln's orders of April 19 and 27, Ford realized that the lower Río Grande region would be the only practicable point of entry for goods and of outlet for cotton, the only means the Confederacy had of establishing its credit abroad. Since the Brazos Santiago and Point Isabel installations at the river mouth could not be successfully defended against naval attack, obviously Fort Brown, about twenty miles above the Gulf and just outside Brownsville, was the key to control of the lower river. The fort was habitable for a small force but hardly defensible: walls, parapets, and ditches had almost crumbled away, and its approaches were too overgrown with mesquite to offer a field of fire for either artillery

[26] *Ibid.*, 914–17, 927; *O. R.*, Ser. I, Vol. 1, 577–78; Vol. 4, 136–37; Ford to Capistrán, November 9, 1861, War Department Collection of Confederate Records, Carded Records and Correspondence Re: John S. Ford, 2d Regiment Texas Cavalry (2 Texas Mounted Rifles) (Confederate), National Archives, Washington, D. C. Hereafter cited as War Dept., Ford Records.

or infantry. Ford began reconditioning the post on April 19, assisted by Judge Israel Bigelow and other Brownsville citizens. While the troops worked to restore the defenses, civilians hired and directed by Bigelow hacked away at the mesquite with pick and spade, ax and grubbing hoe. The hot, arduous labor was somewhat lightened by merchant Jeremiah Galvan. In his warehouse were several barrels of whisky, left behind by the federal quartermasters. Periodically the "jigger bucket" passed among the toilers.[27] Gentler hands also were busy rendering aid of another kind. Mrs. Bigelow and a group of Brownsville women assumed the task of making a Confederate flag for "Old Rip"'s men. It was ceremoniously presented by the Judge, and Ford received it with appropriate remarks. Then the banner rose to the peak of the Fort Brown flagpole, whence it flew while the Confederacy held the lower river.[28]

Activities now were enlivened by the temporary return to the Río Grande of Juan Cortina. Under his urging, Mexican residents of Zapata County pronounced against the Confederacy, an action more anti-Texan than it was pro-Union, for it offered an excuse for predatory operations north of the Río Grande. Early in April, after hanging the secessionist county judge, the *pronunciados* began a thorough devastation of the Texas frontier above Brownsville. The bandits were defeated in a series of sharp engagements, the decisive fight coming on May 23 at Carrizo, about sixty miles below Laredo, when Cortina himself was repulsed and pursued. Soon thereafter, perhaps at Ford's request, General García went upstream for pointed words with Cortina, who again disappeared from the valley to await a more favorable opportunity.[29] The quick suppression of the outbreak was irrefutable testimony to Ford's diplomatic skill and to the command competence he had shown in the dispersal of his horsemen.

May brought several changes to Ford's situation. For one thing, no longer was he under the orders of the Committee of Public

[27] Ford, "Memoirs," V, 1004–1005.
[28] *Rio Grande Sentinel* (Brownsville), June 26, 1861.
[29] Ford, "Memoirs," V, 923–25, 927, 919–20, 1002–1003.

Safety. Its work ended when military responsibility for the Confederate District of Texas was assumed on April 12 by Colonel Earl Van Dorn, whom Ford had met in 1859 as a United States cavalry major at Camp Radziminski. By late May, Van Dorn had decided upon two lines of defense for Texas' western frontier, the first extending from Red River to the junction of the North and Main Conchos, the second stretching from Fort Inge to Fort Bliss, including on the way Forts Quitman and Davis, Camp Stockton, Forts Lancaster and Clark, and Camp Wood. Van Dorn placed Ford in command of the second line, with orders to remain on the lower Río Grande, expressing "perfect confidence" that, under Ford's direction, the Río Grande line would be well guarded.[30] Ford was instructed to muster into Confederate service the infantry companies he had taken to the river. His own regiment of mounted riflemen was recruiting in San Antonio to bring it up to full strength. He planned to use the recruits to supplement the units of Nolan, Donelson, and Littleton, on duty along the Río Grande, but as four companies they ultimately marched to El Paso under Ford's subordinates, Lieutenant Colonel John R. Baylor and Major Ed Waller, to resist a possible Union thrust from New Mexico.

Probably before he received Van Dorn's orders, "Old Rip" had experienced what his misogynistic friends might have termed another "change of command." In Brownsville, on May 31, 1861, the grizzled Colonel took as his third wife Addie Smith, of less than half his years.[31] He was not to be separated from his young bride by Van Dorn's suggestion that border heaquarters be moved to Fort Clark. Before Ford could comply with his orders in detail, Van Dorn had been promoted and transferred east, and the command had been assumed by Brigadier General Paul O. Hebert, with Colonel Henry E. McCulloch becoming Ford's immediate superior, commanding the Sub-Department of the Río Grande. Ford remained at Fort Brown.[32]

[30] O. R., Ser. I, Vol. 1, 574–75, 577–78.
[31] Brown, "Annals," Ch. XXII, 44.   [32] O. R., Ser. I, Vol. 1, 577–78.

Throughout the summer and fall of 1861, Colonel Ford kept the river frontier quiet. Mexican raids became appreciably less frequent and less destructive, and goods flowed freely between Brownsville and Matamoros. But early in the fall arose the design, obscure in origin, to replace Ford with an officer holding a Confederate commission. Ford himself felt that the intention grew out of political animosity. On August 18, he wrote to O. M. Roberts that he desired a Confederate commission and that he believed his shortage of supplies for the border troops was being made a political football in San Antonio by Governor Edward Clark's opponents.[33] When he again wrote to Roberts, on September 30, he displayed irritation with the situation and showed some suspicion of the Governor.

> I have been for some time, satisfied of the existence of a plot to slander and disgrace me. The friends of Gov. Clark were reported as the disseminators of charges against me, which were false. If he was not a party concerned he held his peace when his silence was an injustice to me and gave weight to the detractors. The small fry officials of San Antonio were exceedingly active in circulating falsehoods and condemning me on orders originating from their prolific imagination.[34]

That Ford was not then relieved of the border command probably was due to the favorable reporting of Juan A. Quintero. Cuban-born Quintero, whose abilities history unfortunately has largely overlooked, had been sent to Monterrey as the Confederate commercial and confidential agent. He was *de facto* ambassador to the northeastern Mexican states and performed his duties with much honor to himself and the Confederacy. On October 18, in a long report on the border situation to R. M. T. Hunter, Confederate secretary of state, Quintero commented that "Col. Ford is a gentleman of fine intellect and an old veteran. He is thoroughly acquainted with the Mexican character and Spanish language and

[33] Ford to O. M. Roberts, August 18, 1861, Roberts Papers.
[34] Ford to Roberts, September 30, 1861, Scrapbook III, *ibid*.

ought by all means remain permanently at this post. He can be of *great service* to our government."[35]

Even so, Ford would lose his command because of his own dogged loyalty combined with the vagaries of Mexican and Texan politics. The first incident of the series which was to result in his removal came in November of 1861. Mexican President Benito Juárez appointed Jesús de la Serna to be governor of Tamaulipas, whereupon General García and the Matamoros garrison protested the appointment and revolted. To quell the uprising came General José Carbajal, Ford's old friend and nemesis-to-be. Seeking to compromise and knowing of Ford's friendship with Carbajal, García requested "Old Rip" to carry proposals to the Carbajal camp. Ford complied with the request, but Carbajal refused to negotiate, declaring his intention of restoring Juárez' authority. After the discussion, Ford by request reviewed Carbajal's troops and estimated their chances of success. He assured the General that a vigorous, unrelenting assault on the city would result in quick suppression of the *pronunciados*. But, as he had done in a similar situation a decade earlier, Carbajal ignored the advice and wasted the winter and his men in committing small detachments to unco-ordinated, ineffective skirmishes.[36]

Early in 1862, Ford was called to McCulloch's headquarters, leaving Colonel P. N. Luckett, Third Texas Infantry, in charge of the river district. About March 1, Ford arrived back on the border, to "the general satisfaction" of border residents, Quintero noted.[37] McCulloch not only had given Ford command of all troops on the border, but also apparently had instructed him to do everything possible to maintain trade relations with Mexico in the face of the threatened federal blockade. Immediately upon his return, Ford moved to place the King and Kenedy steamships under neutral registry to assure their uninterrupted operation. Ford found a changed situation in Matamoros, requiring a new

[35] Quintero to Hunter, October 18, 1861, "Pickett Papers," Box L, MS Division, Library of Congress. Hereafter cited as Pickett Papers.

[36] Ford, "Memoirs," V, 927–28.

[37] Quintero to William M. Browne, March 4, 1862, Pickett Papers.

series of negotiations. Juárez, to solve the Tamaulipas problem, had placed the state under the rule of General Santiago Vidaurri, already virtual dictator of Nuevo León and Coahuila. To represent him in Matamoros, Vidaurri had sent a Colonel Quiroga, from whom Ford obtained Mexican registry for some of the Texas steamers. Next Ford turned to the British consul in Matamoros, a certain Blaker, and was able to have other vessels registered under the British flag, a particularly advantageous maneuver since the British frigate *Phaeton* was patrolling the Mexican coast south of the Río Grande and would prevent United States interference with the steamers.[38]

In March, Carbajal disturbed the border situation. Unwilling to accept Juárez' decision regarding Tamaulipas, he attempted to seize Matamoros. When his assault on the city was beaten off, he and his men fled to Texas, surrendering their arms to Ford as they crossed the river. The fugitives encamped a few miles above Brownsville, and Carbajal promptly began recruiting a force to drive Quiroga out of Matamoros. Arms for the malcontents were provided by Mifflin Kenedy and other Brownsville merchants. When Quiroga demanded that Ford extradite Carbajal for trial for treason, Ford refused, and Mexican-Confederate relations deteriorated swiftly. On March 28, Quintero reported that "threatening communications have been passed between Col. Ford and Col. Quiroga and our *friendly relations with the Mexican frontier are fast dying away. . . . I apprehend serious difficulties*."[39] Ford reported, too, on April 3, that "We are on the verge of a war with Mexico," and expressed the opinion that if war came, he could not reasonably be expected to conduct a successful defense with only 976 men of all arms.[40]

The situation was aggravated in April when Carbajal's men fired across the river on Mexican troops. Quiroga again demanded extradition of Carbajal, and again Ford refused. In retaliation, Vidaurri, on April 17, levied a duty of two cents a pound on Texas

[38] Ford to Browne, March 14, 1862, *ibid.*; Ford "Memoirs," V, 893–94.
[39] Quintero to Browne, March 28, 1862, *ibid.*
[40] Ford to Browne, April 3, 1862, *ibid.*

cotton entering Mexico (a duty later reduced to one cent a pound because of Quintero's protest). In the meantime, word of the controversy had reached San Antonio, and on the same day on which Vidaurri's duty took effect, McCulloch sent orders to Ford to surrender Carbajal to Quiroga.[41] Ford was now, in the Texan phrase, "between a rock and a hard place": he could extradite Carbajal in obedience to Confederate authority, as represented by McCulloch, or he could obey the dictates of sentiment and refuse to surrender his old comrade to certain death before a firing squad. Friendship won, and when it did, Ford irreparably compromised his command position. He informed Carbajal of McCulloch's order, and the old revolutionary suspended his disquieting preparations for a descent on Matamoros. Possibly Ford believed that when Carbajal ceased to agitate, the whole affair would blow over; it did, but too late to benefit "Old Rip."

April 29 finally brought visual proof of the Lincoln blockade. On the morning of that day the U.S.S. *Montgomery* (Captain Charles Hunter) hove to at the river mouth. Hunter sent notice to Captain W. H. Brewin at Brazos Santiago that he would wait a day to permit the evacuation of women and children from the small settlement before opening fire. He also extended an invitation to any Texan who felt so disposed to meet with him and swear allegiance to the Union government, an offer which resulted in much swearing of a kind not exactly expected by Hunter. Brewin withdrew his command beyond range of the *Montgomery*'s guns and sent Ford word of the situation. Ford replied to Hunter on the next day, expressing regret that circumstances did not allow the Texans to meet the federals at sea, but bombastically asserting, "If you will come ashore you shall be met as brave men ever meet the invaders of their soil, who come to execute the edicts of a despotic government."[42]

Hunter could do little more than force the evacuation of Brazos Santiago. He must have been sorely frustrated to see the King and

<hr />

41 Quintero to Browne, April 17, 1862, *ibid.*

42 *War of the Rebellion: Official Records of the Union and Confederate Navies,* Ser. I, Vol. 18, 458.

Kenedy vessels discharging cargo off Bagdad, on the Mexican side of the river mouth, while riding complacently under the neutral flags that Ford's efforts had provided for them. When Hunter proposed to interfere, he was promptly overawed by the skipper of the *Phaeton*, who told him precisely what would happen if the *Montgomery* attempted to patrol the Gulf Coast south of the river.[43] The *Phaeton* was big, the *Montgomery* small; Hunter offered no further difficulty.

"Old Rip"'s tenure of command had less than a month to run. In May, McCulloch was superseded as commander of the Western Department of Texas by Brigadier General H. P. Bee, who came, as he said, "specially assigned by the President to the command of the Rio Grande."[44] Bee was among those whom Ford suspected of instigating criticism against him in the preceding summer. Ford was recalled from field service to San Antonio, and the border troops were assigned to Colonel Luckett. Carbajal soon left the border, obtaining passage to New York, where he remained until the Civil War ended. Finally, Vidaurri, dismissed for ignoring Juárez' order to close the border to Confederate trade, found sanctuary at the Benavides home in Laredo.

Resentful over his transfer to an office assignment and reluctant to leave his pregnant wife at her father's home in Brownsville, "Old Rip" was certain that his reassignment was another attempt by jealous political enemies to get him out of the service. Probably he knew that his transfer from the Río Grande had been urged, as the only way of averting war with Mexico, by his old enemy William B. Ochiltree, while a delegate to the Provisional Congress of the Confederate States. If Ford was the object of such a plot, he did little to improve his situation in the developments of the autumn. His regiment was mustered into Confederate service and then furloughed in September, when the companies that had been with Baylor and Waller in New Mexico had returned. Citing the conscription law of April 16, Bee thereupon ordered the regiment to reorganize on October 8 and to elect its field officers.

[43] Ford to Browne, March 14, 1862, Pickett Papers.
[44] *O. R.*, Ser. I, Vol. 9, 730.

Claiming that his selection by the convention could not be set aside by the conscription law and that Bee was violating the law's intent—a position Ford later admitted "perhaps was not well founded"—"Old Rip" was not a candidate for the colonelcy.[45] The reorganized regiment was redesignated the Second Texas Cavalry and it chose as its colonel Major Charles L. Pyron, who had ably commanded the western companies at Valverde and Glorieta Pass in New Mexico.[46] Pyron received a Confederate commission. Ford was never to receive one and, consequently, was never regarded by the Confederate War Department as one of its officers.

Ford's new duties were to tax his administrative capacities. On April 16, 1862, the Confederate Congress had enacted legislation requiring all white male citizens between eighteen and thirty-five years of age to enroll for military service. Enrolling officers with the rank and authority of captains in the Confederate Army were appointed for each county, and district camps of instruction were authorized to provide some basic military training for the enrollees. On June 2, Ford assumed the dual role of commanding officer of the Houston conscript camp and of superintendent of conscripts of the Department of Texas, responsible in the latter capacity for the successful operation of the conscription program in his state.[47] In July he transferred his headquarters as commandant of conscripts to Austin, where he would exercise the authority of the office until November.

In the absence of precise instructions, Superintendent Ford had to formulate a policy for exemptions from conscription. He exempted all those whose employment or occupation bore directly upon the manufacture, transportation, or procurement of goods for the Confederate or Texas government. Believing that those possessing the most material wealth had the most to fight for, he exempted overseers but conscripted plantation owners. Holding

[45] Ford, "Memoirs," VII, 1201.

[46] Ford to Roberts, September 30, 1861, Roberts Papers.

[47] E. W. Winkler (ed.), "Checklist of Texas Imprints," *Southwestern Historical Quarterly*, Vol. LIII (July, 1948), 75; *O. R.*, Ser. I, Vol. 26, pt. 2, 382.

that no man should be forced to take up arms to oppose his own principles, Ford never knowingly approved the assignment of a Union sympathizer to a Confederate combat unit.[48] He applied the Conscript Act impartially, instructing his enrolling officers that the law would not be "diverted from the great ends for which it was enacted to suit the views of any one. It shall not be used to aid the schemes of office-seekers or office-holders, as long as the present Superintendent remains upon duty."[49] Spurning offers of bribes, he administered conscription with a fairness that, he believed, generally satisfied his fellow Texans. But before the announcement in Texas in December of the famous supplementary "twenty nigger law" of April 21, 1862, and the resultant feeling that the crisis had become "a rich man's war and a poor man's fight," Ford had resigned the superintendency to become a private citizen.

About the first of November, shortly before Ford resigned from the Conscript Bureau, Mrs. Ford joined her husband in Austin with their infant daughter, Lula (May Louise), born on August 15. For the next four months, Ford held no official position. His memoirs do not account for his activities during the period, but he frequently was in San Antonio, to keep in touch with events and to be readily accessible should the state and the department of Texas need his services.[50]

Although most Texans appreciated Ford's administration of the Conscript Bureau, they felt that his more useful talents of military command were being wasted. Their attitude resulted in petitions for his promotion to brigadier general. As early as September 20, 1861, W. S. Oldham, L. T. Wigfall, and others in the Confederate Provisional Congress had directly requested President Jefferson Davis to commission Ford a brigadier. On November 6, Texas Supreme Court Justice George F. Moore wrote to Postmaster General John H. Reagan urging him to work toward

[48] Ford, "Memoirs," V, 1007; VII, 1200.
[49] Ford, Order No. 3, July 4, 1862, Ed Burleson Papers. Burleson served as one of Ford's enrolling officers.
[50] Ford, "Memoirs," VII, 1201–1202, 1207.

the same end. Reagan forwarded the request on December 11 to Secretary of War Judah P. Benjamin. Francis W. Latham, now Confederate customs collector at Brownsville, Captain Matthew Nolan, and a number of other South Texans addressed the President on Ford's behalf on December 17, 1862, asking, in addition to his commissioning, that he be assigned to command along the Río Grande. On February 16, 1863, three petitions for "Old Rip"'s advancement were dispatched: one to Davis from Texas congressmen, another to the Texas Congressional corps from the Texas legislature, and a third to the Secretary of War from a group of East Texans. The last petition mentioned that Ford had resigned as superintendent of conscripts to "shoulder his rifle and take his place in the ranks," and requested that the Confederacy make better use of him, since "it would be the delight of Texans to follow such a leader."[51] Davis and Benjamin, however, apparently felt that vacancies in the rank of brigadier should be filled either by men already holding Confederate commissions or, in exceptional cases, by influential politicians. Since Ford possessed neither qualification, the efforts on his behalf were unavailing, although for a time his prospects apparently were bright, for General Bee wrote in some agitation to learn if it were true that Ford had been made a brigadier general and would replace him on the Río Grande line.[52]

"Rip" Ford's destiny lay higher than the ranks. In San Antonio he soon became acquainted with Major General John Bankhead Magruder, whose application of histrionic talents to military operations had so bewildered George B. McClellan on the Yorktown line during the Peninsular Campaign. "Prince John" Magruder, at San Antonio on November 29, 1862, had taken command of the newly created District of Texas, New Mexico, and Arizona, under the Confederacy's recently established Trans-Mississippi Department. Magruder found use for Ford when Major J. P. Flewellen, anxious for field duty, resigned as superintendent of conscripts. On March 21, 1863, Magruder appointed Ford, to

51 War Dept., Ford Records.
52 O. R., Ser. I, Vol. 26, pt. 2, 42.

whom he referred as "an officer of great merit," to resume the position.[53] Not until the appointment had been made did the General learn that his appointee was not a Confederate officer. He then sought a commission for Ford. President Davis denied Magruder's request, but did confirm the appointment. Magruder, however, publicly recognized Ford as a colonel, addressed him as such, and until the close of the war authorized him to act as such. Furthermore, Ford was paid by the Confederate departmental paymaster at the $210 monthly scale for Confederate Army colonels.[54]

Ably assisted by his old friend Captain William C. Walsh, Colonel Ford entered anew on the task of equitable administration of the conscription laws. He found a situation which, however legal, was in his eyes manifestly unfair to Texans under arms and detrimental to civilian morale.

There was a number of men of conscriptable age who managed to keep out of the army by reason of small offices they managed to hold, and other sharp practices well known to the ardent patriot who stayed at home with his wife. These gentlemen were the most eloquent accusers of those officers who lost fights, no matter what the difference in number and position. They abused everything and every body wearing the Confederate uniform; and from the lips out were excelsior soldiers. These censorious citizens did great harm to the Confederate cause.

To forestall the evils arising from the conduct of such people, Ford and his adjutant, Captain John J. Dix, wrote a constitution for and established the Sons of the South, a society whose members came from the troops of the Confederacy. The constitution, emphasizing the subordination of military to civil authority, characterized the membership as "the friends and assistants of the poor and the distressed." The order exercised its influence on Austin meat market proprietors to force prices down to levels at which

[53] Magruder, unnumbered General Order, March 21, 1863, War Dept., Ford Records.

[54] *Ibid.;* Confederate Army pay vouchers, *ibid.;* Ford, "Memoirs," V, 1008, VII, 1203–1204.

the poor could purchase. It provided a fund through which disabled soldiers or their widows or orphans might be supplied with food, fuel, and clothing, and Ford led the way in contributing to the fund.[55] He also published and distributed widely in Texas pamphlets describing the aims of the group and on occasion spoke publicly to urge the establishment of new branches of the parent society. Old Texian Samuel Maverick, in San Antonio on September 27, 1863, heard Ford deliver a "beautiful address" on the order.[56] In a short time the Sons of the South had general dissemination among troops in Texas and in some Confederate units outside the state.

Ford's Conscript Bureau responsibilities occasionally went beyond office routine, since "in Texas there were a number who avoided conscription." Some of these people congregated in a camp in the hills west of Austin, living by hunting and by the aid of friends. When these evaders were blamed for the murder of a respected Gonzales County citizen, irate men of the county formed a company to exact revenge. To prevent illegal violence, Ford hastily collected a small party of citizens and soldiers and rode into the hills. Although his group successfully surrounded the camp of the sleeping Unionists, one of his party, possibly in secret sympathy with the fugitives, fired two rapid shots which awakened the sleepers. They escaped in the dark up a bluff so precipitous that it had not been guarded. During the autumn, Ford made several such expeditions, which without bloodshed broke up other hidden concentrations of Unionist sympathizers, most of whom, Ford believed, eventually offered themselves for conscription. The rest fled to Mexico or to other parts of the state, and Confederate authority thus was restored in and around Travis County.[57]

While "Old Rip" exhorted his enrolling officers to better efforts or rode the river brakes after Unionists and draft dodgers,

[55] Brown, "Annals," Ch. XXII, 43.
[56] Ford, "Memoirs," VII, 1203–1205; Rena Maverick Green (ed), *Samuel Maverick, Texan: A Collection of Letters, Journals, and Memoirs*, 372.
[57] Ford, "Memoirs," VII, 1204, 1208–1209.

federal operations were laying the basis for his return to field command. Ambitious Major General Nathaniel P. Banks, Union commander of the Department of the Gulf, had developed plans to occupy Texas. In the fall, by a feint against southeastern Texas, he forced Magruder to concentrate his district strength in that area, leaving Generals Bee and James E. Slaughter to defend the Río Grande Valley with only Colonel James E. Duff's Thirty-third Texas Cavalry at Fort Brown and the small regiment of Colonel Santos Benavides above Ringgold Barracks. Banks then collected Major General N. J. T. Dana's Thirteenth Army Corps at New Orleans and embarked it for the mouth of the Río Grande. At noon on November 2, 1863, Major John Bruce's Nineteenth Iowa Infantry unfurled its colors on the beach of Brazos Island. By November 5, the rest of the corps had disembarked, and on the next day, as Duff's troopers withdrew northward, Banks established his headquarters at Fort Brown. The end of November saw Union occupation firmly consolidated from the Gulf to Río Grande City, where Colonel E. J. Davis had led his First Texas (Union) Cavalry and the Thirty-seventh Illinois Infantry on a reconnaissance in force. Bee's command, weakened by the defection of Captain A. I. Vidal's company,[58] assembled at the King Ranch, except for Benavides' regiment, which had retired above Río Grande City. The Confederate supply link between Matamoros and Brownsville was cut, increasing by half the cost of goods from Mexico, since they now must enter Texas above Laredo.[59] Furthermore, Magruder could not reinforce Bee, as the transfer of enough men to offset Dana's four thousand troops would disastrously weaken the district defense in the face of what appeared to be a major Union invasion from Louisiana, a ruse which Banks ably maintained. Such, then, was the situation which called John S. Ford from the bureau to the border.

[58] *O. R.*, Ser. I, Vol. 26, pt. 1, 399, 423–25, 447–51.
[59] *Ibid.*, 876–78; Ford, "Memoirs," VI, 1018, 1034.

9

The Río Grande Expeditionary Force

FEDERAL OCCUPATION of the lower Río Grande Valley had caused Judge Bigelow, Jerry Galvan, and other Brownsville men to revert quickly to Union allegiance, but most of the valley citizens clung to the Confederacy and called in December for help from their most reliable troubleshooter, "Old Rip" Ford.[1] In his eager hands, their demand became the lever with which he pried from reluctant Confederate officialdom authority for his largest, most effective command—the Río Grande Expeditionary Force.

Personally sympathetic though he was with Ford's plan to collect a force to liberate the valley, Magruder hesitated to assume responsibility for what his superiors would consider an illegal force commanded by an uncommissioned officer, especially since his requests for a Confederate commission for Ford had been rejected by both the War Department and the Trans-Mississippi Department. Ford, meanwhile, issued calls for recruits from among conscription-exempt Texans and left Austin for San Antonio, incessantly prodding Magruder to issue official sanction for the campaign. Confident that he could collect a command on state authority, he was also aware that he would need Confederate units to raise his strength to match the estimated seven thousand Federal troops based on Brownsville.

The able persuasion of Major A. G. Dickinson, C.S.A., district adjutant general and commandant of the San Antonio garri-

[1] *O. R.*, Ser. I, Vol. 26, pt. 1, 881; pt. 2, 415, 530.

James E. Slaughter, nominal Confederate commander
on the lower Río Grande in the last year of the Civil War.

Lew Wallace, general and politico, who attempted
to negotiate a separate peace with Texas.

son, finally pushed "Prince John" to a decision. On December 22, Magruder dispatched a long, confidential order to Ford, giving "Old Rip" command of all troops at San Antonio and to the west and south of that station. Major Albert Walthersdorff was ordered in from the Blanco County frontier with his two-company Ranger battalion; Colonel S. B. Baird's Fourth Arizona cavalry regiment, largely Texan in personnel, was assigned to the expedition; county enrolling officers were to send their new conscripts to Ford; and, finally, he might muster as many companies as he could raise among men exempt from conscription. The last source would provide the bulk of Ford's command, since these men were to be enlisted for short terms with the understanding that they would not be ordered to serve outside the state.

Magruder also provided that Major Matt Nolan and his riders from the Corpus Christi region and Captain A. J. Ware, commanding a battalion near San Patricio, would join Ford's column as it moved south. When the force reached the river, it would assimilate Colonel Santos Benavides' small regiment and Captain George H. Giddings' command, based on Eagle Pass.[2] Finally, Ford was told to create the impression that the force was destined for Indianola, to help repulse a threatened invasion from Louisiana, but to inform Colonel Duff secretly that reinforcements soon would be on the way south.[3] "Old Rip" tried to disguise his destination, but so open was the secret that he complained that new recruits arriving in San Antonio came clamoring to know how soon they would march for the lower river. At the same time, he reported that the counties were responding well to his call for volunteers and that he intended sending his old border friend, H. Clay Davis, to Mexico to organize additional units from among Texas refugees in Matamoros, Reynosa, Camargo, and other Mexican frontier towns.[4]

Until mid-March Ford was immersed in the various tasks of

[2] *Ibid.*, pt. 1, 529–31; Vol. 53, 922–23.
[3] *Ibid.*, Vol. 26, pt. 1, 525–26.
[4] *Ibid.*, 543–44.

staff and command organization and supply procurement, while simultaneously directing operations of the units already in the field to the west and south. Magruder had given him an almost free hand in the selection of subordinates. Unable to obtain Dickinson for his executive officer, Ford left the post unfilled, but otherwise assembled a staff which promised competency. Captain C. H. Merritt, released by Major Simeon Hart of the district cotton bureau at Ford's request, was quartermaster. Captain W. G. M. Samuels came down from Henry McCulloch's command in North Texas to be ordinance officer. From Magruder, Ford drew a chief of staff, Major Felix Blücher, grandnephew of Field Marshal Blücher of Waterloo fame; conversant in five languages, a surveyor intimately acquainted with the country south of the Nueces, Blücher would be a valuable acquisition—if Ford could keep him sober. Ford's choice for tactical officer fell on Walthersdorff, an awesome giant who could without apparent effort, lift and hold at arm's length a two-hundred-pound recruit.[5]

Ford attempted, unsuccessfully, to acquire the Ranger company led by the English adventurer, Captain R. H. Williams. Williams, well acquainted with Ford, was pleased at not being assigned to Ford's command, for he "had no very high opinion of the man," and characterized Ford as "the most inveterate gambler and the hardest swearer I have ever met, even out West; indeed, his power of 'language' when the luck went against him was almost grotesque in its resourcefulness." Unaware of the frustrations Ford was experiencing, Williams was critical of what appeared to him to be the Colonel's procrastination.

> With a Colonel's commission in his pocket, and supposed to be earnestly engaged in raising a regiment for State service, he was generally to be found in one of the most notorious gambling dens in San Antonio "dealing" monte with all the riff-raff of the place, whilst youngsters of his own regiment stood around "bucking" at him; *i.e.* backing his luck.
>
> Notwithstanding all this, I am bound to say that "Old Rip" as he delighted to be called, was fairly popular with most of the people,

[5] Ford, "Memoirs," VI, 1039–42; *O. R.*, Ser. I, Vol. 53, 922–23.

being hail-fellow-well-met with everybody, free with his money, and equally free with his six-shooter.[6]

Ford's memoirs, as we have them, are silent about such interludes.

Actually it appears that Ford drove himself and his staff unsparingly to get the expedition afoot. To his own growing impatience now was added that of Magruder, and to Captain E. P. Turner of Magruder's staff Ford recounted the difficulties delaying his movement.

> I regret not having been able to take the field ere this. I have had serious obstacles to surmount. Exhausted resources, a population almost drained of men subject to military duty, oppositions from rivalry, and the nameless disagreeable retardations incident to an undertaking of this character are all too well known to the major-general commanding.

Most of the rivalry Ford mentioned came from Colonel Baird of the Fourth Arizona. Baird, whose organized companies were guarding the Indian frontier under Lieutenant Colonel Dan Showalter, was recruiting in the San Antonio region when ordered to report to Ford. He arrived in San Antonio on February 4, 1864, and was promptly ordered to take his new recruits and assume command at Fort Merrill, on the Nueces. Holding a Confederate commission and feeling that he outranked Ford, Baird refused to obey, even when Magruder sustained Ford's authority. Baird eased an ugly situation by obtaining a transfer, command of the regiment devolving upon Showalter, who by then was bringing the frontier companies to Ford.[7]

Less easily resolved was Ford's commissary problem. A devastating drought in 1863 made procurement of food and forage difficult. While waiting for the grass to green up, Quartermaster Merritt's men scoured the country for corn, ably assisted by Captain John Littleton's knowledge of every bypath in the region. Where others failed to find provisions, Littleton regularly appeared with

[6] R. H. Williams, *With the Border Ruffians: Memoirs of the Far West, 1852–1868* (ed. by E. W. Williams), 365.

[7] *O. R.*, Ser. I, Vol. 34, pt. 2, 946–47, 961–62; Ford, "Memoirs," VI, 1036.

wagonloads of corn, whose reluctant owners were impressed to haul the grain to the Helena depot for grinding. A chief obstacle to the procurement of corn and transport lay in the specie short-age, but there were Confederate bills in plenty, and those farmers who refused such payment found their goods and services requisitioned by Ford, acting with Magruder's authorization. Unceasing effort had its result. By the winter's end, the command was ready.

On March 17, Alamo Plaza saw the Expeditionary Force pass southward. Marching fast, within the week Ford camped at Banquete, where Showalter was to join him. There dispatches from Colonel Benavides reported an unsuccessful Union attack on Laredo on March 19. Waiting no longer for Showalter, on March 26, Ford led his slowly increasing force westward to join Benavides. Four days later, on San Fernando Creek, the Arizona companies came in. On April 9 the march resumed toward Los Ojuelos, where Ford expected to meet Benavides at the Ranger headquarters of a decade past. Now Nolan and a big company were flung far to the east and south, to cover the left flank and to keep an eye on the coast, particularly on Corpus Christi, where a Union reconnaissance group had landed. By an indirect route, dictated by the necessities of forage and water, Colonel Ford led his main command down to Laredo.

Union partisans had made the Federal commanders vaguely aware of Ford's movements. Major General John A. McClernand, at Thirteenth Corps headquarters at Pass Cavallo, knew that Ford's men had occupied Corpus Christi and heard also, from Major General J. F. Herron, commanding at Fort Brown, of a general rumor that Ford would attack Brownsville. Herron discounted the rumor, however, since the best Union estimates placed Ford's force at a greatly outnumbered 650 men.

Banquete, Laredo, and Brownsville formed the approximate points of an irregular, inverted right triangle, tilted slightly to the left, with the Río Grande an erratic hypotenuse. This triangle would contain most of Ford's operation. His Expeditionary Force reached Laredo and Benavides on April 15, minus the Fourth Arizona scouting eastward and the remainder of Nolan's battalion, under Captain T. E. Cater, screening the westward line from its Los Angeles base, dispositions guaranteed to prevent any surprise Union movement against Ford's supply line.

The possibility of a Federal surprise troubled "Old Rip" less, however, than the tangled international political situation of which he learned at Laredo. Mexican politics had taken several devious turns during his absence from the valley. At the Benavides home in Laredo, Ford found the fugitive Mexican general, Santiago Vidaurri, sympathetic with Maximilian's *Imperialistas*. Ford simultaneously endeavored to cultivate Vidaurri's good will and to placate the Juárez government, as Magruder had directed.[8] Now governing Tamaulipas was "Rip" Ford's former antagonist, opportunist General Juan Cortina. Ford learned that Governor Serna, after having successfully resisted Carbajal's attempts against Matamoros, had been replaced by General Manuel Ruiz, at Juárez' order. While Union forces marched on Brownsville in November, 1863, Miramón-supporter-in-exile General José M. Cobos had led a small army across the river to capture Matamoros and imprison Ruiz. Cobos' force was commanded by Cortina, who had assembled it. Therein lay Cobos' downfall. He invested Matamoros on November 4; three days later he died before a firing squad for, according to Cortina, plotting against the legitimate Juárez government. Ruiz was immediately released but, fearing that he was marked for Cobos' fate, fled to Brownsville. With no rivals, Cortina thereupon proclaimed himself military governor of Tamaulipas, a position in which the harassed Juárez administration found it expedient to sustain him.[9]

In April, circumstances involving Mrs. Ford presented another facet of the character of the enigmatic Cortina. In that month, Addie Ford and her small daughter arrived in Matamoros, having come down by stage in March from San Antonio via Eagle Pass and the Mexican side of the Río Grande. Mrs. Ford had hoped

[8] *O. R.*, Ser. I, Vol. 34, pt. 1, 647–48; pt. 2, 1106–1107; pt. 3, 129–30, 176–78, 754, 775–76.

[9] *Ibid.*, Vol. 26, pt. 1, 399–404.

to visit her mother in Brownsville, but was warned by her sister Lu that Union officers intended to take her into custody if she should cross the river. Addie's wrath was allayed somewhat by an unexpected visit from Cortina and his staff. The General offered to supply her with whatever funds she might require or with any other items for her comfort. In spite of her polite refusals, the offers were repeatedly renewed. The eventual permission granted her to visit Brownsville safely may, under the circumstances, be attributed to the intercession of Cortina, who was on good terms with the Union officers at Fort Brown. As he told Ford later, he had not forgotten the Ranger Captain's courteous and considerate treatment of his own mother and sister during the Cortina War.[10]

Meanwhile, Ford looked with anticipation toward Brownsville, two hundred miles away. Within a week after reaching Laredo, he began his march down country, leaving Benavides to guard the upper river. By April 23 he was moving on his first objective, Río Grande City, fretfully wondering why Giddings' command had not appeared from Eagle Pass. Ten days of steady splashing through the spring rains past the campsites of Los Angeles, Los Ojuelos, Comites, and Abritas brought his sodden column to Ringgold Barracks on the edge of Río Grande City. Ford entered unopposed; the Federals had withdrawn downstream to Edinburg.[11]

Now Ford went with Captain Granville Ouray to Matamoros to obtain information about the activities and intentions of the enemy around Brownsville. To promote Confederate interests in Matamoros, the Colonel also detailed Lieutenant Colonel J. J. Fisher, who had resigned similar rank with Juárez to join the Confederates at Río Grande City.[12] By the end of May, Colonel Ford was on friendly terms with Mexican authorities in Camargo, who had begun to suppress the depredations of Vidal and other renegades. Colonel John M. Swisher was already in Mexico purchas-

10 Ford, "Memoirs," VI, 1044–45; V, 907.
11 O. R., Ser. I, Vol. 34, pt. 3, 807–808.
12 John S. Ford, General Orders, 1863–1865, Museum of the United Daughters of the Confederacy, Austin, Texas. Hereafter cited as Ford, General Orders.

ing arms from Union deserters, cotton again was beginning to move across the border, and Ford optimistically was negotiating to increase his small artillery arm by the purchase of field guns from Cortina.

General Cortina, although aware that his force was too weak for prolonged resistance, had decided to hold Matamoros as long as possible against the Mexican imperial columns advancing slowly toward the Río Grande. To avoid losing his artillery to the *Imperialistas,* he had begun bargaining for its sale to Ford through Francis Latham, representing Confederate commercial interests in Matamoros.[13] Ford was eager to buy, but Cortina, trying to decide whether allegiance to Juárez or to Maximilian would best profit him, could not be brought to a final settlement.

Multiplying difficulties held Ford for six weeks at Ringgold Barracks. He was plagued with the difficulties of supply procurement, finally being forced to impress cotton which he sold in Mexico for coin to pay for goods acquired both there and in Texas. His troop organization also was disrupted by the expiration of short-term enlistments and by the transfers to other commands of some of his units. Particularly annoying to "Old Rip" was a lack of co-operation exhibited by Lieutenant Colonel Oliver Steele of Waul's Legion, commanding a camp at Gonzales, and Ford appealed to General Slaughter for help:

> I may labor under erroneous impressions, but I am led to believe that had Lieutenant-Colonel Steele offered an opposition as persistent and determined to a Federal officer's intentions and plans as he has to mine, he would have done the country good service. His reported intermeddlings reach me almost daily. If these reports are true . . . I have an undoubted right to request the major-general commanding to again protect me from officious interference.[14]

The jealous rivalry which had hampered Ford's earlier operations was yet alive, it appears.

In June came a rumor that the Federals had evacuated Brownsville. To test its validity, Ford conducted a reconnaissance in force,

[13] *O. R.,* Ser. I, Vol. 53, 998–99; Vol. 34, pt. 4, 684–85.
[14] *Ibid.,* Vol. 41, pt. 2, 994–96, 1001.

following an arc designed to bring his riders to the river road between Brownsville and a Union cavalry picket at Las Rucias Ranch, about twenty-six miles above Fort Brown. Ford set out with sixty men on or about June 21 for John Young's ranch, on the river below Edinburg, where he was to meet Fisher with the latest Matamoros intelligence. Showalter's Arizonians, with the battalions of Captain Refugio Benavides and Cater, were sent directly overland to Como Se Llama Ranch on the Arroyo Colorado north of Edinburg. Ford arrived at Showalter's camp on the night of June 23, spent the next day drying beef for emergency rations in case of a forced retirement, and in the false dawn of June 25 marched south under a lowering sky for the river road. He struck it at mid-morning slightly below Las Rucias. Countrymen verified the presence of the Federal outpost and Ford moved on the picket through the concealing chaparral. The enemy, forewarned and expecting attack, had not guarded the road to Brownsville, believing that Ford was coming from upriver with only the detachment he had taken to Young's ranch. Consequently, the Texan advance party hit the Federals sooner than either expected. When fired upon, Captain James Dunn charged with the small advance detachment and the engagement became general.

Under rolling thunder which brought a slashing rain, Showalter led his regiment to support Dunn, and Ford sent in the battalions of Cater and Benavides. The defenders, troopers of Companies "A" and "C" of Colonel E. J. Davis' First Texas (Union) Cavalry, commanded by Captain P. G. Temple, fought desperately from the *jacales* and brick headquarters of Las Rucias, having been told that the Confederates would treat them as traitors. The short, hot fight ended with the flight of those Federals who could escape to the cane thickets on the Mexican side of the Río Grande. As the firing died away, Giddings and his men arrived, having been detained up the river by Colonel Benavides.

Ford's operation was a complete success. Only eight of the more than one hundred Union cavalrymen, including Captain Temple who "left early," rejoined Herron at Fort Brown. The raiders took thirty-six prisoners, counted twenty dead enemies, including some wounded who drowned while trying to escape across a small lagoon, and acquired saddles, arms, wagons, and some twenty horses, prizes doubly valuable to a force operating so far from the upstate depots. Of the 250 men "Old Rip" had taken into battle, only three had been killed and four wounded. Captain Temple's official file, found during the fight, revealed that Davis' regiment was under orders to embark for New Orleans. The possibility of a counterattack, then, was remote, but Ford withdrew deliberately upstream to Edinburg, where for a day and a half he waited for Union retaliation before returning to Ringgold Barracks. No reprisal came, since General Herron now estimated Ford's strength at twelve hundred instead of the four hundred actually at hand, and he decided to await an attack on Brownsville—such strategy would give him better use of his infantry and artillery.[15]

Except for a thin screen of cavalry pickets, the way was now open to Ford. However, having no accurate estimate of Federal strength, "Old Rip" exercised prudence. For several weeks the force remained at Ringgold Barracks, preparing ammunition pouches, accumulating stores, wagons, and pack animals, and waiting for new companies to report to replace the ninety-day recruits. Regularly the Texan patrols scouted down the river road, but lack of grass and forage prevented them from effectively pursuing Mexican gangs engaged in driving stolen livestock across the river. Finally on July 19, his command reorganized and his supplies packed, Colonel Ford and fifteen hundred men moved out on the hundred-mile march to Brownsville.[16]

The first Union opposition developed on June 22 at the Ebonal Ranch, scene of the old Heintzelman-Cortina fight. "Old Rip" placed half the column in reserve and, though too ill to mount unaided, drove out the Union picket, pressing it hard down to the Brownsville city limits. His march upstream interrupted by a brief

[15] *Ibid.*, Vol. 34, pt. 1, 1054–56; pt. 4, 559–60; Ford, "Memoirs," VI, 1080–85. Warning of Ford's reconnaissance was carried to the Federals by the mulatto son of a white man named Weber, a neighbor to Young.

[16] *O. R.*, Ser. I, Vol. 41, pt. 2, 1001; Ford, "Memoirs," VI, 1009, 1102.

clash between his rear guard and a Federal scouting party, he halted for the night in a hastily prepared position astride the road. Next morning, leaving a picket on the road, he brought the two echelons of the Expeditionary Force together at Carricitos Ranch, twenty-two miles above Brownsville.

Having outrun his supply line, Ford was two days at Carricitos awaiting stores from Matamoros. Governor Cortina, although apparently favoring the Union cause, allowed his friends to engage in a lucrative trade with the Confederates, provided no Mexican goods crossed the Río Grande below Edinburg. Consequently, the further Ford moved down from that village, the longer and more exposed his communications became. He himself likened the region to "a kind of sack, and should the Federals by any sort of management have gotten a portion of their force above the Confederates, escape would have been extremely difficult, if not impossible." Prudence was expedient, the more so since Ford had learned that Herron had been ordered to evacuate Brownsville. Thus it appeared to the Colonel that his prime mission, expulsion of the Federal forces, would come about without his having to hurl his horsemen against the fire of entrenched enemy infantry and artillery.

Herron, however, was in no hurry. When a month dragged by with no evacuation begun, the Expeditionary Force, on July 25, moved down on Brownsville behind Showalter's advance guard. Ford halted the column a short distance above the town and sent dismounted riflemen forward to engage the Federals. The principal Texan firing line was in a depression with the inviting title of Dead Man's Hollow, half a mile above the western municipal limits. Ford's advance lines drove the Union defenders into town but, as he refused to move his men within artillery range and the Federal troops refused to advance beyond its protection, "A good deal of long taw firing was done . . . ," with no noticeable effect. Late in the evening, Ford called his men into camp a short way upstream.

From Matamoros, Confederates had come hurrying across the river to take a hand in the fight, among them Dr. Combe of the old Río Grande Squadron and elderly Colonel John M. Swisher, a San Jacinto veteran. Both fearlessly exposed themselves, particularly Swisher, who was mounted on a horse belonging to Combe. When a Union shot narrowly missed the old man, Combe called out, "Take care, Swisher, or you will get my horse killed."

Momentarily unappreciative of Combe's facetiousness, the old Colonel indignantly spluttered, "D-a-m your horse, don't you care if I get killed?"[17]

Several days of desultory outpost firing followed, but when Showalter, on the morning of July 30, carefully reconnoitered the town he found the Federals gone and the citizens, led by E. W. Cave, organized to preserve order. Reconnaissance of Fort Brown revealed that Herron had abandoned it too, and a trail of discarded equipment, leading eastward, indicated both the direction and the speed of his withdrawal. Captain W. N. Robinson and a part of Giddings' command followed the trail until they caught up with the Federal rear guard about fifteen miles below Fort Brown and drove it in on the main body. That night Robinson reported the Union troops to be concentrating on Brazos Santiago. On the next morning, after an absence of more than two years, "Rip" Ford again flew the Confederate banner over Fort Brown, where his family soon joined him.

Addie Ford's arrival was timely, for the illness which had beset him at Ringgold Barracks now had weakened him to the point where he was unable to sign his name.[18] While nothing exists to indicate the nature of the ailment, it may have been of a recurring kind which had caught him twice with Hays in Mexico, again during the Ford-Neighbors expedition of 1849, and possibly a fourth time during Ranger service in the early 1850's. That his condition had been a matter of concern to his superiors may be indicated by the comment in Bob Cotter's brief message to Governor Runnels at the close of the Canadian River expedition that "Capt. Ford is in good health and good spirits," a remark hardly

---

[17] Ford, "Memoirs," V, 1016–17; VI, 1101–1103.

[18] *O. R.*, Ser. I, Vol. 41, pt. 1, 185–86. During the period of severe illness, orders were signed by Captain James H. Fry, Ford's acting assistant adjutant general.

worth including in so short a communication unless there was specific reason for it.[19] The most recent attack previous to the one he now experienced was that which had brought him low while awaiting Magruder's approval of the Expeditionary Force.

Showalter, Ford's senior lieutenant colonel, had been given temporary command of field operations, but he, too, now claimed illness, and on July 31 Ford placed the Fourth Arizona under Fisher until Showalter recovered.[20]

Bedridden though he was, Ford still controlled the situation. From his cot he issued, over the signature of his adjutant, Captain James H. Fry, a stream of orders designated to consolidate the Confederate position and to keep the Federals under surveillance. He sent Showalter's regiment toward the Gulf to watch the Unionists. Showalter, recovered from his brief illness, bivouacked within six miles of Brazos Santiago and opened a daily series of outpost skirmishes. To this operation "Old Rip" gave close attention, since Showalter's "illness" had been a drunken condition which had prevented capture of the Union wagon train as the enemy withdrew from Fort Brown.[21] Furthermore, since drought had depleted pastures in spite of unusually heavy spring rains, Ford had to disperse all but about eighty men to locations where their horses could graze and recuperate. Several companies were detailed to operate a courier service from Fort Brown to King's Ranch, providing the Colonel with twelve-hour delivery of communications received there through messengers from sub-district headquarters at Houston.

As his strength returned, Ford opened a correspondence with General Cortina, expressing gratitude for considerations shown Confederate refugees and promising to reciprocate should Mexican developments reverse the General's situation.[22] With the Union withdrawal, Cortina had lifted his restrictions on the trans-

[19] Cotter to Runnels (n. d.), 1858, G. L.
[20] Special Order No. 110, Ford, General Orders.
[21] Ford, "Memoirs," VI, 1107–1108.
[22] Quoted in Ford, "Memoirs," VI, 1110–11.

river trade and apparently was in full sympathy with the Confederates. Ford still hoped to purchase Cortina's artillery, since rumors now indicated a major Imperialist effort against Matamoros, but still Cortina was undecided whether to run or fight. Ford also found it necessary to defend himself to Brigadier General Thomas Drayton, temporarily district commander, against the complaints of other commanding officers whose men had joined Ford. Some of Duff's men had deserted to Mexico, whereupon Magruder promised pardons to those who would return for service. F. W. Latham in Matamoros was in charge of arrangements and apparently informed the deserters they might join any Confederate command they wished. Most of them came to Ford, knowing that the Expeditionary Force, because of its peculiar composition and status, would not operate outside Texas. Men of other commands took advantage of the situation to leave their outfits, saying that they were going to join Ford. Of the latter sort, he claimed to have received few recruits; most of them simply went home or crossed into Mexico.[23]

On August 22, on his own authority, Ford assigned to Latham the duty of Confederate consular representative in Matamoros. Such an official, Ford foresaw, would be necessary. Events were shaping to determine whether *Imperialistas* or Juárez would control the lower river, and foreigners in Mexico would need the protection of their consuls. Already a French fleet, bearing an Imperialist force, tugged at its anchors off Bagdad (Boca del Río), the seaport village on the Mexican side of the river. On August 24, Ford sent Fisher and Major Waldemar Hyllested, district provost marshal, to Captain A. Véron, the French naval commander, to learn what would be the French attitude toward the Confederates, particularly those in Matamoros. Véron received the emissaries with courtesy and, to Ford's delight, assured "Old Rip" that he would see "that all persons and property covered by the flag of your nation are duly respected."[24] Ford's jubilant

[23] *O. R.*, Ser. I, Vol. 41, pt. 2, 994–96; Ford, "Memoirs," VI, 1115.
[24] *O. R.*, Ser. I, Vol. 41, pt. 2, 1089; pt. 3, 910–11.

report to department headquarters shows that he believed Véron's reply tantamount to French recognition of the Confederacy.[25]

Ford's pardonable jubilation was diminished almost immediately by other matters. There arose an unpleasant argument involving command prerogative. Colonel Benavides, hoping, apparently with some justification, to be promoted to brigadier, began acting in an independent capacity, occasionally countermanding Ford's orders for the disposition of certain troop units. Ford's complaints to higher headquarters were emphatic and explicit, and his messages to Benavides were not those of graceful diplomacy.[26] Furthermore, the unpredictable course of Juan Cortina in the face of the Imperialist threat presented a serious problem.

Late in August, as Mexican Imperialists under General Tomás Mejía moved north toward Matamoros, French troops landed at Bagdad to skirmish against Cortina's outposts. Showalter's men, based at Palmito Ranch on the southern rim of Palo Alto prairie, showed unrestrained enthusiasm for the French and thorough dislike for Mexicans by occasional long-range sniping over the river at Cortina's men, action which Showalter vehemently denied later. Their conduct probably was responsible for Mexican firing, a few days later, on Ford's men in the defensive work of Freeport, just above the Brownsville limits. Cortina, possibly encouraged by an understanding with Leonard Pierce, United States consul in Matamoros, and Colonel H. M. Day of the Ninety-first Illinois, commanding an estimated twelve hundred Federal troops on Brazos Island, now displayed hostility toward the Confederates. Ford heard a rumor that Cortina had been promised a commission as a United States brigadier general if he should capture Brownsville, an operation worth attempting should it become evident that he could not hold Matamoros against the Imperialists.

25 Ford to Captain J. E. Dwyer, August 29, 1864, Letter Book, August 24, 1864–December 30, 1864, of John S. Ford, Colonel Commanding Expeditionary Force, Museum of the United Daughters of the Confederacy, Austin, Texas. There are several books for different periods. Hereafter cited as Ford, Letter Book, with appropriate dates.

26 Ford to sub-district headquarters (n. d., but likely September 3–6, 1864), *ibid.*, August–December, 1864; Ford, "Memoirs," VI, 1126.

Pierce may have assured Cortina that if he crossed to strike at Brownsville from above, Union troops at Brazos would move up against Ford. At any rate, with the noose slowly tightening about him, on September 3 Cortina closed the river traffic to the Confederates and wheeled artillery pieces into position directly opposite Brownsville.[27]

When word came from Dr. Combe in Matamoros of Cortina's intentions, "Old Rip" sent George Giddings to reinforce Showalter, with orders to hold the lower line if at all possible.[28] An estimated six hundred Mexicans, with artillery, had gone upstream to cross and strike down the Río Grande City road. Ford was sure that if the enemy hit him front and rear, other Cortina men would swarm across the river from Matamoros.

The Union attack materialized on September 6, when Day's infantry and artillery moved to the mainland and engaged Showalter at Palmito. Cortina's artillery opened a heavy fire, from across the river, on the Confederate flank and the Fourth Arizona broke quickly. Ford refused to comment on the manner of Showalter's hasty retreat, but Colonel Day reported his foe as "flying in confusion."[29] Giddings arrived to rally the broken regiment, relieving Showalter at Ford's order, and organized a new defensive position several miles above Palmito.[30] A later investigation of the affair revealed that once too often Dan Showalter had tried to wash away in whisky the memories of an unfortunate love affair. His dismissal by Ford being upheld by a court-martial, the Fourth Arizona went under command of its major, F. E. Kavanaugh.[31] Kavanaugh would hold the line; for Day, although his troops were joined by certain Cortina units, was uncertain of numerical su-

[27] Ford, "Memoirs," V, 1022–23; VI, 1125; Ford to Dwyer, September 8, 1864, Ford, Letter Book, August–December, 1864; *Reports of the Committee of Investigation*, 151. The latter source is useful for events; careless printing makes it unsafe regarding specific dates.

[28] Ford to Showalter, September 6, 1864, Ford, Letter Book, August–December, 1864; Ford to Giddings, September 6, *ibid.*

[29] O. R., Ser. I, Vol. 41, pt. 1, 742.

[30] *Ibid.*, pt. 3, 946–47.

[31] Ford, "Memoirs," V, 1023, 1026–27; VI, 1142, 1158–59; Ford to Dwyer, September 8, 1864, Ford, Letter Book, August–December, 1864.

periority. Too, the western road was a morass after heavy rains; Day stood fast at Palmito.

Ford, meanwhile, had spent the day in amateur theatricals. He had been able to collect no more than three hundred men at Brownsville, but, borrowing a leaf from Magruder's operations manual, he made his numbers appear much greater by keeping his men continually on the move, sometimes in their coats, again in shirt sleeves. He himself remained constantly in view from Matamoros, his grizzled, curling hair and beard identifying him unmistakably to the watching Mexicans. As night came down, bringing with it the severest thunderstorm of the year, he turned his attention toward the safety of his family, now increased by the birth of a second daughter, Addie. He sent them to the sanctuary of a Brownsville convent maintained by the Sisters of the Incarnate Word. Mrs. Ford, it appears, was of the same mettle as her husband; before dawn she had returned to share his dangers.

The precarious military situation was no secret at Fort Brown. For once, as he impatiently paced his headquarters throughout the stormy night, Ford wondered about the morale of his command. Shortly before dawn he went to awake his troopers. Splashing to the nearest barracks, he thrust his head inside, summoned the sleepers, and stepped back into the dark to watch their reaction. Promptly, positively it came. A weathered former mountain man leaped erect from his blankets, slapping his chest and issuing the defiant rooster crow of his breed. "Hurra boys," he bawled, "by G-o-d, Old Rip is going to fight." Ford's uncharacteristic pessimism evaporated as he strode off to the other barracks.

Dawn came but not the anticipated attack. The rolling river, at high flood stage above Brownsville, had prevented the Mexicans from crossing. Had the dynamic Cortina led the complement, an effort might have been made, but the General had remained in Matamoros, faced with a near mutiny. His ranking colonel, Servando Canales, had flatly refused to lead his regiment against John Ford, his *compañero* from the days of the Plan of La Loba.

Ford's sharp note demanding an explanation for Cortina's hostile conduct drew an evasive reply, and the cannon which had frowned so ominously toward Brownsville shortly disappeared.[32] Ford now turned his attention to the Palmito situation. Giddings, now a colonel since his unit had increased beyond battalion strength, sent word on the morning of September 9 that he was moving down to meet a Union advance. In forwarding Giddings' report, Ford noted that he himself was preparing to defend Brownsville, in case of Giddings' repulse, "until the last brick is knocked from its place."[33] In the early afternoon, the Federals fell back about eight miles before Giddings' attack, leaving arms, equipment, and casualties "by dozens" upon the field. After halting briefly while his left flank swung around through the chaparral to pin down the Union right rear, Giddings again moved in to open a two-hour fight which ended at sundown. Failure of an ammunition train to reach him early in the morning caused a delay which permitted his enemy to slip back to Palmito, where he encountered their pickets at dusk. On the morning of September 11, his reconnaissance force maintained a running skirmish with the Federal rear guard below Palmito, but he held off from a major attack, choosing not to expose his men to artillery fire while crossing the intervening swampy terrain.

He had no need to attack next morning. The Federals continued their retreat across the narrow channel to Brazos Island and the shelter of their guns, and Giddings was able to report that "The river is now free and open to trade so far as the Yankees are concerned."[34] He had lost only a few killed and wounded and three missing. Ford estimated the Union casualties, including desertions, at the possibly exaggerated figure of 550. Among Giddings' prisoners were men of the *Exploradores del Bravo* regiment of Colonel Echarzetta's corps in Cortina's army. When informed by Colonel Day that they were United States volunteers, Ford treated the Mexicans as prisoners of war rather than as brigands.[35]

At the request of the again-ailing Colonel, who anticipated a

[32] Ford, "Memoirs," V, 1024; VI, 1129–31.

[33] Ford to Agent Ross, September 9, 7 P.M., 1864, Ford, Letter Book, August–December, 1864.

[34] Quoted in Ford, "Memoirs," VI, 1134–38.

[35] *O. R.*, Ser. I, Vol. 41, pt. 3, 947; Ford, "Memoirs," VI, 1142.

Union counteroffensive, General Drayton temporarily moved his Western Sub-District headquarters from Houston to Fort Brown. Drayton did not interfere with Ford as field commander nor with the latter's negotiations with Cortina, who had become increasingly more tractable since Giddings' victory. On September 23, Cortina invited Ford to Matamoros to discuss a resumption of political and commercial intercourse between the two governments. When Ford's Texans learned that he had accepted the invitation, they feared treachery and excitedly forbade him to go. "After considerable expostulation," he won their consent by buckling on his pistols and stationing riflemen in buildings directly opposite the Matamoros ferry landing, where the meeting was to occur. Cortina greeted "Old Rip" with the characteristic Mexican *abrazo*, and the two commanders quickly reached an agreement to resume the former amicable international relationship. Drayton, confident that the border was in competent hands, ratified the Ford-Cortina pact and returned to Houston.

Within the week, however, a new situation across the river erased the agreement. The opportunistic Cortina agreed to surrender Matamoros without a fight if the Imperialists would accept his allegiance and if they would occupy the city with Mexican troops only. Captain Véron, on behalf of the French, accepted the terms, and on September 29, Mejía's army marched in, almost interning "Rip" Ford in the process.[36] Ford, assured by Cortina that Mejía would not enter until September 30, had come over in another attempt to buy Cortina's field guns. He caught the ferry barely ahead of the Imperialists and believed for years afterward that Cortina had connived to effect his capture. Ford did not flee alone; certain of Cortina's officers accompanied him. Colonels Julian Cerda and Mariano Hidalgo and Major José Puente refused to renounce Juárez. They crossed with their commands to Texas, sold their arms to Ford, and were granted sanctuary while awaiting an opportunity to return to their homeland under more favorable circumstances.

[36] Ford to Ross, September 9, 1864, Ford, Letter Book, August–December, 1864; Ford, "Memoirs," V, 1028–29; VI, 1143; *O. R.*, Ser. I, Vol. 41, pt. 3, 721–22, 958.

Now that Ford and his Texans had ridded all the lower valley except Brazos Island of Federals, the Confederate War Department felt the time had come for its officers to resume direct authority in the region. Ford's military achievements were beyond logical criticism, and his diplomacy, which had re-established the vital flow of goods to the severed, western portion of the Confederacy, was all that Richmond reasonably could expect. Nevertheless, in late October, Lieutenant Colonel Matt Nolan appeared at Fort Brown with orders from district headquarters to remuster into Confederate service Giddings' regiment and another organized by Ford from independently recruited companies of conscription-exempt men. Nolan was to assign sufficient remustered men to Benavides' regiment to raise it to brigade proportions, thereby clearing the way for Benavides' promotion to brigadier general, a step logical enough to the Confederate War Department since the promotion might strengthen the loyalty of the Mexicans in Confederate ranks. Protesting bitterly, Ford pointed out to Nolan that many of his men, after deserting to Mexico, had returned on condition that they would serve only under him, and that many men in both regiments were neither subject to conscription nor enlisted for any specified time. He warned Nolan that should an attempt be made to carry out the remuster, most of these men would refuse to remain, the entire command would be demoralized and the area again be vulnerable for Union occupation. Since his orders demanded that he make the attempt, Nolan rode with Ford to Giddings' camp, where they explained the mission. Convinced by the indignant reaction of Giddings' men that Ford had accurately analyzed the situation, Nolan made no further attempt to fulfill the assignment. Benavides, however soon came down to Fort Brown to discuss the matter with Ford, but returned to Río Grande City after disclaiming any intention of depleting Ford's units for his own ends.[37] The friction among commanders was allayed somewhat after Brigadier General James E. Slaughter established his Western Sub-District headquarters at Fort Brown about the first of November. By the end of the year he had re-

[37] Ford, "Memoirs," VI, 1143–44, 1146, 1164–67.

organized the sub-district assignments, leaving Ford to command the Southern Division from Fort Brown and creating a Western Division, comprising the Río Grande City–Laredo area, under Benavides.[38] The Northern Division, including Corpus Christi, became Pyron's responsibility. Although Ford's area of command had been reduced, all efforts to dismiss him and to dismember his unusual regiment had failed.

With his routine now principally that of administration, Ford soon established cordial relations with Mejía, whose character he greatly admired, and the stocky Indian was as amenable to Confederate overtures as Cortina had been. Ford's own sympathies in Mexican affairs, on account of his sincere dislike of autocracy, lay with Juárez; his official attitude, however, was dictated by the necessities of the Confederacy, and to that end he negotiated with admirable success.

Day's troops at Brazos Santiago now offered only occasional outpost skirmishes, although the situation at the river mouth remained a tense stalemate, so much so that when Commodore Raphael Semmes, the John Paul Jones of the Confederacy, appeared at Brownsville on his circuitous way to Richmond, Ford's characteristic prudence saw that the Commodore rode northward with no less than a twenty-trooper escort.[39] The tension eased, however, in the spring of 1865 when an unusual agreement effectively took the lower Río Grande area out of the Civil War.

The border truce grew out of the mixed ambitions of the Indiana politician, editor, author, and major general of volunteers, Lew Wallace. Shunted from field service under suspicion of dilatory tactics at Shiloh, he later had been appointed to the Union's Middle Department, with headquarters in Baltimore, because Lincoln needed his political support. Anxious to regain the public eye and interested in Mexico since Mexican War days, Wallace saw in the Maximilian-Juárez struggle and the Confederate reoccupation of the lower Río Grande Valley an opportunity suited to his

[38] *O. R.*, Ser. I, Vol. 41, pt. 4, 1138; pt. 1, 1311–12.
[39] Special Order No. 169, Ford, General Orders.

aspirations. He hoped, given enough official latitude, to restore lower Texas to the Union, perhaps the entire Trans-Mississippi Department as well, and at the same time to provide for Juárez a combined Union-Confederate force to drive imperial troops from northern Mexico. By the beginning of 1865, he apparently had communicated his plan to General Grant, but became more insistent in the middle of January upon the arrival in Baltimore from Matamoros of an old Indiana friend, S. S. Brown. Wallace wrote to Grant on January 14, explaining the situation at Matamoros and Brownsville as Brown had pictured it and suggested that, under the pretext of making an inspection tour, he be allowed to attempt negotiations with the Confederates and Juárez' party. With the approval of President Lincoln, to whom details of the missions probably were presented in deliberately vague form, and of Secretary of State William H. Seward, Grant on January 22 issued the order which sent Wallace westward to develop his intrigue.

Exactly a month later, Wallace reported optimistically to Grant from New Orleans. Union officers there had informed him that morale and discipline were low among Texans on the lower Río Grande, a condition which Slaughter had gloomily admitted, and that they were eager for the war to end. By March 6, Wallace was at Brazos Santiago, whence he had sent a civilian deputy, Charles Worthington, to Matamoros to negotiate with Slaughter. Worthington officially asked Slaughter to agree to discuss with Wallace, under a flag of truce, the mutual rendition of criminals. He reported that his actual mission, that of obtaining Slaughter's agreement to discuss "other matters," was successful. Consequently, on March 11, Wallace and Worthington met Slaughter and Ford at Point Isabel, across a narrow strait from Brazos Island. The tents and some $600 worth of "refreshments" which Wallace brought may have contributed to the amity and concord of the conference, which extended late into the next afternoon.[40] To his wife Wallace wrote that if his Indiana constituents could have seen him and Slaughter "lie down to sleep upon the same blanket,

[40] *O. R.*, Ser. I, Vol. 43, pt. 1, 512, 837–38, 1276–79, 1353–55; Vol. 46, pt. 2, 201.

as quietly as two children in the same little bed, I fear my character for loyalty would be forever lost—certainly I could never get to Congress from the 8th Judicial District."[41]

Hoping to arrange a separate peace with the Confederate Trans-Mississippi Department, Wallace proposed that if the Confederates would cease opposition to the federal government and take an oath of allegiance to the United States, they would be granted full amnesty. Those who spurned the oath would be permitted to emigrate, without interference, to any country they might select. There would be no interference with private property legally held at the beginning of the war, except that the final disposition of slave property would be determined by the United States government.

No surrender of Confederate arms was called for, probably because these would be important to the Mexican project which Wallace now outlined to the Confederates and to which he reported them fully receptive. He explained that military aid could not be sent to Juárez until a formal treaty had been enacted with the Trans-Mississippi Department. Slaughter expressed the opinion that the best way for Confederates to assure themselves of a welcome return to the Union would be to come dragging behind them a number of conquered Mexican states. To this suggestion Ford offered no comment, but he must have seen that once the war had ended, the desire for French recognition of the Confederacy would be irrelevant and that, no longer required to pretend friendship for the Imperialists, he could throw himself wholeheartedly into a struggle for democratic principles. Privately Ford told Wallace that he suspected Kirby-Smith of negotiating with Maximilian, possibly with a view to Imperial annexation of Texas. What, Wallace wondered, would be Ford's attitude if such an attempt should be made? Without hesitation came "Old Rip"'s answer: he would lead a counterrevolution against Kirby-Smith.

Wallace made it clear to Ford and Slaughter that while he had no official authority to make his proposals, he was confident that

[41] Quoted in Irving McKee, *"Ben-Hur" Wallace, the Life of General Lew Wallace*, 93.

his government would accept such an agreement, since Lincoln, Seward, and Grant had sanctioned his journey. Furthermore, should Lincoln prove recalcitrant, he might be supplanted by a military dictatorship willing to compromise. Wallace reported the Confederate commanders anxious to find some basis on which they could withdraw from the war with honor, and consequently showing deep interest in his proposals.

Very early in the interview I made up my mind that both General Slaughter and Colonel Ford were not only willing but anxious to find some ground upon which they could honorably get from under a failing Confederacy. In justice to them, I will add that both went into the rebellion reluctantly. I will say further that General Slaughter placed his dispositions to bring about an accommodation upon grounds of humanity and an unwillingness to see his State invaded and ruined and the war decline into guerrilla murders. He and Ford insisted that they could procrastinate the final result indefinitely, but at the same time frankly admitted that if that were done the North would ultimately conquer the South as a desert. When I urged that in the present situation of the war west of the Mississippi that they could not reasonably hope for assistance from Richmond and their eastern armies; that they were practically isolated; that as a consequence their highest obligations were to their Trans-Mississippi army and citizens, whose honor and welfare they were charged with and alone bound to regard, they agreed with me without hesitation and asked me to give them such propositions as would cover those objects and at the same time be likely to prove acceptable to our government.

It was agreed that Ford should carry the propositions immediately to General E. Kirby-Smith, commanding the Trans-Mississippi Department. Ford was to go first to Galveston, where he would arrange for the landing of Wallace and E. J. Davis of Cameron County, now a Union brigadier general. The three then would seek an interview with Kirby-Smith. The optimistic Wallace wrote Grant that his propositions ultimately would be accepted, particularly because of the co-operation of Ford, who was, he believed, "politically the most influential Confederate soldier in

Texas." This comment alone indicated how little understanding of the Texas situation Wallace actually had achieved.

For reasons not officially recorded, Slaughter suddenly absented himself from headquarters, leaving Ford nominally as well as actually in command and thus making it impossible for the Colonel to proceed upon the agreed mission.[42] Ford sent Wallace's proposals "under the seal of secrecy" to Kirby-Smith by Colonel Fairfax Gray. When they reached district headquarters, Major General J. G. Walker ignored the seal, opened them, made them public, and sent reproving letters not only to Ford and Slaughter but to Wallace as well. Walker wondered (logically, it would appear) that an officer of Wallace's rank should "be reduced to the necessity of seeking an obscure corner of the Confederacy to inaugurate negotiations." Stung by the reproof, Wallace retorted that he doubted that "accident or policy has located all the sane men of your Confederacy in its obscure corners," and requested that the proposals be forwarded to their original destination. But, as Wallace commented to Grant, Walker belonged to the "last ditch school," and with the acrimonious exchange of correspondence the ambitious peace negotiator's mission closed. He abandoned his waiting outside Galveston harbor, returned to Baltimore, and there, on April 18, wrote his final report to Grant, admitting his failure and, recalling the number of masts he had seen behind the Galveston breakwater, implying that Walker was making too great a personal profit from blockade runners to desire an end to hostilities.[43]

Although he reported immediately after the interviews that he suspected Wallace of trying to divide the Confederacy, Ford observed much later that he felt the South should have accepted the proposals.

> The suggestion of Gen. Wallace that the armies should not be disbanded until after a formal treaty of peace had been concluded

[42] O. R., Ser. I, Vol. 43, pt. 1, 1166–67, 1276–82; pt. 2, 459. More details of the Mexican scheme were explained to Ford by Wallace in several private conferences of which Slaughter apparently was ignorant.

[43] Ibid., pt. 1, 1275–76; pt. 2, 457–58, 462; Ford, "Memoirs," VII, 1181.

and ratified was a true one. The days of reconstruction as things occurred in the South, were terrible proofs of the evils arising from the contrary course. . . . Better it would have been for the Confederate States to have accepted the terms proposed by Gen. Wallace than to have disbanded its armies, surrendered at discretion, and become the prey of unprincipled men.

During the Point Isabel conversations, Wallace incidentally remarked that since military operations along the Río Grande could not possibly alter the outcome of the war, he felt that hostilities there should cease by mutual agreement. The Confederate officers concurred. For the next two months the rival commanders respected the agreement, allowing a "no man's land" between them in the vicinity of Palo Alto prairie and Palmito.[44] On May 12, however, almost five weeks after Appomattox, the opposing forces clashed at Palmito Ranch in the last battle of the war.

At that time, Colonel Theodore H. Barrett (Sixty-second Colored Infantry) temporarily commanded the Brazos garrison. Besides his own regiment, his troops included the Thirty-fourth Indiana, the Morton Rifles (a New York regiment), several dismounted companies of Colonel John L. Haynes's Texas Cavalry, made up largely of deserters from the Confederate ranks (Haynes himself was a Brownsville man), and several artillery companies. Barrett, having seen little if any combat service, was obsessed by a desire "to establish for himself some notoriety before the war closed." In the absence of the post commander, Brigadier General E. B. Brown, Barrett requested permission to make a demonstration against Fort Brown, but was emphatically refused by department headquarters. Ignoring the advice of Lieutenant Colonel David Branson of the Indiana regiment, Barrett resolved to attack Ford's command anyway.[45]

At sunup of May 12, Barrett sent his colored infantry upriver. At dusk they were halted at Palmito by Giddings' regiment. When the Federal movement was reported to Fort Brown, "Old Rip"

[44] Ford, "Memoirs," VII, 1174–81, 1185–86, 1189.
[45] *New York Times*, June 18, 1865. The cited material is a letter of May 17, 1865, by a quartermaster officer of the Thirty-fourth Indiana.

sent couriers speeding through the night to call in his cavalry companies, which had been scattered so their mounts could graze. He then sat down to supper with Slaughter, intending to explain his plans to the General. To his dismay, he found that Slaughter, whose military capacity seems to have been limited to writing critical reports about his subordinates, was completely demoralized by the news; he had seized every vehicle he could find, had loaded his personal effects into a confiscated carriage, and had decided to order a general retreat. "Rip" Ford's blue eyes gleamed frostily across the table as he issued his flat defiance of the fearful General: "You can retreat and go to hell if you wish. These are my men and I am going to fight."[46]

Ford's artillery horses were grazing some twenty miles up the river, but by eleven o'clock next morning the rattling, jouncing caissons spun onto the Fort Brown parade ground, whereupon "Old Rip" and his cavalry mounted and moved out. A four-hour march brought him within four miles of Palmito, where he found Giddings' men retiring slowly before the heavy fire of the strong Federal skirmish line, Indiana and New York riflemen commanded by Lieutenant Colonel Robert G. Morrison, regiments tired by an all night march with Barrett to overtake the advance. Concealing his mounted men in a clump of timber, Ford waited until the infantry had drawn the Union skirmishers far ahead of their main body. Then he sent Captain W. N. Robinson into an infantry counterattack on the Federal left flank, while two other companies pressed on the right and the Texas field guns, including an Imperialist battery loaned by Captain Véron for the occasion, opened a devastating blast.[47]

As balls from the Union Springfields lashed the thickets around them, "Old Rip" addressed his impatient Texans. "Men, we have whipped the enemy in all previous fights. We can do it again." The troopers roared eagerly; Ford bawled "Charge," and with three hundred horsemen he swept in to cut off the Federal skirmishers. Over the deep roar of their galloping assault shrilled the Texas yell, "the earnest voice of every man to every other one

[46] Ford, "Memoirs," VII, 1190.   [47] *New York Times*, June 18, 1865.

238

in the line for united action to gather as one man. Such a yell exploded on the air, and coalescing into one combined sound, has been distinctly heard three miles across the prairie, over the reports of the musketry and cannon of the raging battle."[48]

The Union skirmish line had advanced too far from its support when halted by the disastrous fire of Ford's field pieces. Through the torn ranks plunged Ford's charge, riding down the battle-hardened New York and Hoosier infantrymen and taking prisoners by the score. Colonel Barrett departed precipitately without ordering the skirmishers to retire, although he recalled the rest of his force. Three times during the seven-mile retreat to the protection of their guns at Boca Chica Point the Union troops made temporary stands, and thrice "Rip" Ford's bellowing cannon sped them on their way anew while the Texas horsemen stormed against the stumbling rear. With dusk dropping, Ford suspended pursuit as the remnant of the shattered Federal command splashed across a marshy inlet to Brazos Santiago.[49]

As an anticlimax, General Slaughter now came spurring up at the head of Captain W. H. D. Carrington's battalion, having been detained, Ford later learned, by the threat of a Cortina attack on Brownsville. Finding that Ford flatly refused to continue a profitless pursuit, Slaughter led the battalion on to Boca Chica Strait, where, to Carrington's amazement and probable disgust, the vainglorious General rode into the slough and emptied his pistol at the retreating Federals, three hundred yards away.[50]

To avoid any surprise retaliation, Ford withdrew his men into bivouac ten miles below Fort Brown. Then he summed up the results of the fight. Considering the magnitude of the encounter, his own casualties were negligible: he had no dead; of Giddings'

---

[48] Captain W. H. D. Carrington, quoted in John Henry Brown, *History of Texas*, II, 435–36; O. M. Roberts, "History of the War in Texas, 1861–1865," (MS, Roberts Papers, Barker Center, U. T.).

[49] *New York Times*, June 18, 1865. Barrett later preferred charges against Morrison, who was exonerated by a court-martial for which Ford crossed from Matamoros to testify; Ford, "Memoirs," V, 1031–33; Brown, *History of Texas*, II, 431–36.

[50] Brown, *History of Texas*, II, 431–36.

regiment, longest under fire, there were seven wounded, only one seriously; there were even fewer casualties among the men "Old Rip" had led into battle. By contrast, the Federal units had suffered heavily, the Thirty-fourth Indiana alone losing 220 of its complement of 300. Ford had captured 111 enlisted men and four officers, all of whom he paroled and permitted to return to the Brazos garrison because of the expense of feeding them. One trophy which the Texans proudly displayed was the regimental colors of the Indianans. Their color sergeant, in the last stages of the retreat, had wrapped the flag around him and plunged into the slough. Killed as he swam, he sank to the bottom, from where a Texan dragged the body and returned with the flag.[51]

Among the captives were some from the Sixty-second (Colored) Regiment, who were "agreeably surprised when they were paroled and permitted to depart with the white prisoners." However, there is conflicting testimony concerning certain other prisoners. Some twenty years later, with an eye toward posterity, Ford wrote of these:

> Several of them were from Texas. This made no difference in their treatment. Some were taken who had deserted from the command on the lower Rio Grande. The most of these were allowed to escape on the march up to Brownsville. The confederate soldiers were unwilling to see them tried as deserters. . . . Several of the prisoners were from Austin and vicinity. They were assured they would be treated as prisoners of war. There was no disposition to visit upon them, or any of the captured, a mean spirit of revenge. The right to choose, to follow the bent of opinion, was recognized and accorded.[52]

Not so did the paroled prisoners report. Reaching Brazos Island on May 17, with the memory of the combat still vividly before them, they stated: "There was a company of Texans [probably Haynes's men] made up mostly of deserters from the rebels. As fast as these were captured they were shot down. Neither would

51 *New York Times*, June 18, 1865. It may have been this Indiana flag which Ford later took to display over his house in Matamoros for protection.
52 Ford, "Memoirs," VII, 1197.

the deserters surrender, for they knew it would be death, and so died fighting." The paroled men reported that they themselves were well treated, and provided the thought-provoking information that "the rebel general had told one of our captains that if the white regiment [the Morton Rifles] had come up alone they would have surrendered to us, but that they would never surrender to niggers. They said they believed the war was played out, but thought this was a good opportunity to give us a whipping."[53]

Several days after the battle, Ford received from General Brown at Brazos Island the news that the Confederacy east of the Mississippi had collapsed and that the war was, in effect, at an end. "Old Rip" at first expressed pointed disbelief, but when examination revealed the reports irrefutable, he vented an impressive oration of lyric profanity. As gradually he came to realize the absurdity of the situation, his expletives gave way to a ringing roar of laughter.[54] Yet, until Kirby-Smith, commanding the Trans-Mississippi Department, should capitulate, Ford would faithfully exercise his trusteeship of the lower Río Grande Valley.

Peace again came to the river, and with it an exchange of courtesies. A few days after the battle, half a dozen Union officers rode in to pay a friendly call. A visiting major accompanied Ford home for a refreshing glass of eggnog. As the guest smacked his lips over the welcome beverage, he commented, "If my wife knew I was at the house of a Confederate colonel, and accepting his friendly hospitality, she would be so mad she would hardly speak to me." To provide his visitors further entertainment and also to cause consternation among the French over the river, against whom he probably retained resentment because of their government's failure to recognize the Confederacy, Ford and his adjutant, Captain Dix, arranged a visit to Matamoros for their congenial enemies. One Sunday morning when Ford knew that Mejía had scheduled a review of his Imperial troops, the mixed group

[53] *New York Times*, June 18, 1865. However the son of Judge John Hancock, a Texas Unionist who had helped to organize the regiment, was among those paroled by Ford.

[54] Hobart Huson, *Refugio, A Comprehensive History of Refugio County from Aboriginal Times to 1955*, II, 119.

of Americans crossed to the Mexican bank of the Río Grande. Stationing themselves across the plaza from Mejía's reviewing position, they watched the Mexicans march by. To Ford's amusement, as each rank passed, the soldiers craned to gaze at the mingled knot of blue and gray uniforms, the ranks consequently assuming the form of an arc rather than retaining their proper straight alignment. When the review ended, Ford took his guests to breakfast, deliberately selecting the restaurant operated by John Clinch, where the French officers habitually dined. Calling for a room in the rear of the French dining room, Ford coolly led his party past the Frenchmen, who sprang to their feet in amazed wonder to see the American enemies in friendly concourse. The buzzing which arose indicated that Ford had sprung a signal diplomatic surprise. The French, feeling secure from United States interference while the Civil War continued, besieged Ford upon his exit, to learn the implications of the visit. Inwardly delighted, the bronzed Colonel only increased their confusion by blandly assuring them that the situation across the river was still unchanged—he was merely entertaining a few friends.[55]

In the brief time remaining to the Confederacy on the lower Río Grande, Ford and Slaughter took positions widely separated concerning what the future course should be. Slaughter and a few adherents desired to resist to the last and then cross over to join the Imperialists, eventually pursuing the latter aim. Ford and most of his men, other considerations apart, favored the Juárez government and hoped for an early peace and the possibility of participating with Union troops in driving out Maximilian's forces. This much General Brown learned through official correspondence with Slaughter and secret communications with Ford. By late May, even Slaughter recognized the inevitable and took steps to get as much out of the situation for himself as possible. He was on excellent terms with Mejía, who had offered to send his lancers over the river in civilian clothes on May 13 to help Slaughter defend Brownsville from Cortina. Now that the war was over, Slaughter transported his artillery to Matamoros and sold it to

[55] Ford, "Memoirs," VII, 1197–99.

Mejía. Almost immediately, Ford and his men learned of the transaction. They seized Slaughter and confined him until he negotiated the transfer of some $20,000 in silver (most of the price of the guns) to "Old Rip," who then released him and distributed the money among the Texans for more than a year's arrears of pay. Ford retained $4,000 as his own pay, an amount less than that actually due him. On May 26, by Slaughter's last order, command of the district was transferred to Ford, who thus became the last Confederate authority on the lower river.[56] On the same day, with his men drifting away to their homes or crossing the river with him, Colonel John Ford took his family to Matamoros, where, with Mejía's consent, he had rented a house.[57]

Ford's last official act for the Confederacy came with the surrender of Kirby-Smith and the Trans-Mississippi Department. Kirby-Smith capitulated on June 2, and on that day Magruder, commanding the District of Texas, designated Ford as one of the officers to arrange with Union occupation commanders the paroles of former Confederates. The Federal commander at Brownsville was General Frederick Steele. Through the able liaison of Lieutenant Richard Strong of Steele's staff, a cousin of Mrs. Ford, a friendly relationship between Steele and Ford quickly sprang up, and "Old Rip" was able to carry out his last assignment without molestation. He worked at the task conscientiously, arranging for the paroles of many refugees in Matamoros, including Richard King, Mifflin Kenedy, and Major Blücher, who earlier had been cashiered for drunkenness.[58]

[56] *Ibid.*, 1211; *New York Times*, June 18, 1865; *O. R.*, Ser. I, Vol. 43, pt. 2, 564–65, 727–28, 813–14, 827–28, 841; Slaughter, Unnumbered Special Order, May 26, 1865, Ford, General Orders.

[57] Ford, "Memoirs," VII, 1212. Mejía supported Ford in resisting the demands of a French officer that the house be surrendered for troop use. Ford afterward told Mejía that if he had endorsed the attempt of the French officer, he (Ford) "would have at once crossed the Rio Grande, and the Imperials would have been lucky to get good sleep for one night even."

[58] Magruder, unnumbered order, June 2, 1865, *O. R.*, Ser. I, Vol. 43, pt. 2, 727–28; Ford, "Memoirs," VII, 1214. Blücher had been in Matamoros since the preceding fall, having been dismissed as chief of staff by Ford for drunkenness on September 30, 1865. Ford, Letter Book, August–December, 1864.

Ford's own parole, listing his home as Austin, became effective on July 18, 1865,[59] but he did not immediately take advantage of it. For more than a month after his work ended he remained in Matamoros, wondering what to do now. Dissatisfied though he was with the results of the war, he could see no future for a Southerner in a foreign land, and, as he explained later, he felt that honor dictated that he share the problems of the men who willingly had followed where he led. Abandoning a first impulse to remain an immigrant, he settled down in Brownsville in the late summer of 1865 and began to search for threads which he might weave into a postwar career.[60]

[59] War Dept., Ford Records.

[60] Ford, "Memoirs," VII, 1213–14. The fact that Matamoros was threatened with a siege by Cortina probably accounted for Ford's moving his family back to Brownsville as early as he did.

10

The Postwar Years

THE SUMMER OF 1865 found John S. Ford in seemingly hopeless circumstances. Two years of campaigning had left him too broken in health to provide for his family, and the Mexican silver dollars he had retained as his colonel's pay soon vanished. Border ties, however, were strong; Richard King, appreciatively remembering "Old Rip"'s services to border men and the border, came secretly to his aid, and monthly, for two years, Ford found his rent paid and $250 deposited mysteriously to his bank credit.[1]

As his health improved, there came an opportunity for Ford to capitalize on his military prowess. José Carbajal, who had been in New York negotiating with Lew Wallace for a military force to go to Juárez' aid under the guise of a colonization scheme, reappeared in Brownsville in the spring of 1866 and opened discussions with General Mejía in Matamoros. Mejía wished to withdraw in the face of rising anti-Maximilian sentiment. Upon the promise that he could depart with the honors of war, he removed his imperial troops from the city on June 2. Immediately Carbajal marched in and proclaimed himself the *Juárezista* governor. Cognizant that his position was precarious, he turned for help to his former brigadier, remembering that when Ford called for volunteers, eager Texans seemed to spring from the very earth. Accordingly, he offered Ford the rank of brigadier if "Old Rip" would join him with one of his characteristic fighting units.

Ford was willing, provided he could obtain official permission

[1] Lea, *The King Ranch*, II, 241–42.

to cross into Mexico. He sought consent from Major General Philip H. Sheridan, who had established his headquarters at Fort Brown preparatory to moving against Napoleon III's French troops if they stayed in Mexico. To Ford's request, Sheridan replied that he did not favor permitting those with unfriendly sentiments toward the United States to go abroad. Ford's response was that he had no intention of enlisting any man inimical to United States interests or disloyal in sentiment, but Sheridan had no right to expect that men who had been defeated in a great war should be satisfied with their defeat. Permission for the project was extracted when, at the end of Ford's guileless statement, the famous cavalryman grumbled grudgingly, "Well, go long. I suppose you will do right."[2]

With more than one hundred rapidly assembled adventurers, Ford crossed the Río Grande to take up garrison duties at one of the small forts forming the Matamoros defense perimeter. But unanticipated difficulties soon arose. On August 12, while Ford was visiting Lew Wallace at Carbajal's headquarters, the General burst in to inform them that a counterrevolution had erupted. Ford stepped into the street, hailed a carriage, and rattled away to his fort. Carbajal quickly sought refuge in Brownsville. The insurgents, declaring for Servando Canales, Carbajal's foster son, seized the confused Wallace but released him at the end of the two-hour bloodless *coup d'état.*[3]

Ford feared an attack from the Mexican troops, who resented Carbajal's favoritism toward the Texans. Instead there came a deputation to request that he confer with Canales. When the two old friends sat down to discuss the situation, Ford learned that Canales intended to adhere to the Juárez government. He readily accepted the rank of brigadier with the new Tamaulipas administration, a change of allegiance most confusing to his Austin acquaintances.[4]

---

[2] Ford, "Memoirs," VII, 1217–18.

[3] McKee, *Wallace,* 105; Bancroft, *Works,* XIV, 252–55.

[4] *Southern Intelligencer* (Austin), September 6, 1866; Ford, "Memoirs," VII, 1219.

The situation actually was more complicated than either Canales or Ford realized at the time. Juárez, displeased by the liberal terms Carbajal had granted Mejía, on August 5 had ordered Santiago Tapía to replace the old General. When news of Tapía's appointment finally reached Matamoros on October 2, Canales refused to honor it. His refusal to relinquish command placed Ford and his Texans in a compromising position: if they continued under Canales, they would be committed to fight the administration they had come to support. The Texans, restless anyway because they had not yet seen a payday, informed Ford that they intended to release a Juárez emissary imprisoned by Canales. After conferring with his officers on board a steamer Carbajal had converted into a gunboat, Ford agreed to attack Canales' headquarters on the main plaza, although his heart was not in the operation.[5] The attack was a night affair, launched during a booming thunderstorm. Convenient illness kept Ford from the scene, but when the assault was repulsed after a great deal of wild, harmless firing, "Old Rip" supervised the safe crossing of his men to Texas soil. The Texans then disbanded, content to let the Mexican rivals find their own solution to the Tamaulipas question. To his indignation, Ford learned that the attempt against Canales was seen by certain other Texans as a freebooter's effort to plunder the Matamoros treasury for the pay promised but never issued to the volunteers.

The doings of General Ford and Admiral Osborn [B. S. Osbon], the one commanding an army of 175 Americans and 13 Mexicans, and the other a gunboat, manned by eight as gallant tars as ever drank rum, are notorious. They were to capture Matamoros, seize the treasury, and pay themselves the wages due. It is not to be supposed that if successful, they would have been careful to return the odd change that might have been left over. A terrific storm arose, which drove the gunboat to the American side, where her gallant crew got drunk as princes. The navy was drunk, and Ford had to abandon his undertaking. Canales got out his cannon and threatened, although the boat was in sanctuary on the American side. Thereupon

[5] Ford, "Memoirs," VII, 1220.

the brave Admiral surrendered her to the American authorities, by whom she is retained a subject for litigation.[6]

Such was one view of Ford's final militant excursion into Mexican political affairs.

Thereafter Ford occupied himself in his own community. For a time he served as an editorial assistant to Somers Kinney of the Brownsville *Ranchero*, later transferring his services to the rival *Courier*. During the winter of 1866–67, he served as foreman of the federal grand jury in the Brownsville district. He was on good terms with Generals Frederick Steele, Alexander McCook, and Henry Clitz, successive Federal commanders at Fort Brown, and placed his invaluable knowledge of the border at their disposal. When his health permitted, he was employed as a guide for the cavalry companies which patrolled continually in an effort to suppress the tremendous wave of cattle theft plaguing the border. Finally, in 1868, Ford and Jesse E. Dougherty formed a partnership and began to publish the *Sentinel*, under Ford's editorship. Under such partisan direction, especially in the times of Reconstruction, the early years of the press were bound to be stormy ones, as "Old Rip" later intimated.

> The paper was democratic, opposed to the election of Gen. Grant as President of the United States, the election of Edmund J. Davis as governor of Texas, and to all the wild and oppressive measures of the Republican party, and other unconstitutional heresies they advocated and passed into laws. He [Ford] was for a time deprived of the right to vote.[7]

This temporary difficulty into which his caustic pen led him is the only instance recorded by Ford of any personal restriction during the Reconstruction period. However, there is evidence that his life was not a placid one, for the following item appeared in the Corpus Christi *Advertiser* of February 25, 1870: "As we go to press the mail from Brownsville brings the intelligence that the Sheriff of Cameron, Krause, attempted to assassinate Col. John S.

[6] *Flake's Daily Galveston Bulletin*, October 26, 1866.
[7] Ford, "Memoirs," VII, 1221–28.

Ford, editor of the *Sentinel*, firing a shot at him from his revolver." No further dispatches indicate the fate of the foolhardy peace officer, and Ford's memoirs ignore the affair.

Ford's horizon of activity widened after the passage by Congress of the Amnesty Act in May, 1872. As Democrats returned to power in the Texas legislature and began repealing Radical Republican laws, Democratic journals resumed unfettered publication. His partisan labors in South Texas resulted in Ford's selection as a delegate to the Democratic national convention in Baltimore.[8] On July 9, 1872, he sat among those who pledged their support to the Liberal Republican standard bearer, Horace Greeley. It must have been difficult for an original organizer of the Texas Democracy to accept the convention's decision, but his writings do not reveal his feelings in the matter.

Although concerned with politics in 1872, Ford was also involved in another problem of grave importance: the restoration of order and of safety for property along the Río Grande. So greatly had Mexican depredations on Texans increased that Congress in that year sent a committee to the border to gather testimony for a report on the extent of lawlessness.[9] Border residents paraded before the committee with their claims for indemnification for stolen property. Ford appeared to represent a certain Champini, a stage-line operator and rancher who sought payment not only for 150 goats stolen in 1867 but also for what should have been their natural increase over a five-year period. After the committee, advised by ranchers, had derived a formula for determining the reproductive capacity of goats, Ford and Major R. H. Savage of the committee attempted to ascertain Champini's possible total loss. Journalist Alex A. Sweet, who was present at the hearing, observed that both men were somewhat dismayed at the enormity of the final estimate. Ford, when Savage ended his calculations, was still scratching his ear and muttering subdued

[8] Ernest William Winkler (ed.), *Platforms of Political Parties in Texas. University of Texas Bulletin No. 53* (1916), 144.

[9] 44 Cong., 1 sess., *Index to Reports of Committees of the House of Representatives*, II. Hereafter cited as *Index to Reports*.

curses. When he thought Ford had completed his estimate, Savage asked for it. "Old Rip"'s irritable response was:

> Damn the goats! . . . they seem to me to multiply in the most unreasonable way. Let me see. A goat has three kids in March and two in September. Then the March kids have young when they are eighteen months old, and by that time—well, in short I make it two million five hundred and twenty-one thousand and eighteen goats. The Lord help us! If figures don't lie, and the goat business ain't stopped, in ten years, sir, Texas won't hold her goats.

A German farmer who had remained in the committee room after presenting a claim for five stolen mules listened intently to the discussion. He turned excitedly to the committee, after Ford's remarks, with a new demand: "Schentlemens, I vants natural ingreese on mine mooles, by tam! It was not fair to giff ingreese on der goats, and not on der mooles. I vants dot schentlemans vot gounted der goats to poot some off dot figuring on mine mooles."[10]

Even though the investigating committee collected considerable evidence of crime along the border, no federal action resulted and the situation grew increasingly worse. It was, in effect, a continuation of the Cortina War of 1859–60, temporarily interrupted by the United States Civil War but now swollen to such proportions that neither state nor federal officials could control it. The raiders decimated alike the herds of the large-scale ranchers like Richard King and those of the stockman who owned but a few cows. Murders were commonplace. "Hide-peelers," who slaughtered cattle and skinned them on the spot for their hides, developed a lucrative business. To check their activities, the state appointed cattle and hide inspectors to examine all hides and cattle sold and to determine if the skins bore the brand of the seller. Ford served as the inspector for Cameron County,[11] using his position to provide the military with information about the activities of the raiders.

In December, 1873, Ford suddenly left Brownsville for Austin,

10 Alex E. Sweet and J. Armoy Knox, *On A Mexican Mustang Through Texas: From the Gulf to the Rio Grande*, 550–51.

11 Webb, *Handbook of Texas*, I, 618.

where a new crisis was in the making. The situation which magnetically drew him to the capital was the final clash between the Radical Republicans, led by Governor E. J. Davis, and the resurgent Texas Democracy. It stemmed from a dispute over the constitutionality of the gubernatorial election of 1873. The Reconstruction constitution of 1869 provided that "all elections for State, district, and county officers shall be held at the county seats of the several counties until otherwise provided by law; and the polls shall be opened for four days, from 8 o'clock A.M. until 4 o'clock P.M. of each day." When the Democratic Thirteenth Legislature met in January, 1873, it repealed the basic laws of the Radical program and enacted its own. Resting its authority upon the phrase, "until otherwise provided by law," in the constitutional article governing elections, the legislature altered the election law to provide that each precinct "shall constitute an election precinct," and "That all elections in this state shall be held for one day only at each election, the polls shall be open on that day from 8 o'clock A.M. to 6 o'clock P.M." This statute, changing both the place of holding elections and the time during which the polls should remain open, was approved by Governor Davis. In May the legislature provided for a general election for state officials to be held on December 2, 1873, and in due time Governor Davis issued a call for the election in accordance with the new election law. The Radicals renominated Davis for governor, and the Democrats, in their first real state convention since the Civil War, nominated Richard Coke of Waco.

The campaign, an all-out contest of strength between the two parties, resulted in an overwhelming Democratic victory. Davis and his supporters then endeavored to have the election invalidated because the polls had been held open for only one day in violation of the constitutional requirement that they be kept open for four days. In a test case they brought into court on December 16, Joseph Rodríguez of Harris County was indicted for having unlawfully voted twice in the recent election, and he sought to show that he had committed no offense because the law under which the election had been held was unconstitutional. The Radical-Reconstruction Court, on January 5, 1874, agreed, holding that the statement following the semicolon in the above quoted sentence from the constitution was not in any way qualified by the language immediately preceding it; thus the election was null and void. This was the "infamous," "semicolon" decision.[12] Davis thereupon announced his intention of continuing in the governor's office and appealed to President Grant to sustain him by force if necessary. Intending to tolerate no further frustration at Radical hands, the Democrats of Texas, ignoring both the court decision and Davis' threat, streamed toward the capital to prevent the "republican despots" from making "dishonored slaves of thousands of Texians."

In Austin, Ford found the Democrats in a state of suspense, waiting for Davis to make the first move so that they might not be accused of aggressive tactics. On January 12, 1874, learning of Davis' announcement that he would continue as governor even though Grant had refused his request for federal troops and had advised him to accept majority rule, the members-elect of the legislature met to decide on a course of action. On the next day, the Senators elected John Ireland president pro tem until Lieutenant Governor-elect Richard B. Hubbard could be sworn into office and the House chose Guy M. Bryan as Speaker. A joint committee then informed Davis that the Fourteenth Legislature was in session, although he had stated that he would not recognize the newly elected body.

On January 13 and 14, Ford and several of his old friends were among the apprehensive citizens from all parts of Texas jamming the state house. The election returns were obtained without resistance from the office of the Secretary of State on January 15, and the legislature-elect proceeded to count the ballots. Richard Coke was declared governor by a vote of 85,549 to Davis' 42,633, and Hubbard, lieutenant governor. That night the two executives were inaugurated enthusiastically in the Hall of Representatives.

[12] Ernest Wallace, "Documents of Texas History," (unpublished MS, Texas Technological College, Lubbock, Texas); Abner V. McCall, *History of the Texas Election Laws*, XIX–XX; *Ex parte Rodriguez*, 39 Tex. 706 (1873).

That Davis intended to retain office until April 28, under a dubious constitutional interpretation by the Radical Supreme Court, seemed obvious that night when his adjutant general appeared in the capitol basement with a mixed white-Negro detachment of state troops to block entry and exit of the new state officers. Immediately after the inauguration ceremony, Governor Coke appointed Henry E. McCulloch as temporary adjutant general until his regular appointee, William Steele, should arrive. Fortunately for Coke and the party, McCulloch soon acquired the services of the Travis Rifles, a local volunteer militia company which Davis had summoned to the capitol. When the company arrived, Lieutenant A. S. Roberts, its commander, suggested that the men be sworn as a posse under Sheriff George Zimpleman. The latter assigned them to McCulloch, who disposed them about the legislative chambers.

Early the next morning, McCulloch gave up his temporary office because of illness. Coke thereupon ordered Speaker Bryan to protect the building and grounds adjacent to the Hall of Representatives. As Bryan, head bowed in thought, threaded his way through the throng back toward the Hall, he encountered William N. Hardeman. The sight of him suggested a solution. Inquiring for "Old Gotch" (W. P. Hardeman) and "Old Rip," Bryan was told that they were there.[13] He asked Hardeman to find the two and to report with them to the Speaker's rostrum. When the trio presented themselves before the House, Bryan told them, "You love Texas, you have seen much service in her behalf during three wars, you are experienced and accustomed to command men. A great crisis is now upon Texas. Never has Texas needed your services more than now. I trust you fully, I know no men I would prefer to you for discharge of the duties I will entrust to you." He then appointed the three assistant sergeants at arms and charged them with the protection of the legislature, public buildings, and grounds, assuring them that he would sustain their actions and provide what they needed. He strongly emphasized the need to preserve peace, adding that "if one drop

[13] Ford, "Memoirs," VII, 1247, 1250–51, 1277–80.

of blood is spilled—God alone knows the consequences and the end."[14]

On January 16, Coke demanded that Davis surrender to him, as duly elected governor, the executive offices, state papers, and public property. The increasing tension and excitement almost erupted into violence when Mayor T. B. Wheeler was arrested by Negro police at the state armory while attempting to persuade them to surrender the place. However, his release was negotiated without a clash, for, circulating among the aroused crowds, "Rip Ford counseled moderation and firmness."[15] "Old Gotch," too, at the statehouse, was busy averting a clash between Davis' militiamen and the Travis Rifles, on one occasion seizing in the nick of time the musket of a sentinel intending to shoot a militia captain "just to see him kick."

On the next day, after Coke indignantly had spurned Davis' suggestion that the matter be submitted to arbitration by either the President or Congress, the furious Democrats determined to take affairs into their own hands. To the enraged Coke partisans, the armory, with its Negro garrison, symbolized political injustice and stirred their anger somewhat in the manner that the Bastille once had infuriated a Paris mob. They congregated on Congress Avenue, bent on the capture of the armory and the annihilation of the Davis troops. It was then that John S. Ford performed his most significant public service. The swelling mass of angry men drew his attention as he came down the street from the capitol. Hurrying to the scene, he mounted the steps of a house before which the crowd was milling and quickly caught its attention. In his most forceful, persuasive style he harangued the throng, telling his listeners that he was acting under the orders of Coke, who had instructed his supporters to avoid any aggressive action. "If the radicals and darkies attack us we will give them the worst whipping ever inflicted on any set of men since the world began. If we fire the first shot we will again be placed under

[14] Guy M. Bryan to W. P. Hardeman, March 2, 1891, quoted in Ford, "Memoirs," VII, 1257–62.

[15] *Daily Herald* (San Antonio), January 17, 1874.

a military government, and God only knows when we shall be again free." At that point a Coke adherent appeared at Ford's elbow to state that he had come, with Hardeman's permission, to collect a company for the governor. Ford shouted the information to the crowd, asking that all "gentlemen who wish to aid Gov. Coke in sustaining himself in his constitutional and legal position as Governor of Texas, and in the fair and impartial administration of the laws, will please fall in on Maj. Royleston and obey his orders." The men rushed to comply, and were marched away to the capitol. Ford then ordered a nearby detachment of the Travis Rifles to join the volunteers at the statehouse. The crowd disintegrated, its violent intentions diverted into less dangerous channels by Ford's convincing spontaneity, and, as it dispersed, the most critical phase of the crisis passed safely away. By preventing a clash, Ford had deprived the Radical leaders of any grounds to urge military reoccupation of Texas. Eighteen years later, W. P. Hardeman expressed to Ford the opinion that "the service we rendered Texas on that occasion was worth infinitely more than all others, and I say now that if the row had commenced, in my opinion not less than 20,000 people would have been killed in two weeks—and Texas would not have recovered from it in fifty years—few even of those in the Capitol at the time realized the danger."

Recognizing the futility of further attempting to thwart the public will, Davis that night ordered his militia from the capitol and the armory and vanished from the scene. With tension relaxing, the Senate at the end of January discharged its assistant sergeants at arms, but, on the basis of a rumor that certain Radicals had expressed an intention to seize the capitol at night, the House retained Ford and the Hardemans until February 7. During that time the three slept undisturbed in a capitol office.[16] On the seventh, the danger obviously past, Speaker Bryan summoned his old reliables before the platform of the House and gratefully commended their efforts:

[16] Ford, "Memoirs," VII, 1270, 1281–82, 1285.

Faithful servants of Texas, I have asked you to come here, that in the presence of the Representatives of the People of Texas, in their name as Speaker, and in the name of every man, woman, and child in Texas to thank you for the invaluable services you have rendered them for, but for you, Texas might have been drenched in blood, and remanded back to military rule, which in my humble judgment you have largely contributed to avert by your consummate tact, true courage, and patriotism. You are now discharged.[17]

To the general applause of the representatives, the three old warriors departed from the Hall.

After April 21, Ford set out for home.[18] An embellished account of his role in the capital crisis had probably preceded him, for the admiring Brownsville citizens made him their next mayor.[19] Twenty-one years earlier, in another frontier town, "Old Rip" similarly had served in the dual capacity of mayor and editor, but now these responsibilities must share time with another task calling for his peculiar abilities—the border situation. Without hesitation he turned to it.

Ford's facility in the bastard Spanish of the river frontier had caused Latin-American citizens of Cameron County to seek his aid in translating into English their petitions for redress of grievances suffered in the border raids.[20] So adept was he that in 1875 the circuit court for the Eastern District of Texas employed him as its official translator, a labor which, in view of the continuing depredations, became practically a full-time occupation in itself. His familiarity with the border language and border people was one reason for his inclusion on a permanent committee composed "of the most reliable and prominent citizens of Brownsville . . . ," charged with the responsibility of investigating frontier disturbances and reporting them, with a petition for relief, to the legislature. In March, 1875, Ford and his old rival, Santos Benavides, testified before a joint legislative committee regarding the basic problems of the border. In spite of Ranger successes in lessening

17 Bryan, to Hardeman, *ibid.*, 1257–62.

18 Brown, "Annals," Ch. XXXIII, 57–58, states that Ford marched in the San Jacinto Day parade in Austin in 1874.

19 Webb, *Handbook of Texas*, I, 618. 20 *Index to Reports*, 125–56, *et passim.*

thievery, 90 per cent of the normal number of cattle between Starr County and the Gulf had disappeared since the Civil War; raiders rode without fear across the border because of intelligence provided by intimidated Mexican-Americans; and 105 Texas citizens had been murdered by depredators in the preceding three or four years. While the strong hands of Mexican state administrations had held stealing to a minimum above Laredo, there could be no redress expected from Mexico along the Tamaulipas frontier, for Juan Cortina, now in the double capacity of mayor of Matamoros and commandant of the frontier troops, not only protected the bandits but also actually encouraged them to raid north of the Río Grande. Both Ford and Benavides expressed the opinion that settlement in lower Texas had been "badly discouraged" as a result of bandit operations and recommended that the legislature provide a remedy.[21]

In the late summer of 1875, Ford temporarily suspended his preoccupation with frontier troubles to take part in a state constitutional convention, designed to replace the Radical Republican organic law with one more representative of Texas majority attitudes. Heeding Governor Coke's warning against antagonizing Congress, the Texas Democrats had waited until the Congressional elections in November of 1874 returned a Democratic majority to the House of Representatives. When it was then safe to proceed, the Texas legislature enacted a bill calling for a constitutional convention. Coke approved the bill and accordingly issued a call for the election of delegates who were to meet in Austin on September 6.[22] Ford attended as a delegate from the Twenty-ninth Senatorial District. When the convention was organized, he was made chairman of the Committee on State Affairs and was also assigned membership on the committees on Suffrage, Municipal Corporations, Printing and Contingent Expenses, Apportionment, and Frontier Affairs.[23]

[21] *Ibid.*, 50–59, 167–70.
[22] S. S. McKay, *Seven Decades of the Texas Constitution of 1876*, 23–76.
[23] *Journal of the Constitutional Convention of the State of Texas, 1875*, 5, 7, 9, 35, 228.

Chairman Ford's Committee on State Affairs recommended that the constitution permit legislative measures for the maintenance of public roads by a system of citizen labor rather than by a tax levy. The committee also recommended the retention of a state geologist, repair of the capitol building, and pensions for veterans of the Texas Revolution. Individually, Delegate Ford suggested the constitutional exclusion of judges from participation in political affairs; encouragement of immigration; provision for local option for sale of liquor; creation of the office of commissioner of insurance, statistics, and history; and granting of gubernatorial authority to lease or sell public lands to the federal government for military installations. The convention journal reveals that Ford consistently voted for all propositions designed to promote public education and to benefit the frontier residents.[24] The definitive account of the debates in the convention shows that Ford spoke at length only once during the entire session. On that occasion he characteristically paid tribute to West Texas and predicted a glorious, prosperous future for the area.[25] His speech was a reflection of his impressions of the region gained at the time of his search for Comanches in 1859.[26]

On November 24, the final day of the convention, Ford joined with other delegates in petitioning Congress to compensate Texas citizens for losses due to the bandit forays.[27] On returning to Brownsville, he found no improvement in the border situation, nor could he foresee any. Yet, in January, 1876, he became a major contributor to the development which eventually ended the outrages. Revolutionary activity had broken out against the unpopular regime of President Sebastián Lerdo. Before the end of the month, former *Juárezista* General Porfirio Díaz, the leading revolutionist, appeared in Brownsville, seeking funds to finance his revolt.[28] He was referred to "Old Rip," who bluntly stated the terms of American aid: "You are no doubt aware of the trouble

[24] *Ibid.*, 3–821, *et passim.*
[25] S. S. McKay, *Debates in the Constitutional Convention of 1875*, 117.
[26] Ford, "Memoirs," IV, 760–61.
[27] *Index to Reports*, 171–74.
[28] Testimony of General E. O. C. Ord, January 12, 1876, *ibid.*, 34.

General Cortina is causing on this frontier. If you will give your word that, if successful in the revolution you are to inaugurate, you will order Cortina to be removed from this frontier, Americans will loan you money."

Díaz promised, and donations soon were forthcoming. Among them was one of fifty thousand dollars provided by a respected, naturalized citizen, Don Sabas Cavasos, a half-brother to Cortina.[29] Since the Lerdo administration had supplanted Cortina with a more loyal commander in Matamoros itself, Díaz was unable to win over the city. In June, with his American-provided war chest, he embarked on the circuitous voyage which led him to Vera Cruz and the campaign that brought him to the presidency of Mexico.[30]

Díaz' success was to be Cortina's disaster. Once his administration was on firm footing, the new President placed his own men along the border, assigning the Matamoros command to Cortina's bitter enemy, Servando Canales. Although Cortina eventually had declared for Díaz, certain of his operations had aroused distrust, and it was, doubtless, with enthusiasm that Canales prepared to dispose of the old border lord. Ford, in the confidence of all the border leaders, warned Cortina of his impending danger; but the latter, who not long before had been arrested and released, shrugged off the warning as being based on an inferior knowledge of Mexican character. Nevertheless, on his first subsequent visit to Matamoros, Cortina was arrested, tried, and sentenced to be shot. When Ford learned of the sentence, he visited Canales to intercede for Cortina's life. He pointed out to the Matamoros commander that, because of the known enmity between the two, the sentence, if carried out, would cast dishonor on Canales, and and he begged that Cortina be sent, along with the findings of the court-martial, to Mexico City for Díaz' final disposition. At the conclusion of Ford's plea, Canales turned to his staff and asked,

[29] Ford, "Memoirs," VII, 1237–38.
[30] Salvador Queredo y Zubieta, *El Caudillo: continuación de "Porfirio Díaz, ensayo de Psicología Histórica"* (*Septiembre 1865–Noviembre 1876*), 243–44; José C. Valades, *El Porfirismo, História de un Regimen: El Nacimiento* (*1876–1884*), 15.

in amazement, "Did you hear what that white-headed old man said? If there is a man in the world more opposed to Cortina's mode of doing things than Col. Ford I do not know of him."[31] Ford won his case; Canales adopted the suggestion. Díaz concurred with the verdict and sentence, but, with the mixture of sentiment and practicality which sometimes characterizes Latin-American decisions, substituted for the death penalty a parole valid so long as Cortina should remain within the limits of Mexico City. The old renegade purchased a small estate in the suburbs and there remained until his death in 1894.[32]

There was a reason behind Ford's surprising intercession on Cortina's behalf. During the Civil War the two men apparently had reached a binding personal agreement of an undisclosed nature.[33] It may have been to this mysterious compact that Ranger Captain S. H. McNally referred in Washington when he said, in testimony before a Congressional investigating committee, that the only instance he knew of any restitution of plundered property was when "General Cortina himself did deliver some stock, as a personal favor, to a particular friend of his, one of his compadres on this side, who was an American."[34] It is noteworthy also that throughout Ford's memoirs there appears in connection with Cortina's name an admixture of violent censure and grudging admiration.

In the spring of 1876, the border electorate showed appreciation for Ford's labors by sending him to the state senate, where he represented District Number Twenty-nine in both the Fifteenth and Sixteenth Legislatures. That he preferred a public office of a more permanent nature he made clear in a letter to state Supreme Court Justice Oran M. Roberts. While waiting for the electoral commission to decide the disputed Hayes-Tilden election, he wrote requesting support for a place in the customs service, should Tilden's claim to the presidency be upheld.

31 Ford, "Memoirs," VII, 1239-40.
32 Miguel Angel Peral, *Diccionario biográfico mexicano*, 191.
33 Ford, "Memoirs," VII, 1239.
34 *Index to Reports*, 14.

My friends have put me forward for the position of Collector of the Customs for the District of Brazos Santiago, provided Mr. Tilden is inaugurated.

If you can consistently with your sense of propriety write a letter recommending me, and get others of your court to sign it, you would oblige me very much. If you do so, direct it to Senator Coke, Washington.

The letter also revealed that, after thirty years, "Old Rip" still felt that the only solution to border troubles was for the United States to extend its supervision south of the river: "Mexican affairs are unsettled and will no doubt remain so. The revolutions have paralyzed business and impeded industrial pursuits. The elements of reform, if there, can be made available with difficulty. A protectorate will become indispensable, in my opinion."[35]

His hopes for the collectorship blighted by the inauguration of Rutherford B. Hayes, Ford continued to work at the frontier problem. Late in 1877, after journeying some two hundred miles by horseback up and down the river to learn the current attitudes and opinions of the border citizens, he was summoned to Washington to testify as an expert on frontier affairs before the House Committee on Foreign Affairs. To the committee, on January 21 and 25, 1878, he expressed the opinion that only force could quiet the disturbances and he recommended that United States recognition of the Díaz administration be suspended until Díaz had shown his ability to restore order on Mexico's Río Grande frontier. At the time he testified, Ford was not optimistic over Díaz' chances of success.[36] Upon his return to Brownsville, he found increased Mexican hostility toward the United States. Its proportions, by August, reached a degree so alarming that he wrote hurriedly to General E. O. C. Ord, commanding the Department of Texas: "Reports have reached here that a rupture with Mexico is almost certain. Will you authorize Gen. Alexander to arm a citizen organization to defend Brownsville in case of emergency? The Mexicans on our front are organized. Should they assume the offensive

[35] Ford to Roberts, February 6, 1877, Roberts Papers.
[36] *New York Times,* January 26, 1878.

we are prepared for defense." Ord could only reply that Ford should "appeal to the Governor, who alone possessed authority to extend the privilege asked."[37] Mexican resentment probably had been aroused by a War Department order permitting United States troops to cross into Mexico in pursuit of bandits. That the order was not rescinded until 1880 may be due, in part, to Ford's earlier testimony.

In the summer of 1879, Ford's legislative duties placed him in Austin at a time most convenient for the state administration. An embarrassing situation had arisen concerning the state Deaf and Dumb Institution. The superintendency of the institution had been assigned to Henry McCulloch as a sinecure for the old Ranger's long years of stalwart service. Complaints of maladministration became so frequent that a legislative sub-committee investigated his operations.[38] Although McCulloch vigorously protested its subsequent report, the committee's findings and its answer to McCulloch so clearly revealed his ineptness and laxity that he resigned as of September 1, 1879. Whether Ford asked for the superintendency or accepted it at the request of Governor O. M. Roberts is not known, but on August 30, "Old Rip" submitted his resignation from the state senate and on September 1 assumed the office McCulloch reluctantly relinquished.[39]

Apparently Ford had received advance notice that the position would be his, for he had already begun to prepare himself for his duties. With the thoroughness which characterized his earlier military operations, he set himself to learn sign language, which would enable him to communicate with the wards of the institution. On one occasion, as he gesticulated earnestly before a mirror in his capitol office, a friend passing down the corridor glanced through Ford's open doorway and halted in amazement. The Senator, unconscious of a witness, continued his gestures while the friend

[37] *United States Army and Navy Journal and Gazette of the Regular and Volunteer Forces,* Vol. XVI (1878–1879), 78.

[38] *Management of the Deaf and Dumb Institution. Reports of the Sub-Committee of Investigation, and the Evidences and Reply to General Henry E. McCulloch's Defense of Himself and His Administration of the Institution.*

[39] G. L., Governor O. M. Roberts; Brown, "Annals," Ch. XXXV, 19.

watched with increasing concern, certain that the old man had lost his mind. Finally, when Ford passed his hand quickly across his throat, the observer could contain himself no longer. Springing into the office, he cried: "My God, Colonel Ford, what are you doing?"

"Fool," was the angry reply, "don't you see that I am studying the sign language?"

"Oh! no!" replied the other. "But what did you mean by drawing your hand across your neck as you did just now, as if you were cutting your throat?"

"Fool!" responded Ford, "that signifies 'cat' in the sign language."

Some time later, to a query about the truthfulness of the incident, Ford answered testily, "No, it's a lie. I didn't tell him it signified 'cat,' I told him it meant 'hog.' "[40]

Upon assuming his new duties, Superintendent Ford found a few unpretentious buildings and a student body of fifty-four children at the hilltop location south of the Colorado River. A believer in practical education, Ford quickly made curriculum changes which placed emphasis upon instruction in trade skills. Although an experiment in the teaching of mattress making had little success, the programs in bookbinding, shoemaking, cabinetmaking, and printing showed excellent results. Ford was especially pleased with the progress of student printers, and reported that if they could complete their course, they would be able to compete favorably with the non-handicapped. Evidence of the interest in typography was the regular appearance of the school newspaper, *The Mute Ranger*, largely subsidized from Ford's own pocket. To its columns the Superintendent and other old frontier veterans occasionally contributed accounts of early adventures, making it a rich source of Texas history.

Ford's persistent efforts on behalf of his charges resulted also in the expansion of the physical plant to include a new building, as well as enlargement of the old ones, to accommodate a broadened curriculum and an increasing enrollment of more than ninety

[40] Rena Maverick Green (ed.), *The Swisher Memoirs*, 59.

pupils.[41] In May of 1883, while the institution was abandoning its wells and beginning to receive the service of city water mains, the board president, Dr. R. M. Swearingen, was receiving bids for the construction "Old Rip" had so continuously and convincingly advocated. The Superintendent, however, was to be deprived of the satisfaction of witnessing the fruits of his labors. Although a steward had been added to his staff to aid him with purchasing, clerical work, and the supervision of state property, Ford's enthusiasm for his job made it more and more rigorous in its demands. In the fall of 1883, illness—perhaps of the nature of the attacks which previously had intermittently plagued him—so enfeebled him that he realized he was no longer able to superintend the institution. On December 6, Superintendent Ford submitted to the asylum board his resignation from the position which he had filled to the obvious satisfaction of the public. When the resignation became effective on December 31, 1883, it marked the end of almost half a century of official service to Texas.[42]

41 *Twenty-third Annual Report of the Superintendent of the Texas Institution for the Deaf and Dumb for the Fiscal Year Ending August 31, 1879. John S. Ford, Superintendent;* also annual reports Nos. 24–27, 1880–83.

42 Bonds and Oaths File, Texas State Library, Archives Division, Austin; *Statesman* (Austin), December 1, 1883.

II

A Paladin Passes

UPON RESIGNING the superintendency of the Deaf and Dumb Institution, John S. Ford moved his family to San Antonio, where he spent his declining years. His slender figure, surmounted by a mass of white hair and beard, became a familiar one at the Menger House and other Alamo City meeting places, and citizens noted him respectfully as the worn Ranger, gold-headed cane in hand, slowly paced the town's busy plazas and pleasant byways, occasionally halting to gaze keenly around him, an ineradicable habit acquired in the border wars.[1] When Frederic Remington came to San Antonio in the early 1890's to interview the "old originals" among Texas frontiersmen, he found this "connoisseur" of desperate ventures "a very old man, with a wealth of snow white hair and beard—bent, but not withered . . . with stiffened limbs." He was introduced to Ford as to one who could "tell stories that will make your eyes hang out on your shirt front," and Ford did not disappoint him.[2]

During his last years, Ford occupied himself in preparing his memoirs (a project begun while superintending the Deaf and Dumb Institution) and collecting materials for a history of Texas, adding to those he had been acquiring since the 1850's. Out of his interest in Texas history grew the idea of a state historical association. In the spring of 1874, while in Austin after the installation of the Coke administration, Ford had met with other "Old Tex-

[1] Martin, "Last of the Ranger Chieftains," 39.
[2] Remington, "How the Law Got into the Chaparral," 60.

ians" in an effort to found such an organization,[3] but it was not until the final year of his life that he saw this particular ambition brought to fruition. Meanwhile, as his health permitted, he contributed occasional reminiscences to the San Antonio newspapers and corresponded with old comrades. He also exchanged letters with his old rival, Juan Cortina,[4] and, it is said, journeyed to Mexico City in 1891 to visit the caged warlord.[5] In 1894, Ford was an active member of the Alamo Association, and in that year his brief history of the Alamo fight was published in pamphlet form as a part of the Association's efforts to obtain donations for the erection of a suitable monument to the martyred commands of Travis and Bowie.[6] Finally, in February, 1897, O. M. Roberts, F. R. Lubbock, John H. Reagan, and other interested parties met at the state university to plan the founding of a state historical society. Ford came to Austin on March 2 for a meeting which resulted in the establishment of the Texas State Historical Society, under Roberts' presidency. No believer in the equality of the sexes, Ford stalked in disgust from the meeting when the other charter members refused to alter the proposed constitution to distinguish between "members" and "lady members," and it took the best persuasive efforts of Professor George P. Garrison, of the university history staff, and Francis Lubbock, the next day in Ford's hotel room, to convince the old veteran that his support was vitally important to the society.[7] Even then, members were not positive of his co-operation until he wrote to Roberts on March 20, "I anticipate remaining with the 'Texas Historical Society' as long as I can do anything to promote the interests of Texas history." How long that would be, he added, he was not sure, since "indications of age have already developed, and there is no means of guessing when the end may come. The only thing I can do is

[3] Brown, "Annals," Ch. XXXIII, 56.

[4] "News Items," *Southwestern Historical Quarterly*, Vol. XVII (July 1913–April 1914), 430.

[5] Lyman L. Woodman, *Cortina, Rogue of the Rio Grande*, 106.

[6] John S. Ford, *The Origin and Fall of the Alamo*.

[7] Bride Neill Taylor, "The Beginnings of the State Historical Association," *Southwestern Historical Quarterly*, Vol. XXXIII (July 1929–April, 1930), 1–17.

to await the finality with becoming complacency and fortitude."

Deploring the paucity of documentary and manuscript materials, Ford feared that the actual Texas story might never be made known.

The proper history of Texas is yet unpublished. The men who enacted the great deeds, rendering the Lone Star Republic famous, have generally died without writing what they aided in doing. Jonas Harrison wrote articles which stirred the heroic people and helped to strengthen the resolution to resist tyranny, but where are they? R. W. Williamson was an outspoken advocate of a free government. He did more than any one man to nerve our people to strike out for liberty. He has been gathered to his fathers, and where are the evidences of his wonderful exertions. They are almost lost to the world. Gen. Thomas J. Rusk—brave, eloquent, and fearless—our Secretary of War when the revolution was at its most fearful height, after the Alamo and Goliad and their defenders had fallen; after the mistaken members of the Consultation had illegally attempted to turn Gov. Smith out of office, and to invade Mexico. Where is the historian who lived in these days of trouble and danger. Col. Frank Johnson wrote a history of Texas. He was an officer of the Texas army, was defeated at San Patricio. His work has never seen the light and perhaps never will.

Gen. Rusk was at the battle of San Jacinto. He made an official report to President Burnet, and left no individual, private, account of that wonderful contest.

Gen. Stephen F. Austin, the "father" of Texas, wrote a great deal. Up to the present time no one has assumed the responsibility to edit and publish his papers and his life.

Who can tell us of the career of Richard Ellis, the president of the Convention of 1836? They met at Washington on the Brazos, and declared Texas independent on the second day of March, 1836. How little is known of the members of that memorable and distinguished company of men?

Who has written a comprehensive life of Travis? of Bowie? and the heroes of the Alamo? What has been done to revive a correct memory of David G. Burnet? of Gen. Edward Burleson, who commanded the Texas Troops in 1835 when Gen. Cos surrendered San Antonio to him?

The failure of Texans to exploit the achievements of the past, Ford believed, lay in the fact that they had been better actors than scribes: "The Texians have proved themselves good soldiers. If we look at their utter neglect to record what they have done in war, and in the matter of legislation, we must conclude that they are not willing writers."[8] But he, at least, belied the pattern by contributing an article to the first issue of the society's journal.[9]

The indications of age to which the old adventurer had referred became increasingly evident in the following months. A stroke, on October 1, brought John Ford low. With the grim determination that characterized him in his frontier battles, "Old Rip" fought his most unrelenting foe for more than a month, but each temporary recovery was followed by a relapse. Finally, at seven-thirty on the evening of November 3, 1897, the border captain lost his last fight. On the next day, "the last of the ranger chieftains, . . . whose name for nearly half a century [had] been a household word in Texas,"[10] was eulogized by his Presbyterian pastor and then laid ceremoniously to rest beside the San Antonio River by his Masonic brethren and his sorrowing comrades of the United Confederate Veterans.[11] Into Texas sod disappeared the last Ford of his line.[12]

With the passing of John Salmon Ford, a new generation of

8 Ford to Roberts, March 20, 1897, Roberts Papers, Scrapbook I.

9 John S. Ford, "The Fight on the Frio, July 4, 1865," *Quarterly of the Texas State Historical Association,* Vol. I (July, 1897–April, 1898), 118–20. The article describes a Kickapoo raid in the Leona River area.

10 *Daily Statesman* (Austin), Sunday supplement, November 7, 1897.

11 *Ibid.,* November 4, 1897. Ford had become a church member after moving to Austin.

12 Ford's oldest daughter, Fannie, during the Civil War married a Mr. Thomas in Austin. Her grandson, L. R. Cowan, is a Brownsville attorney. Of the children of Ford's third marriage, Addie was married in 1882 to Samuel Delgado de Cordova, a son of the Phineas de Cordova from whom Ford had purchased the *South-Western American;* a grandson of "Old Rip," F. H. de Cordova, is a Corpus Christi resident. Another daughter, May Louise (Lula), became Mrs. Joseph W. Maddox. John William, "Rip" Ford's only son, was born in 1870 but died before reaching maturity, killed, according to one story, by the accidental discharge of the first Colt revolver he had the opportunity to examine. Lillian, an adopted daughter of John S. and Addie Smith Ford, became Mrs. R. A. Votaw, Sr., and was last reported (May, 1959) living in Robstown, Texas.

Texans lost one of its strongest links with a historic past. For half a century he had marched in the Texas vanguard as an important actor and keen observer of every significant political and military incident involving Texans since their successful revolution in 1836. His official services to the governments of the Republic and the state were many and varied: volunteer trooper; surveyor of her public lands; spokesman, in the Texas Congress, for her frontier people; adjutant of her finest Mexican War regiment; Ranger captain whose command had made secure life and property in South Texas; a senator in both her pre– and post–Civil War legislatures; a protector of her frontiers from the Río Grande to the Red River; and a military diplomat who without bloodshed had negotiated the evacuation of federal troops from Texas at the time of her secession from the American Union. He had been instrumental in bringing Texas into the United States; he had played a major role in removing her from that federation. Even more important was his part, after the Civil War, in restoring to its rightful place in Texas affairs government by will of the people. As a final though unspectacular service, he had lifted a Texas eleemosynary institution from a discreditable condition to one of which his state could be proud.

His services were equally valuable and extensive in days when he occupied no position of state or national responsibility. As a dedicated physician he had nurtured the health of his East Texas and Travis County patients; as an equally dedicated frontier editor he had nurtured their spirits, championing not only popular causes but also others which he felt were right, even though his stand might leave him virtually alone. He enjoyed both the signal honor of being named to the group which established the Democratic party organization in Texas and that of being specifically sought out to serve in the crisis which, in 1874, resulted in his party's restoration to power in the state. He had, at the demands of his fellow citizens in 1849, made an arduous, health-wracking, thousand-mile ride to seek a road for their commercial advantage; as a war-worn, aged veteran, almost three decades later, he had spent countless hours in the saddle trying to achieve conditions which would permit his South Texas friends to live with life and property secure.

A survey of the scope and multiplicity of Ford's services reveals at least two occasions on which Ford's absence might have provided a different destiny for Texas. In 1861, it was astute planning which sent Ford, rather than either of the McCullochs, to the Río Grande frontier. The "Old Alcalde" in Texas history, O. M. Roberts, was positive that Ford's diplomacy not only made possible the peaceful evacuation of United States troops from the lower river but also kept the Confederacy from becoming involved in a Mexican war. Perhaps more significant was Ford's service during the Coke-Davis crisis of 1874, when his skillful dispersal of a dangerous mob forced Davis to surrender without having been provided with an excuse to justify military reoccupation of the state.

Because his role in the Reconstruction dispute has been relatively unpublicized, Texans most frequently remember "Rip" Ford as a frontier military commander. He acquired his martial knowledge through reading treatises on the art of war and testing their theories in the field. His close friend, Roberts, wrote that Ford, "unlike most of our frontier officers, . . . had studied war as a science, had a fine military library, and had for years devoted himself to it. And then he had system, good business habits. Was a man of action, not of words, of caution in devising, and of intrepidity in execution."[13] That Ford was no rash glory seeker was obvious when, in 1861, he, "by the generalship of prudence and patience succeeded far better, than if he had adopted a reckless adventure, that, though it failed, might have given him a reputation of a gallant officer in the action."[14] But when the time for prudence was past, he could fight, as his old subalterns attested. Captain W. H. D. Carrington of the Río Grande Expeditionary Force, in an account somewhat colored by his enthusiasm for his old colonel, wrote:

[13] Journal of O. M. Roberts, quoted in Ford, "Memoirs," V, 955.

[14] O. M. Roberts, "The History of the War in Texas—1861–1865," MS, Roberts Papers.

On a more extended sphere of action he would have been the Murat of the Confederacy. His tactics were peculiar. . . . He believed that his cavalry in a fierce charge was invincible. Hence, whenever the right time arrived, he hurled squadron after squadron of his troopers on the foe with irresistible force.[15]

With similar fervor, Lieutenant Charles L. Martin of an earlier border regiment, designated Ford's place in Texian ranks.

In all the history of Texas since 1836, not one of the many able and active men who helped shape and achieve its destiny, stands forth more prominent than John S. Ford. Not one rendered more efficient service; not one gave more of his life, his labor, his devotion, his valor and his ability to the good of the State, its advancement, development, progress and prosperity than he.

"No monument," Martin wrote further, "may ever be erected to honor his resting place, but he will live forever in the hearts of men who love honor, honesty, virtue, valor, fortitude, patriotism, and devotion." But, as Martin noted, no monument was necessary, since for "all the statesmen, paladins, and jurists, who, with Ford, gave the best of genius and the prowess of valiant hearts . . . Texas is their monument."[16] That such commentary was not merely posthumous tribute may be shown by the remarks, several months before Ford's death, by state Adjutant General W. H. King: "Colonel Ford . . . is held in deserved esteem by those who value lifelong devotion and able service to the State, and who appreciate modesty, manliness, and uprightness in public and private life."[17]

Those of the rawhide breed who rode, worked, and fought with John S. Ford iterate the theme of his service; indeed, it was the thread which provided unity to the long career of a Texian whose motto was, "Ready; aye ready." Whether at the medical cabinet, in the legislative chair, at the editorial desk, or in the saddle, his fixed principle was service to Texas and her people. As estimated by his contemporaries and the test of time, herein lay the worth and contribution of "Old Rip" Ford.

[15] *Galveston Daily News*, May 7, 1911.

[16] Martin, "Last of the Ranger Chieftains," 40–41.

[17] Dudley G. Wooten (ed.), *A Comprehensive History of Texas, 1865 to 1897*, II, 338.

Bibliography

MANUSCRIPT SOURCES
(Unpublished or incompletely published)

Bickley, George W. L. Papers. Records of the War Department, Office of the Judge Advocate General, National Archives, Washington, D. C.

Blake, R. B. "Sketches of Nacogdoches and Citizens Thereof" (typescript). Archives Division, Texas State Library, Austin.

Brown, Frank. "Annals of Travis County and the City of Austin (From the Earliest Times to the Close of 1875)" (typescript). Archives Division, Texas State Library, Austin.

Burleson, Ed. Miscellaneous papers. Barker History Center, University of Texas, Austin.

Ford, John Salmon. Letter Books of John S. Ford, Colonel Commanding Expeditionary Force. Museum of the United Daughters of the Confederacy, Austin, Texas.

———. "The Memoirs of John Salmon Ford." 7 vols. Barker History Center, University of Texas, Austin.

———. General Orders. Museum of the United Daughters of the Confederacy, Austin, Texas.

———. Papers. Barker History Center, University of Texas, Austin.

"Pickett Papers." Box L., MS Division, Library of Congress, Washington, D. C.

Roberts, Oran Milo. Miscellaneous notes and papers. Barker History Center, University of Texas, Austin.

Rusk, Thomas Jefferson. Miscellaneous papers. Barker History Center, University of Texas, Austin.

Wallace, Ernest. "Documents of Texas History." Texas Technological College, Lubbock.

PUBLIC DOCUMENTS

I. *Federal*

Mexican War Correspondence: Message of the President of the United States, and the Correspondence, therewith communicated, between the Secretary of War and other officers of the government upon the subject of the Mexican War. Washington, Wendell & Van Benthuysen, 1848.

Records Group No. 94. National Archives, Washington, D. C.

Reports of the Committee of Investigation Sent by the Mexican Government to the Frontier of Texas. Translated from the Official Edition Made in Mexico. New York, Baker and Godwin, Printers, 1875.

36 Cong., 2 sess., *House Exec. Doc. 1.* Washington, Government Printing Office, 1861.

30 Cong., 2 sess., *House Exec. Doc. 1.* 2 vols. Washington, Wendell & Van Benthuysen, 1848.

36 Cong., 1 sess., *House Exec. Doc. 52.* Washington, Thomas H. Ford, Printer, 1860.

36 Cong., 1 sess., *House Exec. Doc. 81.* Washington, Thomas H. Ford, Printer, 1860.

44 Cong., 1 sess., *House Index to Reports of Committees.* 1875–76, 2 vols. Washington, Government Printing Office, 1876.

36 Cong., 1 sess., *House Misc. Doc. 38.* Washington, Thomas H. Ford, Printer, 1860.

45 Cong., 2 sess., *House Reports of Committees,* 1877–78, 3 vols. Washington, Government Printing Office, 1878.

31 Cong., 1 sess., *Senate Exec. Doc. 64.* Washington, William M. Belt, 1850.

War Department Collection of Confederate Records. Carded Records and Correspondence Re: John S. Ford, 2d Regiment Texas Cavalry (2 Texas Mounted Rifles) (Confederate). National Archives, Washington, D. C.

War of the Rebellion: A Compilation of the Official Records of the Union and Confederate Armies. 128 vols. Washington, Government Printing Office, 1880–91.

War of the Rebellion: Official Records of the Union and Confederate Navies. 30 vols. Washington, Government Printing Office, 1894–1922.

II. *State*

Annual Report of the Superintendent of the Texas Institution for the Deaf and Dumb, Nos. 23–27 (1880–83). Austin, State of Texas, 1880–83.

Bonds and Oaths File. Texas State Library, Archives Division, Austin.

Executive Record Books. Texas State Library, Archives Division, Austin.

Ex parte Rodriguez, 39 Tex. 706 (1873).

Ford, John S. General Orders, 1863–65. Museum of the United Daughters of the Confederacy.

[Ford, John S.] Letter Book, August 24, 1864–December 30, 1864, of John S. Ford, Colonel Commanding Expeditionary Force. Museum of the United Daughters of the Confederacy, Austin.

Governors Letters File. Texas State Library, Archives Division, Austin.

List of Land Grants. Tennessee State Library, Archives Division, Nashville.

Management of the Deaf and Dumb Institution. Reports of the Sub-Committee of Investigation, and the Evidences and Reply to General Henry E. McCulloch's Defense of Himself and His Administration of the Institution. Austin, State of Texas, 1879.

Sexton's Records. Oakwood Cemetery, Austin, Texas.

Newspaper Sources

Austin, Texas, Newspapers
  Austin Statesman, 1924.
  Daily Statesman, 1897.
  Southern Intelligencer, 1866.
  South-Western American, 1852, 1853.
  State Gazette, 1851, 1852, 1857, 1858, 1859, 1860.
  Statesman, 1883.
  Texas Democrat, 1846, 1849.
  Texas National Register, 1845, 1846.
  Texas Sentinel, 1857.

Bibliography

Texas State Gazette, 1852, 1853.
Texas State Times, 1854, 1855, 1856, 1857.

Galveston, Texas, Newspapers
Flake's Daily Galveston Bulletin, 1866.
Galveston Daily News, 1911.

Houston, Texas, Newspapers
Democratic Telegraph and Texas Register, 1848, 1849, 1850.
Telegraph and Texas Register, 1836, 1839.

Others
Daily Herald (San Antonio), 1874.
New York Times, 1865, 1878.
Picayune (New Orleans), 1860.
Red-Lander (San Augustine), 1841, 1842, 1843, 1844.
Rio Grande Sentinel (Brownsville), 1861.
Texas National Register (Washington-on-the-Brazos), 1844, 1845.

Books

Bancroft, Hubert Howe. *History of California.* 7 vols. San Francisco, The History Company, 1888.

———. *History of Mexico.* 6 vols. San Francisco, 1887.

Biographical Directory of the Texas Conventions and Congresses: 1832–1845. Austin, State of Texas, 1941.

Brackett, Albert G. *History of the United States Cavalry, From the Formation of the Federal Government to the 1st of June, 1863. To which is added a List of all of the Cavalry Regiments, with the Names of the Commanders, which Have Been in the United States Service Since the Breaking out of the Rebellion.* New York, Harper and Brothers, 1865.

Brown, John Henry. *History of Texas: From 1865 to 1892.* 2 vols. St. Louis, E. L. Daniell, 1892.

Cotner, Thomas Ewing. *The Military and Political Career of José Joaquín De Herrera, 1792–1854 (University of Texas Institute of Latin-American Studies, No. 7).* Austin, University of Texas Press, 1949.

Diccionario Enciclopédico U. T. E. H. A. 10 vols. Mexico, Union Tipográfica Editorial Hispano Americana, 1951.

Ford, John S. *The Origin and Fall of the Alamo*. San Antonio, Alamo Monument Association, 1894.

Freeman, Douglas Southall. *Lee's Lieutenants: A Study in Command*. 3 vols. New York, Charles Scribner's Sons, 1942.

Fuess, Claude M. *The Life of Caleb Cushing*. 2 vols. New York, Harcourt, Brace and Company, 1923.

Gammel, H. P. N. (compiler). *The Laws of Texas: 1822–1897*. 10 vols. Austin: Gammel Book Company, 1898.

George, Isaac. *Heroes and Incidents of the Mexican War, containing Doniphan's Expedition. The Cause of the War with Mexico. A Description of the People and Customs at that Time. A Sketch of the Life of Doniphan. Together with Sketches and Portraits of the Heroes of that Struggle*. Greensburg, Pa.: Review Publishing Co., 1903.

Green, Rena Maverick, ed. *Samuel Maverick, Texan: A Collection of Letters, Journals, and Memoirs*. San Antonio, privately printed, 1952.

———. *The Swisher Memoirs*. San Antonio, Mrs. J. R. Blocker, 1932.

Greer, James Kimmins. *Colonel Jack Hays: Texas Frontier Leader and California Builder*. New York, E. P. Dutton and Company, Inc., 1952.

Hitchcock, Ethan Allen. *Fifty Years in Camp and Field*. Ed. by W. A. Croffut. New York and London, G. P. Putnam's Sons, 1909.

Huson, Hobert. *Refugio, A Comprehensive History of Refugio County from Aboriginal Times to 1955*. 2 vols. Woodsboro, Texas, The Rooke Foundation, 1955.

Jenkins, John S. *History of the War between the United States and Mexico, from the commencement of hostilities to the ratification of the treaty of peace*. New York, Miller, Orton and Mulligan, 1855.

Journal of the Constitutional Convention of the State of Texas, 1875. Austin, State of Texas, 1875.

Kenly, John R. *Memoirs of a Maryland Volunteer. War with Mexico, in the Years 1846–47–48*. Philadelphia, J. B. Lippincott & Co., 1873.

Lea, Tom. *The King Ranch*. 2 vols. Boston, Little, Brown and Company, 1957.

McCall, Abner V. *History of the Texas Election Laws*. Kansas City, Missouri, 1952.

McKay, S. S. *Debates in the Constitutional Convention of 1875*. Austin, University of Texas Press, 1930.

———. *Seven Decades of the Texas Constitution of 1876.* Lubbock, Texas Technological College Press, 1942.

McKee, Irving. *"Ben Hur" Wallace, the Life of General Lew Wallace.* Berkeley, University of California Press, 1947.

Members of the Legislature of the State of Texas from 1846 to 1939. Austin, State of Texas, 1939.

Oldham, W. S. and George W. White (compilers). *A Digest of the General Statute Laws of the State of Texas.* Austin, State of Texas, 1859.

Olmsted, Frederick Law. *A Journey Through Texas: or a saddle-trip on the southwestern frontier.* New York, Mason Brothers, 1859.

Oswandel, J. Jacob. *Notes on the Mexican War 1846–47–48. Comprising incidents, adventures, and everyday proceedings and letters while with the United States army in the Mexican War: also extracts from ancient histories of Mexico, giving an accurate account of the first and original settlers of Mexico, etc.; also the names and numbers of the different rulers of Mexico; also influence of the Church.* Rev. ed. Philadelphia, n.p., 1885.

Overdyke, W. Darrell. *The Know-Nothing Party in the South.* Baton Rouge, Louisiana State University Press, 1950.

Paullin, Charles O. *Atlas of the Historical Geography of the United States.* Ed. by John K. Wright. Washington and New York, Carnegie Institution of Washington and the American Geographical Society of New York, 1932.

Peral, Miguel Angel. *Diccionario biográfico mexicano.* Mexico, D. F., Editorial P. A. C., 1944.

Polk, James K. *The Diary of James K. Polk.* Ed. by M. M. Quaife. 3 vols. Chicago, A. C. McClurg & Co., 1910.

Queredo y Zubieta, Salvador. *El Caudillo: continuación de "Porfiro Díaz, ensayo de Psicología Histórica" (Septiembre 1865–Noviembre 1876).* Mexico, Librería de las Vda De C. Bouret, 1909.

Reagan, John H. *Memoirs, With Special Reference to Secession and the Civil War.* Ed. by Walter Flavius McCaleb. New York and Washington, 1906.

Richardson, Rupert Norval. *The Comanche Barrier to South Plains Settlement: A Century and a half of savage resistance to the advancing white frontier.* Glendale, The Arthur H. Clark Company, 1933.

Smith, Justin H. *The War with Mexico.* 2 vols. New York, The Macmillan Company, 1919.

Sowell, A. J. *Early Settlers and Indian Fighters of Southwest Texas.* Austin, Ben C. Jones & Co., Printers, 1900.

Sweet, Alex E. and J. Armoy Knox. *On a Mexican Mustang Through Texas: From the Gulf to the Rio Grande.* London, Chatto & Windus, 1884.

Triplett, Colonel Frank. *Conquering the Wilderness.* New York, N. D. Thompson & Company, 1883.

Valades, José C. *El Porfirismo, História de un Regimen: El Nacimiente (1876–1884).* Mexico, D. F., Antigua Librería Robredo, de José Porrua y Hijos, 1941.

Wallace, Ernest, and E. Adamson Hoebel. *The Comanches: Lords of the South Plains.* Norman, University of Oklahoma Press, 1952.

Webb, Walter Prescott. *The Texas Rangers: A Century of Frontier Defense.* New York, Houghton Mifflin Company, 1935.

———, and others, eds. *The Handbook of Texas.* 2 vols. Austin, The Texas State Historical Association, 1952.

Wilbarger, J. W. *Indian Depredations in Texas. A facsimile reproduction of the original.* Austin, The Steck Company, 1935.

Williams, R. H. *With the Border Ruffians—Memories of the Far West, 1852–1868.* Ed. by E. W. Williams. London, John Murray, 1907.

Winkler, Ernest William, ed. *Journal of the Secession Convention of Texas, 1861.* Austin, Texas Library and Historical Commission, 1912.

———. *Platforms of Political Parties in Texas. University of Texas Bulletin No. 53.* Austin, University of Texas, 1916.

Woestermeyer, Ina Faye and J. Montgomery Gambrill. *The Westward Movement: A Book of Readings on Our Changing Frontiers.* New York, The Appleton-Century Company, Inc., 1939.

Woodman, Lyman L. *Cortina, Rogue of the Rio Grande.* San Antonio, The Naylor Company, 1950.

Wooten, Dudley G., ed. *A Comprehensive History of Texas, 1865 to 1897.* Dallas, William G. Scarff, 1898.

PERIODICALS

Bridges, C. A. "The Knights of the Golden Circle: A Filibustering Fantasy," *Southwestern Historical Quarterly,* Vol. XLIV (1941).

Dykes, J. C. "Buckskin Sam, Ranger and Writer; or, The Life and Sub-Literary Labors of Samuel Stone Hall," *American Book Collector*, Vol. X, No. 7 (March, 1960).

————. "A Bibliographical Check List of the Writing of Samuel Stone Hall," *American Book Collector*, Vol. X, No. 7 (March, 1960).

Ford, John S. "The Fight on the Frio, July 4, 1865," *Quarterly of the Texas State Historical Association*, Vol. I (1898).

Frontier Times, Vol. XV (October, 1937–September, 1938).

Martin, Charles L. "The Last of the Ranger Chieftains," *The Texas Magazine*, Vol. IV (1898).

Muckleroy, Anna. "The Indian Policy of the Republic of Texas," *Southwestern Historical Quarterly*, Vol. XXVI (1923).

Neighbours, Kenneth F. "The Expedition of Major Robert S. Neighbors to El Paso in 1849," *Southwestern Historical Quarterly*, Vol. LVIII (1955).

"News Items," *Southwestern Historical Quarterly*, Vol. XVII (1914).

Oldham, W. S. "Colonel John Marshall," *Southwestern Historical Quarterly*, Vol. XX (1917).

Remington, Frederic. "How the Law Got into the Chaparral," *Harper's New Monthly Magazine*, Vol. XCIV (1896).

Sandbo, Anna Irene. "Beginnings of the Secession Movement in Texas," *Southwestern Historical Quarterly*, Vol. XVII (1915).

Taylor, Bride Neill. "The Beginnings of the State Historical Association," *Southwestern Historical Quarterly*, Vol. XXXIII (1930).

United States Army and Navy Journal and Gazette of the Regular and Volunteer Forces, Vol. XVI (1878–1879).

Winkler, Ernest William, ed. "A Checklist of Texas Imprints," *Southwestern Historical Quarterly*, Vol. LII (1949).

Index

Index